TOTAL
LEADERSHIP

THE PROFESSIONAL PAPERBACK SERIES

The *Professional Paperback Series*, new from Kogan Page, is a major series of practically focused business books aimed at professionals in the middle to senior management bracket. The series covers a wide range of leading edge business topics, including business strategy, organizational theory and design, leadership, marketing, project management and management style. This invaluable series is a mixture of new titles and new or revised editions of best-selling titles. For both practising managers and students of business, the *Professional Paperback Series* will give a boost to their skills and knowledge.

Titles currently available in the series are:

Commonsense Direct Marketing
Fourth edition
Drayton Bird

Transform Your Management Style!
How to Develop and Motivate Your Staff to Achieve Peak Performance
Hilary Walmsley

Total Leadership
How to Inspire and Motivate for Personal and Team Effectiveness
Jim Barrett

Designing Organizations
The Foundation for Excellence
Third edition
Philip Sadler

The Top Consultant
Developing Your Skills for Greater Effectiveness
Third edition
Calvert Markham

The Marketing Plan
A Practitioner's Guide
Second edition
John Westwood

Goal Directed Project Management
Second edition
E S Andersen, K V Grude and T Haug

Creating a World Class Organization
Ten Performance Measures of Business Success
Second edition
Bryan D Prescott

PROFESSIONAL
PAPERBACKS

TOTAL LEADERSHIP

How to Inspire and Motivate for Personal and Team Effectiveness

Jim Barrett

INSTITUTE OF DIRECTORS

KOGAN PAGE

LONDON, UK • NEW HAMPSHIRE, USA • NEW DELHI, INDIA

YOURS TO HAVE AND TO HOLD
BUT NOT TO COPY

First published as part of the Professional Paperback Series in 1998.

Kogan Page Limited
120 Pentonville Road
London N1 9JN

Kogan Page Limited
163 Central Avenue, Suite 4
Dover, NH 03820, USA

British Library Cataloguing in Publication Data

A CIP record this book is available from the British Library.

ISBN 0 7494 2577 6

Typeset by Saxon Graphics Ltd, Derby.
Printed and bound in Great Britain by Clays Ltd, St Ives plc

Contents

Foreword

Although I have used the word 'he' throughout the book, I equally mean 'she'; although I have used the words 'boss', 'subordinate', 'colleague', 'partner', 'parent', I equally mean 'human being'; although I have used the word 'organization', I equally mean 'personal' and 'societal'.

My friends tell me that they have preferred, initially, at least, to 'dip into' the book where their interest has been caught. Please read any chapter in whatever order appeals to you. I hesitate to request that you start with Chapter 1; although some people see this as essential background, others see it as too theoretical. It depends what you want. Therefore, as far as I can, I have attempted to make each chapter comprehensible by itself. However, because I have introduced concepts more or less sequentially, the Glossary is available as a reference. At the same time, I have deliberately created some repetition with the intention of reinforcing a concept in a different context. If you want to begin to get something for yourself which you can use straight away, it may be a good idea to start with Chapter 2 where 'reverse feedback' offers the basic technique. If you want a quick review of the personal as well as the organizational benefits of 'beneath the surface relating', Chapter 11, on making decisions, is the one that best 'draws everything together'. Alternatively, why not use the index as a starting point, finding a subject which appeals to you?

A way of looking at the book is to see it in two parts – the intellectual content and the practical content. The intellectual part deals with all the explanations, while the practical part contains all the exercises. The intention of the exercises is to provide opportunity to connect personal experience and feeling to the theory. Some people prefer not to mix the two, finding that getting into the exercises raises issues that they need further time to dwell upon. It can be tempting to avoid the exercises, which is in itself the best possible reason for doing them.

Author's note

I have borrowed from many authors and extensively from the philosophy of Will Schutz in writing this book. I could hardly fail to do so, since his approach, which he calls 'the human element', has permeated and guided my life. It also is what I pass on to others in my work. The fact that Will's philosophy has its own antecedents leads me to expect that he will forgive me from borrowing from him; anything I have presented in a confused way is likely to be me, not him. I am eternally grateful to gravity for drawing me into his orbit. I have taken what I found useful and total leadership has become my own focus. In the end, people lead their own lives best. If the contents of this book have enabled me, the reciprocal nature of psychology suggests that I may be correct in thinking they might provide something for you.

I would like to thank everybody I have met, whether in business or privately, for the insights they have given me. We have shared so many concerns about management or living and working together, in which the solution, without exception, has been in our understanding of ourselves. A part of them is in this book, somewhere.

Particular thanks to David Wilmshurst who has been a loyal friend and supporter of total leadership over many years. Also thanks to Elaine Ford whose enthusiasm is infectious, Amanda King, Stuart McAdam, Don Oddy, Mike Senior, Stuart Whitter, John Price and John Engestrom for accompanying me at different times, and to so many others who have reminded me of the direction. Finally, I am grateful for the percipience of my wife, Jenny, and I am refreshed to have heard my children, James, Tom, Eve and Harry, comment that 'the way we talk about our problems' has been useful to them.

Introduction

All their thousands of years of additional scientific development have been
wasted in an attempt to achieve size and power when all they needed was to
learn how to co-operate.

A E van Vogt, *The World of Null-A*

The development of our understanding of ourselves and of how we relate
to each other has stood still, whilst our progress in technology is radi-
cally transforming our lives.

Yet, as the millennium turns, there is evidence that relationships,
person to person, organization to worker, society to individual, nation to
nation, have the potential to be harmonious. We now know enough to
make breakthroughs in our relationships that correspond with, even
outstrip, our technological advances. Nor is it necessary to borrow from
technology; chemical manipulation, surgical intrusion, genetic engineer-
ing, organ implanting or cyber enhancement – all these take away from
us, and in the end make us dependent. We already have everything that is
necessary to become as we want to be, not with artificial support, but
through our own volition.

If 'success' is to have any meaning, it must arise from individual
awareness, individual initiating, individual responsibility. To use a
biological paradigm – to change society it is necessary to start at the
molecular, that is, the individual, level. Revolution in our thinking, feeling and behaving will not be brought about by governments or by heads
of organizations, but by individual consciousness and action.

We now have the understanding that can enable this to happen if we
choose. Though our technological accomplishments are wonderful, they
are as naught if our living with ourselves is not self fulfilling. This book
offers a practical process by which understanding can be realized and
fulfilment achieved by everybody in all organizations.

Total leadership means two things. First, it means that everybody is a leader. In other words, wherever you are in your organization, whether boss, subordinate or colleague, it means *you*. Second, that it covers all the relationships you ever find yourself in, whether personal or professional. Since it is so all-encompassing, it is evident that total leadership is *not* what is meant, conventionally, by 'leadership'.

Total leadership means that everybody, no matter whether the organization is a business, a family, a friendship, a political group, government or administration, has a responsibility for leadership. The power of total leadership is that each person individually is responsible to themselves for making it work for them. If it works for them, it works, inevitably, for others.

Total leadership is the term used to describe a process which maximizes the potential of people who have the same purpose, at whatever level or position, in any organization. Awareness of each other is essential to organizational productivity. It is equally essential to the success of our closest and intimate relationships – those we have within our families.

In formal and in informal organizations, the quality of total leadership must be distinguished from reporting arrangements which are often parallel with authority and hierarchy. Conventionally, different roles carry different accountabilities which devolve logically to different levels in some sort of 'tiering' arrangement so that there is orderly sequencing and execution of affairs. But we must be alert to the danger that exists when we create a hierarchy: they can seek to perpetuate themselves for reasons of status rather than efficiency; when they are rigid they become our master rather than our servant; perpetuating the hierarchy becomes the purpose of the organization rather than accomplishing the task itself; historical lines of reporting prevent adaptation to different circumstances.

Therefore, control processes should be limited to what they were originally brought into being for – information exchange; they are the vehicle by which leadership is driven, but they are not what actually does the driving. They should not be confused with the process of total leadership which only has a single level, and, therefore, the flattest possible structure. Furthermore, this process eliminates hierarchy whilst also increasing authority. Thus, the organization's task – to make the most effective decisions – is fulfilled.

1

Total Leadership

The prime responsibility of any individual in the organization is to have the courage not to ignore, but to initiate what he or she is aware of – that is what makes everybody a total leader.

INTRODUCTION

This chapter argues that, for any organization to be effective, everyone in the organization should act as leader. It thus presents a novel, challenging concept of leadership. It argues that any task is completed most successfully when power is replaced with awareness. The leader is defined as the person who initiates his or her awareness of what is happening in the situation.

Since everybody chooses to take responsibility, the organization has the flattest possible structure and, simultaneously, the most robust, adaptable one. It is made possible by individuals engaging in a psychological contract with each other in which conflicts may be resolved. This chapter outlines the principles upon which personal and interpersonal organization may be fulfilled.

THE 'PSYCHOLOGICAL CONTRACT'

Total leadership arises from the agendas that people who are working together agree between themselves, often called the 'psychological contract'. This cannot take the form of a written document, but is an ongoing, 'live' understanding – intangible but absolutely clear and real to those in any relationship.

As people get to know each other and work together, all sorts of assumptions and agreements take place which subtly regulate the way they treat each other. The process of total leadership clarifies those assumptions, hopes and fears. It seeks to prevent the destructive feelings which arise from misunderstanding and unresolved conflict. It is vital in total leadership to confront conflict, and, equally, anticipate conflict, recognizing the power it has to sap the energy of the relationship and, therefore, of the organization.

The psychological contract is adaptable and productive. The predominant feature of the contract is that involved individuals *jointly agree* that they should take the initiative equally in confronting issues that may prevent their accomplishment of the task. This is because each individual is aware that the process by which the task is accomplished is indistinguishable from its outcome. For example, the consequence of negative energy in the process causes failure in task accomplishment.

In making his superior aware of potentially damaging issues, the subordinate is taking the initiative and **leading his leader**. As potentially damaging as the withholding of factual information, is the withholding of conflict about their relationship. Resolving conflict is the primary and major step. It is this quality of the psychological contract which constitutes total leadership.

Total leadership is much more than the subordinate taking responsibility for, acting on behalf of, and in place of, the superior, though it may be all of those things as well. It is more profoundly to do with the willingness of those who work together to confront issues, especially issues connected with the feelings they have about each other, recognizing the power feelings have to distort the relationship, and thus to inhibit organizational achievement.

SUCCESSFUL ORGANIZATIONS

It is only comparatively recently that organizations have come to realize that feelings have massive effects, good and bad, upon team performance and, therefore, upon productivity. People who feel good about each other are more likely to create successful organizations. The reverse is also true. It is perilous to ignore feelings since their power can, literally, destroy organizations.

In total leadership, feelings are brought to the surface and dealt with as part of a constructive process, not allowed to fester or be ignored.

Definition of 'leader': person who initiates their awareness of the situation
Definition of 'organization': one or more persons seeking a shared awareness

There is much misunderstanding about what actually constitutes effective leadership. Sadly, in many organizations, leadership is expected to arise, immaculately almost, once the organization chart has been drawn. And in other ways, for example, by teaching leadership techniques of chairmanship, planning and presentation, many organizations still seek to enhance the 'control' of their leaders. These processes, though they have other virtues, fall short of the productivity that is attainable through total leadership.

To prosper, organizations must be adaptive. Unfortunately, the tendency is for organizations to solve problems the way they have always done. They walk backwards into the future or, as Marshall McLuhan (1997) says, 'We walk proudly forwards looking in our rear view mirror.'

The organization most likely to succeed is the organization that adapts its leadership to tackle the task not, as is so often the case, by attempting to adapt the task to its system of leadership. New circumstances usually require new solutions. Total leadership creates the most robust, flexible and adaptive organizations because it specifically focuses upon conflicts. Total leadership deliberately polarizes differences as the means of creating unity. More of this is explained in Chapter 11 on how decisions are made.

THE MEANING OF 'TOTAL'

Does the word 'total' add anything to the understanding of leadership? After all, leadership may be many things. And it is often seen as opposites: for example, democratic and autocratic, empowering and directive.

The word 'total' is used to define behaviour that is applicable to all organizations and every individual in whatever circumstances.

Total leadership is different from leadership as it is understood in the general, conventional sense: it is more than an aspect of leadership; it encompasses everything that is affected by people who work together; it is total, involving everybody, whether 'appointed' as leader, or not.

Of course, it is certain that some leaders already have been practising total leadership without having given it a name. However, the good thing about naming a concept and a practice is that good ideas are more readily communicated and put into action.

The definition of 'total' is 'complete, comprising or involving the whole'. It is a useful definition because it does not matter at which unit of organization it is applied; it applies equally well to the self, the team, the business or, even, to society.

Most profoundly, the sense in which I use 'total' identifies with the spiritual quest for unity. As Dethlefsen and Dahlke (1990) observed,

If our aim is that unity which encompasses all opposites, then none of us can become healthy or whole so long as we are excluding anything from our consciousness or cutting ourselves off from anything else. In reality all human endeavour serves but one aim: to learn to see the connections more clearly, that is, to become more aware.

The key to understanding the concept and practice of total leadership lies in the attitude of the individual. It is irrelevant whether the individual is the appointed leader, colleague, subordinate, partner, child or parent. What matters is the state of mind and emotional commitment the individual takes to his own life, that is, his attitude to himself and then outwards in his behaviour towards others.

Total leadership is entirely dependent upon the self worth of the individuals who make up the team. When the sense of self is strong, the total leader does not feel displaced if someone else has a better idea, but is pleased that a member of the team is so creative. The total leader does not feel humiliated when a subordinate takes over the running of the team on a particular issue, but feels elevated by the subordinate's success.

If the 'task' is what is involving individuals together, total leadership simultaneously brings together values, psychological truths and processes to ensure that it is fulfilled personally and organizationally. The values of openness and responsibility work most successfully to obtain optimum performance (see Chapter 6). Understanding the psychology of reciprocity prevents misperceptions in the way people regard each other (see 'reciprocity', in Chapter 4). The process of 'reverse feedback' ensures that focus is upon the source of misperception and that the conflict is resolved (see Chapter 2).

'NATURAL' WORK GROUPS

We need to change our view of leadership, basing it upon action, but letting it have nothing to do with status, conferred office or appointment. Total leadership arises from consideration of the nature of the task to be achieved.

A committee is a group of people who represent others, whether or not they have the skills in relation to the issue, and whether or not they are affected by the issue. A 'natural' work group are those people who come together because they are interested in and affected by the issue (see Chapter 11). It follows that the composition of a 'natural' work group, being task specific as opposed to level, role or status specific, is constantly fluid and changing.

Conventional leadership	Total leadership
Conferred office, status or position	Depends upon the task
The leader is always the leader	Everybody is a leader
The person at the top makes the decision and delegates who will make it happen	Everybody makes the decision and the person who cares most makes it happen
Orders come downwards	Everyone agrees from the bottom up
Subordinates need to be told what to do	Subordinates know their jobs best
Feelings are irrelevant to the task	Feelings determine how well the task is completed

STATUS

Decisions enforced on the basis of status are risky ones. Although they may appear to make someone 'look good' in the short term, unilateral decisions almost always backfire, often in ways which could not have been foreseen, and in ways which are difficult to control.

For example, your boss may be talking informally to one of your subordinates. As would be expected, he wants to know how your subordinate is getting on with you, and he is disappointed to hear your subordinate admit, with apparent reluctance, that, 'You are decisive, but not good at using your team'. The comment arises, perhaps unconsciously, as a defensive response to the way they experienced being treated by you: earlier, when you made your decision, you left your colleague out, and now they are leaving you out!

It is always a failure if those who know something about the issue, or those who are interested, are not included. The failure is twofold: first, by not using all the resources available, and, second, because of the inevitable resentment it causes.

Sometimes people do not volunteer what they know in case it challenges their boss's status and makes them vulnerable. After all, a boss has the power to exact harsh penalties upon those who ask questions. Deference to the appointed leader for fear of reprisals remains a predominant behaviour in our organizations. Too often, people who work together are popularly, but erroneously, called, 'team members', although it would be more truthful to call them 'followers'.

The designated leader is not necessarily the best leader for every circumstance. Clutching to the leadership role simply because it seems strong to do so or out of fear that you are not 'looking' like a leader are signs of weak leadership. Furthermore, Mary Parker Follett (1941) has pointed out that authority which is left over from the triumphs of yesterday cannot be assumed to extend to today – it must be won afresh.

Organizations can get fixated on a style which has worked for them and has allowed them to be successful – up until now. It is seductive to preserve what is successful. But the danger is this – preservation is really intended only for what is dead! If we are complacent about how well we are equipped for the future, if we rest upon our past attainments – we can find ourselves out of date. Rather, we should ask, 'Is it still relevant, am I complacent, could I do better?' As Robert Kriegel (1991) advises, 'Always mess with success.'

The *Oxford English Dictionary* associates leadership with status and the 'dignity, office or position of a leader'. It is often difficult to separate the action of leadership from the office which confers authority. This is an essential division for the practice of total leadership.

Webster's New Dictionary and Thesaurus describes 'lead' as 'to show the way by going first; to be at the head of'. It is frequently supposed that people will follow a vigorous, inspired or persuasive individual. Actually, they do so only to the extent that it meets their own requirements; thereafter, they may desert. In this situation, the motivation of the parties, leaders and led, is mercenary, and is therefore temporary and expedient. Total leadership initiates at a deeper level, and refuses to run with followers. It thus ensures the profounder quality of motivation which exists when feelings are confronted as part of the process. This is what is expected in the psychological contract, so that any threats to the contract are explicitly confronted immediately.

Total leadership has nothing to do with conferred office, status or position; it has everything to do with action.

EVERYBODY IS THE LEADER

Is this ambiguous? It sounds like anarchy or communism. To explain, it means that any member of the group takes on a responsibility for leadership as determined by agreement of the 'law' which exists in the 'situation'. To fully understand the 'law' all members act upon their awareness, particularly those times when their awareness is contrary to that of the appointed leader's.

The apparent challenge to the appointed leader's persona is different from what is expected or allowed in a conventional group. Conventionally, power and accountability are given; in total leadership power and accountability are chosen. It implies no subservience. It aims to confront the appointed leader with any matter that may improve the effectiveness of the group, or with any impediment to effectiveness, particularly any conflicts which arise in the situation.

It does not reduce the status of the leader either, but recognizes that status is not best demonstrated by the giving of orders, but through implementing the group's decision at the level of the most senior member. The technical arrangement is that any person has the power of the most senior person present, provided always that this person agrees (see Chapter 11).

It can be dangerous to take metaphors too far, but many training courses on leadership promote a kind of behavioural rigidity. For example, often leaders are exhorted to be 'like helicopters' so that they can have an overview of what is happening on the ground. They are told not to 'come down' and to avoid getting involved in the 'nitty gritty'. The implication is that they lose their authority if they come down – that once in the air, they should maintain their position at all costs.

In contrast, a more flexible, adaptive and confident leader recognizes the advantage in allowing another member of the team, if they know the 'country' better, to take up the helicopter. This is not an abandonment of power on a permanent basis, but a sensible recognition of who should be in the driving seat for any particular phase. The leader has not abandoned control. He can always call the helicopter back down if he wants it when another purpose requires it. The truth is that he allows another person in the helicopter with his authority, not that he has given that authority away.

Total leadership on a team scale creates a psychological phenomenon that Will Schutz (1994) calls 'concordant': the entire team feeling and acting in the concerted way that an individual would, if he were acting on his own. In this situation the most senior member has most fully utilized the resources of the whole team.

In practice, it means that any subordinate checks out the suitability of all suggestions including those of colleagues and the appointed leader. He also adds his own suggestions which he thinks may be improvements to the appointed leader's suggestions. He communicates to the leader those things he feels the leader should be aware of, including those things which he feels initially fearful of saying. Usually, these are the very things which are most important to say. This is an important point because, ultimately, the most senior appointed person is responsible for whatever actions are taken.

The most senior also has to agree with lending his authority to whoever is most suited to lead in that particular situation. Usually this will be the person who knows most about the issue and feels most strongly about it.

The concept recognizes what we know to be the psychological truth: that no single person, not even the appointed leader, knows what is best in every situation; that others apart from the appointed leader are sometimes the best people to take the lead, indeed, fail as team members unless they do take the lead in those situations where they are the most suited to do so.

The concept also recognizes that the appointed leader does not have his status or authority diminished by such events, unless he chooses to perceive it that way, in which case he would probably be unlikely to give up the leadership in the first place. There is nothing in the situation itself which detracts from his status or authority as the leader.

A distinction may helpfully be made between an act of leadership which arises naturally from the situation and those legal and official obligations which are attached to the appointment. When someone else leads besides the appointed leader, the appointed leader has not abandoned his authority, merely lent it.

Leadership implies one leader; in total leadership, everybody is a leader.

WHO CARES MOST?

It is necessary to be clear about what is meant, in this book, by the term total leader: it can be anybody, whether an appointed leader or not. To discern who is actually the leader at any moment, it is necessary to be alert to who is initiating at the 'beneath the surface' level in order to become aware of the situation. Or, to put it in everyday terms, who is taking the initiative to remove any obstacles which are holding the group back?

Appointed leaders are those people who possess, officially, the most power, often reflected in being paid the highest salary. Total leadership is not the preserve of these people. Nor should it be; organizations in which power constantly resides in the hands of the selected few are likely to be rigid, defensive, and uninspiring.

Total leadership arises in any person who takes the initiative because they have the awareness which is necessary to resolve the situation in which they find themselves.

The most effective organizational culture is one which is open, adaptable and robust enough to seek a revolving leadership, thus obeying the dictates, not of an appointed leader, but the law of the situation.

AGREEMENT FROM THE BOTTOM UP

Total leadership works from the top down and is shared between colleagues but, most particularly, it works from the bottom up – when everybody acts as leader, without appointment, simply because they are motivated to do so by feelings of personal responsibility (see Chapter 4).

Leadership implies one direction; total leadership is multidirectional.

Total leadership is a revolving process, although, inevitably, after the group has dealt with many diverse issues, it returns most frequently to the long term, appointed leader. If it doesn't, it is likely that another person who is more 'central' to what is happening in the group should be the appointed leader.

Sometimes people seek to be appointed leader for the wrong reasons: 'I didn't become a leader in order not to be able to do what I want!' In fact, it is impossible to make others do what you want, except, of course, in a depersonalized, task-focused organization, often termed a 'power culture'.

The total leader's power rests entirely upon their ability to harness the motivation of others, and their own, to that of the organization.

Conventionally, there is an expectation for the leader to 'do something'. Not surprisingly, leaders can experience a double edged anxiety as the result of two conflicts: (a) not knowing what to do, but thinking that they ought to know, and (b) not being able to admit that they don't know, because good leaders ought to know.

Note the use of the word 'ought' here. It is similar to the word 'should' or 'must'. They are examples of moral imperatives, coming from outside ourselves and conditioning us to live up to the expectations that others might have of us. Another example is, 'got to'. As Kriegel (1991) says, 'the "gotta's" not only sabotage performance, they also undermine human relationships'.

The total leader is self assured enough to be able to admit that he cannot always have the answers; he is not obliged to 'do' anything. Rather, his leadership is to remove any issue (almost always psychological) that his team experience as blocking what they want to do with and through him. In this way, he harnesses the ideas and the energy from the group rather than relying upon himself.

What the group wants to do is almost always more productive than what the appointed leader or any other individual in the group might want to do.

Furthermore, what the group wants to do has already been 'bought into' since it originates from the group. Therefore, the total leader has no need to 'sell it' to them.

The logic seems inverted, but it makes absolute sense – the total leader is at his most effective when he and anyone in the group initiate equally to resolve any blocks which prevent them carrying out the law of the situation. **It is then that human resources are most fully and effectively employed.** The rationale for this is that

(a) those who do the job know how to do it best, they don't need the leader to tell them
(b) those who report to the leader are the best ones to help the leader be successful and
(c) everybody feels successful if the leader is.

Leadership implies directing: total leadership is initiating.

SUBORDINATES KNOW THEIR JOBS BEST

Many conceptions of leadership extol the virtues of having one leader. They also exhort the leader to keep the leadership at all costs. Some popular guides to leadership are really little more than about 'gamesmanship'. Self-serving 'survival guides' may have consequences which are negative, hindering the development of the individual, team and organization and holding back productivity.

It is staggering that, after so much research into what constitutes leadership, it is a fact that autocracy, diplomacy and gamesmanship are the three apocalyptic horsemen still riding roughshod in most of our organizations. Using guile and aggressive individualism, weak managers are often perceived as strong!

Total leadership is different. It proposes a revolving leadership which is task and talent dependent. Furthermore, it proposes that leadership consists of asking those who are not the appointed leaders to be leaders. It may seem, on the face of it, that I am suggesting that the leader abdicate all responsibility!

Conventionally, the most senior member has the power; in total leadership all of the members assume power.

We may have to examine this seeming paradox in more detail. Does it not seem sensible to give power to the person who has the motivation and skill to deal with the task better than you can? If you have any doubt about this, you act as leader by initiating a discussion about your conflict about giving away power to someone else. That person does not become the leader until you resolve your conflict and you both agree. The feature of this is that you do not give control away – both parties retain control.

The 'task' is what you want to accomplish. The 'situation' is everything of which you are aware or unaware which affects the accomplishment of the 'task'.

You want to have the control that exists when you are sure that the other person *will represent your interests as though they were his own*. For example, this means that if any change in circumstances occurs to what he is empowered to do, he will not make any decision on his own authority unless he previously checks out with you. Of course, as far as small adaptations and amendments go, he may already have your mandate.

A vacuum exists in the absence of the conventional leader. In the absence of the most senior person, total leadership continues to function in the way it always has.

FEELINGS AND PRODUCTIVITY

If people are merely part of a machine-like process, it is unlikely that optimum productivity will be achieved. Even this may not be true, as so many studies have shown that in work situations where people feel subservient to the task, they are endlessly creative in finding ways to impede its progress. It is a way of getting their own back for being dehumanized.

I can think of no organizations where the way people feel about themselves and the way they relate to each other are not important to task accomplishment. In fact, it could be argued that to the extent that people do not feel good about each other, the task never gets done in the way intended.

When people feel good about themselves, sickness and absence from work are low. When people feel good about themselves, they feel good about others. People who feel good about each other form successful organizations.

Productivity is put at risk when people feel bad about each other. Admittedly, there may be signs of endeavour which arises from an element of competition, or from a desire to prove one's worth, whatever you think of that person. But this rarely lasts for long.

When people are absorbed with bad feelings they seek ways of displacing them onto others. Energy is then spent on victimization or defensiveness rather than getting on with the task. Our time is spent trying to 'look good' at the expense of others rather than 'feeling good' as the result of enabling others to feel good about themselves.

The total leadership approach is to confront those negative feelings which prevent us wanting to work together. A negative feeling is a desire to undermine those we work with. It is unconscious because we are not aware that we most of all undermine ourselves. To the extent a person may be absorbed with negative feelings about himself or others, his energy is bound up internally, and his behaviour towards others focuses upon their perceived faults, not upon understanding how to resolve the situation.

Sometimes it is tempting to give up and think that there are just some people that you cannot get on with. Strangely, where apparently incompatible pairs confront the issues which drive them apart, they more often than not discover that they have much more in common that they ever imagined. Usually, what they hated so much in the other person was, in some way, an aspect of themselves they did not like. This is not to say that they are the same as the other person, but that they see something in the other person that they rebel against if they have that in themselves or fear they might have it in themselves.

As will be explained in later chapters, all human beings have the same potential for feeling, it is what they do with their feelings that makes them different. For example, it is difficult for someone who is not 'aware' to admit that they have murderous or lustful thoughts. The fear is so strong that even the thoughts are denied. Awareness will bring recognition of all sorts of 'negative' antisocial or self-harming thoughts, but this is not the same as acting upon them. In fact, recognition of their presence is the best means of controlling them.

It is often the case that the very thing that drives two people apart eventually becomes the very thing that binds them together; they may realize that the person they dislike is the best person to help them understand what they dislike about their self. As they come to understand, feelings of antipathy are replaced by regard, respect and warmth. They like themselves better for overcoming their conflict, they like the other person for engaging with them in the process.

War is the most extreme example of the effect of incompatibility upon productivity. It follows that any increase in compatibility directly increases productivity.

Where the quality of the relationship of people who work together is important to the completion of the task, our responsibility is to enhance compatibility. This cannot be done by waiting for it to happen. Nor can it be achieved by selecting people who seem compatible when they first meet, since situations inevitably arise which will lead people to doubt themselves and each other. For this reason, real or imagined areas of incompatibility must be addressed as soon as possible as they arise. As St Paul said, 'Let not the sun go down upon your wrath.'

THE LAW OF THE SITUATION

Leadership is often thought to rest upon the giving of orders, even though the leader may have involved his subordinates up to the point at which he makes his decision; in total leadership, orders arise from the awareness of everybody as to the natural action to take in order to comply with the law which arises naturally from understanding the situation.

By 'situation' is meant all those reasons, conscious or unconscious, that bring people together to achieve something. The meaning used in this book is an embellishment upon the law originally defined by Mary Parker Follett (1941). This law holds that conflict will be resolved when both parties understand all the factors pertaining to the situation. These factors may be opposing ideas or methods, but might also encompass areas of interpersonal unawareness or personal conflict.

If all of the factors can be made objective and subject to reason, then the resolution of the conflict has its own logic, *independent of the personal power of either party*. If both parties agree on the logic, then action arises from the situation and issues of dominance or compromise are bypassed.

We now have the tools to create a better understanding of **all** of the factors which arise between people and we have a method for making these clear. We can be sure that it is principally the factors that affect us unconsciously that are the most important to deal with. If we do not understand them and the manner in which they operate, they corrupt our thinking without our knowing it, so that our supposed logic is constructed hopelessly on the shifting sands of misperception.

When people try to understand all the factors in a situation, the process is often loaded with defensive (or aggressive) behaviours, through which the aim is to maintain one's own psychological defences. Most management practice, industrial relations, bargaining and negotiations, and much of our day-to-day human relating, is an attempt to make the other person do things as close to the way we want them to as we can. These behaviours are only ever an attempt to distance ourselves from our own unconscious conflicts.

When both parties have some power, even though this is unequal, the result of our attempts to understand is usually a compromise. When this happens, neither party feels satisfied, and the danger is that they wait for a further opportunity to 'get back at' the person whom they perceive as forcing a compromise in the first place. All that is happening here is that the situation was never satisfactorily resolved in the first place. There is still 'heat' in the situation which inevitably, like a bloated corpse, rises to the surface later on. Psychologically, the situation has not been 'completed' upon.

Allowing that situations are continuous and ongoing – even though both parties 'complete' upon the issue – new circumstances may cause the issues to re-emerge in a slightly different form. Therefore, we need a method which allows us to return again to the situation or, more correctly, the 'new situation', with the confidence that we can again discover the 'logic' which resolves the conflicts of both parties.

Discovering the law of the situation depends, ultimately, upon understanding of the self. It is primarily the conflict experienced within the self that prevents awareness of the law of the situation.

Whereas you were previously confused or hostile, understanding the law of the situation dispels misperception and reveals a clear way forward. As part of the process, energy which was previously 'bound up' or 'negative' becomes positive, and the task is completed.

It is essential for you to be aware of how conflicts will distort your thinking. To the extent that you feel you are ignored, not trusted, that others have not been open with you – you will not have found the Law.

The feelings you experience, whether negative or positive, are as logical as mathematics. Feelings can be made clear so that the way they may distort the situation between both parties can be examined. I call it becoming aware of what is going on 'beneath the surface'.

Finding the law leads to these feelings in the situation:
First, 'you see me as significant to you as I am to myself'.
Second, 'you give me control of what happens just as much as you'.
Third, 'I perceive that you have been open about everything which might prevent my understanding of your self and my self'.

What this means, in the end, is that since you will treat me as I would treat myself, we feel as one. We both know what we are going to do about the issue. *The issue of who is the leader has not even arisen.*

Total leadership is initiating, and this is the first, essential step in the logical process of understanding our emotions. 'Initiating' is with who confronts the conflict first. It is with the willingness to risk the denial, hostility or rejection of the other. Then it is the other's turn to show total leadership in recognizing his defences, and to include the other in his deepening understanding as to why this should be. In the situation, both parties can be seen to be 'leaders as helpers'. In effect, they are helping themselves, and in that process also helping the other to become aware.

Since the word 'helper' always contains the suggestion of a defence mechanism, the process of helping oneself or another, if it is being done with awareness, is better described as 'enabling'. Responsibility to one's self therefore leads to a mutually beneficial outcome.

Whereas management by domination is rarely the espoused philosophy of most organizations, it survives in practice. Even consensual management, which is popular currently mainly because it is assumed not to be management by domination, actually is. The fact of the matter is that consensual management is really a form of compromise in which nobody gets what they really want. Or, if some people get what they want this time, they may lose out next time. Consensus is really a form of bargaining in which dominance, persuasion and diplomacy remain the central themes. Consensus therefore remains potentially divisive. Mary Parker Follett (1941) regarded it essential to integrate *all* differences if conflict was to be completely resolved and the task completed.

To the extent that differences are not resolved, the task is not achieved as successfully as it could have been.

The most intractable differences are those which arise from avoiding or repressing the conflicts we feel in any situation. Probably the most intractable conflicts are those which have been shaped by the environment in which we grew up. These are the real issues to be dealt with. It is our fear of tackling these and admitting their impact upon our present, inappropriate behaviour that keeps our dialogue at the 'surface level'. It is at this level that our conflicts have free play, influencing our behaviour without our being aware of what is happening to us and why.

On the other hand, confronting these issues is the only way that will lead to understanding and agreement. Though we may shrink from it, the process allows the person to see their own situation as bound up with, reflecting, and indissoluble from, that of the other person.

Adopting the total leadership process deals constructively with our emotions and creates alignment of our aims and integration of our action. When we discover our law of the situation, we perceive the true self that is the other person, and we experience our shared feelings as a totality. This is another meaning of total leadership, which now includes us both.

Who is actually the total leader depends upon the situation. The task is what has to be completed between us, and part of that task is to be alert to the conflict or potential for conflict that exists in any situation. In the situation, the total leader is the one who initiates his awareness

You will realize by now that this is not a philosophy which seeks to 'socially engineer' the demise of the 'official', legally appointed, elected or nominated leader. These will always exist, indeed, is is impossible to imagine an organization without them. The objective is to make full use of the potential of total leadership that everyone has, whatever their position. Total leadership simply asks what works best and, also, who can most effectively carry out what we want to do?

Most contemporary ideas of involvement and empowerment have their origins in the genius of Mary Parker Follett whose writings appeared so long ago – in the first half of the twentieth century. Though enormous strides have been made, it is only as we begin to turn the page at the end of the century that her ideas are really coming in to their own. And it is through the profound work of Will Schutz(1960, 1979, 1994), who has revealed how feelings operate, that we can now make those ideas a practical reality, in business, in organizations, in government and in all our relationships.

Total leadership is about everyone in the organization initiating what they are aware of – only then does leadership become 'total'.

SUMMARY

This chapter has outlined what is new about total leadership: that it is a process in which the feelings of everybody involved are specifically engaged. Central to the process is the psychological contract which ensures that any situation which might affect completion of the task is resolved. This is crucial to both personal and organizational fulfilment. The following chapters show how to use the process with awareness to achieve what you want.

2

Reverse Feedback

If you understand a man, you agree with him; if you disagree with him, you do not understand him.

P D Ouspensky, Fifth Lecture

INTRODUCTION

When there is conflict between us, the task is unlikely to be completed in the most successful way. It does not matter what the nature of the task is – whether technical or personal – the way we feel about each other always affects the outcome.

If we do not understand each other, we deny ourselves the opportunities that exist in our situation. The 'situation' is all that we are conscious or unconscious of at any moment during our task. Other words for understanding are 'awareness,' 'agree,' 'discover,' 'encounter,' 'conscious', 'truth' and 'unity'.

Though the situation may be distorted by the emotions that we bring to it, the emotions obey precise rules. Rather than accept that emotions will determine our fate, we can comprehend and employ the rules they follow in ways which we consciously determine for ourselves. We can be entirely objective about the process, and, if we get the process right, we have a structured method to resolve our conflicts. As we become aware, what to do about the situation becomes obvious. Personal insight is the first step to self determination. Interpersonally, our mutual understanding makes issues of who is in charge or who is the leader irrelevant – we both are.

The task seems to take care of itself when our relationships are harmonious, but it is vital to become aware of what is happening in our situation immediately we have a perception of ourselves or of another which is negative; it is only negative feelings which cause conflict and prevent us from completing our task successfully.

When there is a breakdown of positive feeling or even the slightest falling away, we might be tempted to tell ourselves we just have to accept that the person is not as likeable as we thought, or that others are bound to let us down in the end. But such temptations are nothing more than excuses, conveniently allowing us to 'cop out' from engaging in the situation.

First of all, if we are not feeling so good about the other person, is our perception of their supposed transgression really accurate? Could we be perceiving the other person through some flaw in ourselves? Whilst it may be comforting to believe it is all the fault of the other person, maybe it is us who are at fault.

For me, Ken Harsham, production supervisor at UK Corrugated, put it perfectly when he said, 'The things that I do not like about me, I prefer to think are you.'

To establish 'how much is you and how much is me', we need to look 'beneath the surface' of what appears to be going on and be willing to experience a deeper level of truth. We can apply the process to our relationship with another person or to the way we treat ourselves. This chapter concentrates upon interpersonal relationships; the personal aspects are pursued more fully later on (see Chapter 9).

RESPONSIBILITY

When teams consist of individuals who function personally and interpersonally in the ways described above, the appointed leader can with assurance concentrate upon his own responsibility. He does not have to worry that subordinates need supervision, prodding or inspection. In fact, he feels the more assured because his subordinates see their job as enabling their superior by removing any impediment which prevents him from being successful in his task. His responsibility is the same to his subordinates and to his superior. Their responsibility is the same to him, to each other, and their own reporting lines.

The reciprocal nature of this behaviour cannot be emphasized strongly enough. By 'enable' is not meant 'carrying' or relieving him or her of the burden of specific tasks, though, of course, it might. It means something much deeper and infinitely more vital to the organization. This much more profound matter concerns the *process* through which the task is undertaken, rather than the task itself. In fact, instead of seeing the task as something which has to be responded to, the process determines that the task is continually redefined and updated.

In the process participants are open about their own conflicts about the situation. The best way to assist *interpersonal* understanding of others is to achieve *personal* understanding. The psychological contract is an agreement to initiate openness about one's perceptions of oneself and others, and particularly, openness in relation to misperceptions, as these are likely to indicate potential conflicts (see also, 'Values and vision', Chapter 6).

Setting out in the first instance to resolve conflicts in others is potentially a projection on to the other person. Such projections represent actions which are carried out without awareness by the initiator of his own conflicts.

Responsibility for another person's integrity and effectiveness is best obtained by initiating awareness of the conflict experienced in the situation with that person. Therefore, make your words relate to yourself and *do not comment directly upon the other person*. This allows the other person to retain control in the situation and to make their own insights, as they become aware of what you, the initiator, are experiencing.

With increased awareness, the other person comes to perceive how his own behaviour may have contributed to the situation. This is for him to discover, not for him to be told by anyone else. 'Telling' usually involves blaming, and blaming sets up defences which make it difficult for both parties to be clear about themselves. Clarity is essential if they are to understand the situation.

The task is attained only so far as openness and responsibility are practised in relation to any matter which, if suppressed, would inhibit the effectiveness of those who work together.

Many people fear openness because they associate it with a brutal, cutting form of truth telling such as that which is summed up in the saying 'honesty can hurt'. This is the kind of openness which is not accompanied by very much awareness; it usually comes over as critical, so that its effect is to distance the initiator from the receiver.

When awareness is included in openness, the initiator implies that he, as well as the receiver, is involved in the situation he finds himself in, and that to resolve it, both parties need to work together to understand it. This, again, is a reciprocal process, which has the effect of drawing the initiator and the receiver closer together in a new, shared understanding.

If openness is practised with awareness, it does not, for example, 'put someone down' or undermine their authority, but seeks to understand what 'beneath the surface' conflicts, in the initiator as well as the receiver, are inhibiting completion of the task.

'REVERSE' FEEDBACK

The usual method of practising 'feedback' is for one person to comment upon the other. The trouble with this is that it is impossible to eliminate some amount of perceptual distortion from the one who is 'giving' to the one who is 'getting'. Even when a two way dialogue is permitted, the same dangers of misperception arise. What frequently happens is that rival participants displace on to each other as much as they can in order to feel that they have 'given as much as they got'. Alternatively, they collude with each other to make only anodyne comments. Either way, they ensure a mutually assured protection by avoiding the issue.

A recently developed method of feedback within organizations is variously called '360 degree', '420 degree' feedback or 'peer review'. This has the advantage in that a number of people comment upon the behaviour of the individual who can then see what common threads emerge. The advantage to the giver is that no one person feels intimidated about giving feedback, since the others are all doing it and because it is often reported anonymously. The advantage to the receiver is that they may discern some truth in consistently emerging themes.

However, none of these methods fully engage the giver and the receiver in the exchange. And none of these methods necessarily resolve the issue between the parties who are involved. Commonly, they merely leave the receiver to 'pick up the message' and to change his behaviour, or direct him to some appropriate training course in which his behaviour may be brought up to expectations. They are 'hands off' processes, nicely sanitized in order that the message may get through, whilst protecting the givers from the difficulty of having to justify what they say. There is no guarantee that the participants will emerge with a better understanding of each other and with a more productive working relationship.

Reverse feedback specifically engages the giver as well as the receiver. In reverse feedback the giver is called the initiator only because this is the person who commences the process, that is, acts as the total leader.

In reverse feedback, the person giving feedback initiates discussion upon their own feelings, *not* upon the behaviour of the other person.

The initiator focuses upon his feelings in the situation with the other person. Since there is no attack, he provokes no defensive reaction. The initiator speaks only of his own self-perception, not of his perception of the other person. He refrains from making any comment, let alone any judgement, upon the other person. He does not point to what the other person has done or should do.

It is pertinent to add at this point that giving positive feedback, that is, pointing out what the other person is good at, is always to be recommended, even though people are often defensive about giving it (see 'Rewards and negative gains', Chapter 8).

In reverse feedback, the receiver feels no threat as there is nothing to justify and nothing to defend. He is not 'back footed' as the result of having to explain and account for his actions. Indeed, because he is being asked to listen, he is in control of the process. He has a choice as to whether to respond to the initiator. He almost always does, as (a) he feels in control of the situation, and (b) he perceives that he will gain in awareness himself as the result of becoming engaged in the process. And, indeed, due to the manner in which he has been engaged in the situation, he gains insight into his own behaviour as a 'mirror' of the initiator's conflict.

As both parties seek, step by step, to resolve the conflicts which arise, or may arise, no sense of blame is attached – the task is only to discover what is happening in the situation they find themselves in. In doing so, they become aware of their individual selves and what has been happening to prevent them working together upon their task as productively as they might have done. The initiator defuses possible antagonism by focusing solely upon his own conflict. By not drawing inferences which might appear to blame the receiver, the receiver remains in control. The receiver makes the choice for himself to engage at the beneath the surface level. At that point, both seek to understand their own feelings and how their own behaviour contributed to the situation. The process becomes a fulfilling one as they gain awareness and are liberated from the burden of conflict. This is the crux at which personal growth takes place. It is when polarized perceptions are connected in an experience of unity. What to do about the situation follows naturally from understanding.

Why is it that the other person chooses to involve themself with your conflict? It is because they would not want to see themselves that way. Their choice is to avoid you or to engage with you. By engaging with you they enable the potential they have in themselves.

Reverse feedback is the only method which can guarantee that feedback has been understood.

CONFLICT

Unfortunately, our roles too often contain explicit directives or implicit expectations. This is what Jaques and Clement (1994) refer to as 'account-abilities'. These originate from outside ourselves, usually from authority figures who expect us to model ourselves upon their example and then, unconsciously, from our own internalization of how we 'should' behave. In organizations, the unfortunate tendency to confuse leadership with control, which exists even in some apparently 'empowering' organizations, tends to absorb and perpetuate the underlying conflicts rather than resolve them.

It would be foolish to deny that conflicts arise in each one of us; it is something that happens to human beings. Fortunately, we can become aware of how we unconsciously project our conflicts and, thus, learn how to make them work for us rather than against us.

Whatever our unique experience, our conflicts are, broadly, of only four types. Although we might use all four, depending upon the pressures of the situation we find ourselves in and also depending upon the conflicts others project upon us, we typically express one conflict more than others (see 'Pressure in enjoyment' in Part 2 of Chapter 3).

To illustrate, let us see how defences might manifest themselves without our awareness in conventional expectations of what our role 'should' be.

DEFENCES

Underlying conflicts you don't resolve may be displaced onto others so you appear to be cross, irritated, blaming or judgemental. You may be said to be a **critic**. What you convey to others is something along the lines of: 'It's all your fault. You're not doing as well as you should. Why should I take responsibility for you?'

Or, you may unconsciously project your conflicts so you appear to be apologetic, servile or a martyr. You might be making yourself something of a **victim**. What you convey is something along the lines of: 'It's all my fault. You're doing your best and I'm letting you down. I can't expect you to take responsibility. I should try harder to take responsibility for you.'

Or, you might identify a need of your own in others – that they want to be appreciated and liked – so you attend to them and make sure that you care for them. When you do not realize that you are almost creating opportuni-ties so that you can assist people, you are making yourself something of a **helper**. What you convey is something along the lines of: 'You cannot be expected to help yourself. My duty is to look after you. I'll take responsibility for you so that you don't have to.'

Or, you may not realize that you are expecting others to compensate for the negative way you feel about yourself. So, you insist that they recognize you and attend to you, in order that they reinforce the image you feel you must have of yourself. You may be said to be something of a **demander**. What you convey is something along the lines of: 'You must treat me as the one who is deserving of attention. I cannot feel good about myself unless you treat me properly. Try harder to make me feel that I am regarded by you.'

There is a lot more about how we defend ourselves from our conflicts under 'Distortions of perception' in Chapter 4. For the time being, let us illustrate by taking the **critic**, whose openness can come across as accusatory, judgemental, blunt or rude. For example, being critical, a person might imply or state that, 'If you ask me the way I see it, a good boss would do it this way...'

Superficially, this statement pretends to be helpful ('. . . reluctantly, I'll give you a word of advice . . .') but is not helpful at all – the real agenda is to let you know covertly that you are not good enough. In other words, what is wrapped up, packaged nicely and offered politely, turns out to be a 'put down'.

The statement fails, because it subtly insinuates that you be blamed for transgressing the giver's expectations. Of course, your most likely reaction is to defend yourself against the implication by rejecting it or attacking back.

What happens is as follows:

	Teller (or giver)	Listener's response (or receiver)
On the surface – superficial truth	'A good boss wouldn't do it that way. . .'	'You couldn't do any better'
	or	or
(About the listener)	'I'll give you some advice...'	'Keep your advice to yourself'

This kind of initiating statement rarely goes any further, because it sets up resistance. Sadly, the bad feelings caused by the words may last interminably. An 'atmosphere' arises between the two which may be summed up in the words, 'we just don't get on'. The opportunity to develop the relationship and work productively on any task is held up.

What is required is an initiating statement which has the promise of deepening the issue so that the beneath the surface feelings can be dealt with. Only through such a process can the conflict be resolved and the negative feeling removed and replaced with positive ones.

The way to do this is for the initiator to talk about himself, as opposed to displacing, projecting, identifying or demanding from the receiver. In the example just given, the initiator's conflict might be that he thinks his boss does not respond to his attempts to assist. His conflict arises from his unconscious desire to avoid feeling that he is not significant to his boss. He therefore displaces his conflict on to his boss. Suppose, instead of the previous comment, he initiated his conflict: I think you feel I am not good enough. I think, why am I bothering?'

	Teller	Listener
Beneath the surface deeper truth – reverse feedback (about the teller)	'I feel I am not good enough and I ask myself, why bother?'	'Tell me more.' 'Is it something I do to make you feel that way?'
Being concrete about what happened or I think has happened	'You did what you wanted (eg after asking me to do it, or asking my advice or making me feel I was involved) without telling me. I feel left out. I needn't have bothered.'	'I didn't know you felt that way. I thought I would burden you if I asked for more help. I thought you expected me to have the courage to make the decision on my own.'
Joint awareness	'Maybe I should have made it clear that I wanted to be involved. Do I sometimes give the impression that I don't want to be bothered, or that you are a nuisance or that I'm not interested?'	'Perhaps, because I'm not always sure what it's OK to ask you about. At the same time, it's maybe that I see you as possibly holding me back that I don't inform you when I should. I think I'm aware I'm taking too much on myself, but don't like to say; I have a problem in seeing advice as criticism.'
Resolution	'I think I brought this situation upon myself.	'It's as much my fault as yours. I should have told

I'm going to make my feelings plainer in future. I hope you'll tell me if I'm being unapproachable. I don't like being that way, in fact, I can see it works against me. And I end up blaming you!'

you I had a conflict about asking you for help because I didn't really think that I was important to you. I am going to remind myself that my feelings of not being important might make you feel that you are not important. The truth is the opposite.

(The 'law' of what to do in this situation has been diiscovered)

'You'd do me a big favour in future if you'd just let me know when I'm putting my "scowl" on or if I seem indifferent about...'

This is all very illuminating. Would you mind pointing out to me in future when I...'

This engagement has involved both parties in the situation and recognizes that, for the conflict to be resolved, both have to take responsibility and work jointly on their perception of how it arises. Responsibility is never solely either the receiver's or the listener's.

In such an exchange, notice how the receiver or listener naturally exchanges roles and himself becomes the initiator when the beneath the surface level is reached. In fact, both people fully share, having identified with each other as both initiators and receivers.

It is only ever useful to talk in terms of your own conflicts and fears rather than about the consequences of your boss's, subordinate's, children's, partner's actions. Saying, 'I feel left out,' is a different message from, 'You leave me out.' Initiating is an invitation to engage, not a challenge to compete.

In an initiating statement, such as, 'I feel left out,' control is retained by the other person. You put yourself rather than him under the 'spotlight'. There is no defensive or aggressive reaction because there is no threat. It shows that you are prepared to go more than half way to meet him. It invites him to help you understand your experience and your situation. It is because he has a choice as to whether to respond or not that he is more likely to do so. And as he becomes more involved, his awareness grows as to the manner in which he may have contributed, along with yourself, to the situation you both find yourself in.

In this non-threatening atmosphere, the receiver can choose to respond by initiating in kind, with his feelings about his own experience. Amazingly quickly, as trust is established and openness becomes the norm, direct comments might be requested about how each other's behaviours are perceived. The atmosphere has become one in which comments are no longer viewed as attack, but welcomed as useful to understanding.

The second message, 'You leave me out,' is critical of the other. A challenge is thrown down which the other person will throw back or may ignore, thus letting you know that he knows better than you whether people will feel left out or not.

The first statement keeps you with him on the 'same side'. The second statement distances you because it says, 'I wouldn't do it that way,' in effect, 'If I was in your position, I'd do it better. You ought to be more like me'.

Note that, in all the foregoing and later remarks and situations which make reference to the 'leader', the words 'colleague,' 'subordinate,' 'partner' or 'human being' could just as easily be substituted.

In any situation the leader is the one who is the initiator.

IT'S THE WAY YOU TELL IT

It is of the utmost importance to be aware of what we say, and the manner in which we say it, to our colleagues, friends, and members of our family. In short, to anybody with whom our relationship is significant. Offhand remarks, not consciously intended to wound, can be the most damaging.

Normally, our everyday communication consists of remarks which, by themselves, seem harmless enough. Often they are calculated to be just below the threshold at which we might explode. They prick and provoke us, but we keep our anger to ourselves, because it seems childish to admit we have been offended or upset by such petty taunts. Even to admit that they have 'got to us' seems an admission of weakness because it may reveal that we actually care what the other person has said.

One way that people often use to try to cope is to 'give back as much as I get'. When this is based upon negative feeling the behaviour is, literally, 'mad', because what happens as a result is Mutually Assured Destruction.

Even the slightest barbs are wounding. Small events are often the worst. We may be furious out of proportion to the event itself. Alternatively, we suppress our feeling because we fear a further riposte, such as, 'Well, fancy being offended by that, how childish'. In this case, the destruction has not only been done, but doubly done. We may grimly go back to work, or try to laugh it off. But the feeling of being abused, not being understood, made to look ridiculous, that is, being a victim, lodges deeply within us.

Later on, when we have an opportunity to 'get back at someone' we do so. We may not be aware of what has led us to behave that way, but even if we do, we may justify ourselves by saying, 'He deserved it.' Unknowingly, we have become a critic as a means of 'getting back at someone' who made us feel a victim. We are only paying them back for the way they made us feel in the first place. But such rivalry and enmity can become bitter, and the consequences for personal, team and organizational effectiveness are disastrous.

Smouldering anger does not create a dynamic, 'buzzing' environment. The energy that should be channelled into personal, team and organizational effectiveness is instead squandered in bickering, trying to get even and all sorts of aggressive and defensive behaviours (see 'negative energy' in Chapters 3 and 11).

It will be obvious by now that individuals who use reverse feedback in their relationship to resolve existing or potential conflicts rely upon openness and trust. These are unusual conditions, rarely fully present in groups of people who work together, although people always wish they were. Any group will always desire greater openness and trust between members; this is almost always what arises from questionnaires which investigate the attitudes of people who work together. They are what people want in their ideal 'cultural climate'.

Unfortunately, saying 'This is what we want' is unlikely to be sufficient to make it happen unless we are aware how to do it. People remain too guarded. Their historical experience makes them wary of trying to bring about the changes they want. And many organizations appear to confuse the survey exercise itself with a practice which will enable adjustments to the 'culture'. Unless there really is a resolution of the cultural conflicts, the exercise will only have demonstrated that people's ideas have been solicited only to be ignored.

The facilitating atmosphere of openness and trust has to be worked at. People have to know that it is feasible and that there is a willingness in their colleagues and in the organization to make it happen. Most of all, the individual must want to make it happen for themselves. Beginning with one's self is the only sure way to bring it about.

OPENNESS AND TRUST

Trust, without some sort of control, could be naive. For example, what would you be getting out of trusting someone who breaks promises? Why should trust be given in any relationship where there is no experience upon which to base it? Trust arises from our experience of the person we know, it is not the same thing at all as a leap of faith!

The best way to engender trust is to eliminate any possible doubt that trust might be misplaced. A person will trust you to the extent that they are convinced that you are as, or more, trustworthy than they are in this situation. They leave you to do something because they know that you are more capable than they are. And if you fail, they can accept the consequences, blaming you no more for the mistake than they would blame themselves.

Trusting someone is your responsibility. Trusting someone because they demand they be trusted is colluding in their defence.

In the same way we might trust a pilot to fly us, so we trust someone with what we initiate with them. When we first do this, there is a fear that the other person may 'throw this back in my face'. Initiating therefore depends upon trusting oneself to take some amount of risk. Initiating openness always appears to be taking a risk. But what we learn is that when the other person feels trusted, they begin to return trust.

Ultimately, trust is about you trusting yourself enough to trust them.

In the beginning, you have to trust yourself to be open. People participate to the extent they feel safe. This is why it is best to take successively small approximations when taking risks, so that threat never appears. When initiating openness, you are not expected to blurt out or expose your innermost soul all at once – they probably won't be able to cope with this unfamiliar behaviour! Instead, it is sensible to go just a little way, and then see if they want to join you, then see if you can both trust yourselves to go a little further. In this way, we can avoid the big risks associated with failing, by taking a sequence of minor risks until we find we have enveloped the major issue – found our way to the causes of conflict and resolved the situation.

Someone must be prepared to initiate in the first instance at the beneath the surface level. That is what total leadership consists of – the willingness to recognize that the buck stops with you, that it is up to you to go first in order to break the barrier, that to be true to yourself, to be the person you want to be, to achieve your life plan, you have to initiate first and lead the way. This is not 'taking over', but is clearing the ground so that you and the other person with whom you find yourself in this situation can go forward, not stand still, not go back, but clear ahead to the vision you have created for yourselves.

Trust is intimately linked with how much control you experience in the situation. From the interpersonal perspective, trusting another person allows them some influence with you and creates a feeling in them that they are in control. From your own personal perspective, you feel sufficiently in control of yourself to welcome that influence.

You trust so far as you remain in control. This is why, if we become aware that we are initiating more than the other person seems able to cope with, we should ask, 'Am I saying too much? or 'Would you like me to stop?' We have probably become aware that they may be feeling defensive or may not want to listen. At this juncture, we put them in control by giving them the choice as to whether they want us to continue. They are much more likely to be involved if it is they who make the choice.

If you are asked to trust to a degree that you feel out of control, you place yourself back in control by initiating your conflict at the beneath the surface level.

BENEATH THE SURFACE

We are not used to relating our experience at a beneath the surface level, especially in organizations, and, fearing to get into unfamiliar territory, we may try to avoid doing so. Thus, we talk about our perceptions of others or argue with them in a vain attempt to persuade them to think as we do. Small wonder we create an environment of defensiveness and aggression. The method for developing trust is to talk about your own feeling, rather than how you perceive the other person.

Our perceptions of others always contain an element of projection of our own fears on to them.

In truth, we attempt to protect ourselves by displacing our fears on to others. To ensure we relate to each other in ways that eliminate the conflicts we feel, and thus allow us to work productively and harmoniously together, we need to be aware of how our feelings dictate our behaviour.

Unfortunately, many of us have been brought up to believe that the expression of feelings makes us vulnerable or look stupid. No doubt our parents and teachers had their own reasons for displacing their own fears upon us, but this is a legacy which has no value. Displacement, like all the other defence mechanisms, appears to be the easy way, but never lasts for very long.

Of course, feelings can blot out our capacity for reasoning – nakedly, feelings are overwhelming. But better to have feelings in any form than suppression of feelings. However, with awareness, we can shape and guide our feelings so that we can take control of them rather than them of us – we need no longer fear that they will swamp us or take us over.

What we can practise, and then employ more frequently as we see how powerfully it can work, is relating to each other in a way that uses 'reflection', involving the initiator and receiver at the beneath the surface level, as in the example given earlier. The technique defuses the situation because, initially at least, it makes 'you' the object of the discussion rather than 'them'.

My own image for initiating at the beneath the surface level is that I shine the 'spotlight' – to demonstrate it is not an interrogation – upon myself rather than the other person.

As the other person is not threatened, they are more likely to listen to you or join you, rather than attack you. The secret is always to initiate by talking about your feelings about yourself when you are with them, as opposed to talking about the way you feel about them. Although, when a climate of trust is established, they may ask you to tell them directly how you perceive them, they will initiate more themselves than they will obtain from you. That is then their choice, it will never arise if they perceive you to be a demander of them.

It is difficult to make the plunge straightaway into the deepest levels of awareness unless you make a concrete 'connection' with how you came to think and feel the way you do. It is useful to start the process with what you are aware of thinking and feeling even though you may also be aware that these may be distorted.

Let us accept the fact that our feelings, whilst they may be misperceptions or distortions of something deeper that is going on, are all we have to go on. To suppress them and say, 'I don't want to talk about them or even admit their presence,' is helpful to nobody, least of all yourself. In fact, it is a form of being a 'helper to yourself' that is called denial. If we at least start with the feeling we are aware of, we will have grasped the thread that eventually will lead us out of the minotaur's labyrinth.

There is a process by which these matters can be worked through and understood. The route to awareness involves our talking to ourselves at a deeper level of truth. We can best understand what is happening to the tides of our emotions through understanding those deeper currents that are flowing in our situation.

Meaning of 'surfaces'	Related concepts
The surface level	The 'conscious' (2 minutes) Partial awareness Thoughts Intellect (left brain hemisphere) Prefrontal cortex 'Defences'
Beneath the surface level	The 'unconscious' (timelessness) What I am aware of Feelings Emotions (right brain hemisphere) Physiological preconscious (most of the sensory nervous system) Insight (objective consciousness)

Research has shown that emotion may exist before a person is aware of it – and that emotion affects their behaviour without their being aware of it. For example, people like things they are not aware they have seen before, having been shown pictures of items at a speed so they have no idea of what they have seen. Similarly, Goleman (1996) refers to research in which people assert they have no fear of snakes even though physiological indicators, such as sweating or skin conductance, clearly reveal anxiety.

Drury (1989) points out the reliance that our Western society places upon scientific and technological solutions, thus developing the right hemisphere of the brain at the expense of the right. Thus, we rely too much on linear thought, on sequential information processing, and not enough on intuition. As Drury points out, 'We operate too much with our heads and not enough through our hearts'.

The limits of continuous consciousness are illustrated by Ouspensky (1974). In his experiment, he maintains that, 'a man can with great effort be conscious of *one subject* (himself) for two minutes or less'. For Ouspensky, consciousness is an illusion. What we would normally refer to as consciousness, he terms 'waking sleepfulness'. However, there are moments in which we can become aware of ourselves, as Ouspenky puts it, 'self-conscious'. These are the moments at which we awake, having had an insight which allows us to see ourselves objectively. For Ouspensky, this is a 'higher level of consciousness' than most people normally attain. For me, it is when we encounter the truth about ourselves (or have an insight, which is the same thing) at the beneath the surface level.

AWARENESS

I prefer to refer to surface levels as opposed to the conscious and unconscious parts of our minds, or to the aware and unaware parts, simply because it is obvious that there is much going on in our conscious or aware minds that we are not, in fact, conscious or aware of. We may believe we are conscious or aware, but are probably deceiving ourselves, such as when we feel we are justified in being angry.

Actually, using the word 'aware' is really using a misnomer because until such time as you make yourself aware of all those things you are hiding from yourself, your awareness is limited. Those very conflicts you are defending yourself against limit your awareness. The task is to bring what we discover beneath the surface level up to the surface level and become aware of what is going on.

Above the surface	I normally focus on *you*
Beneath the surface	I *focus* on what I feel when I am with *you*

Above the surface	I 'project' my feelings on to *you*
Beneath the surface	I understand why I am being defensive

The truth deepens as you move from focusing on the other person and focus instead on what you experience within yourself. Beneath the surface you become aware of how much your thoughts and feelings about the other person are a projection of the way you are feeling about yourself. It is as though you are perceiving an aspect of yourself in the other person. What you perceive as being them is partly them (otherwise there would not be a reflection) and also partly you.

The feelings we have about another person are always reciprocated. If you are blaming the other person for your troubles it seems certain that you are going the wrong way about sorting them out; if they do not want to sort out what you perceive as their 'trouble', perhaps the better thing to do would be to sort out your 'troubles' for yourself.

You discover that your thoughts and feelings about the other person are a displacement or projection of feelings you do not want to experience in yourself. Being aware of the mechanisms you use to defend yourself against your fears, you can more clearly change the situation so that you create behaviours that overcome your fears and lead to positive feelings.

Beneath the surface we become aware of what we are suppressing in our unconscious. The reason for suppression is that we have a conflict we do not know how to deal with. We feel that if we were to express our conflict it would create some sort of pain or anguish, or add in some way to what is making us feel bad about ourself.

In fact, there is a simple, useful way of assessing our situation, which is commonly known to psychotherapists such as Yalom (1991): it is that feeling 'bad', 'sad' or 'mad' always means that we are not being ourself – the only time we are really ourself is when we are 'glad'. The fear of not being able to cope with the conflict (or being anything else but 'glad') makes us 'bury' it beneath the surface in our 'unawareness'.

However much we try to 'turn our back upon' what we do not want to confront, we possess a residual awareness that the resolution of the conflict lies with our co-operating, internally, with ourself or, externally, with the other person. Understanding your conflict is the only way to take control and be free from it.

Our thoughts, feelings and reactions do not simply happen in a vacuum. They arise as a reaction to how we have been treated or imagine we have been treated. As far as our reactions are concerned, what has really happened and what we imagine are the same thing.

The way people behave towards us makes us feel good about ourself or bad about ourself. Good feelings always look after themselves, they are not sources of conflict; in fact, they eliminate conflict, so we do not have to be concerned with them here. The effect of good feelings or, if you like, receiving 'positive feedback' is that it eliminates what you are afraid of.

It is our fear of being the person we want to be, or fear that we cannot cope, that leads us to project our fear onto someone else, and is the cause of our misperception of other people and of our negative thoughts and feelings about them.

When you say or do something to make someone feel good, they unconsciously reciprocate with feelings back to you which make you feel good. In this situation, you are both transferring to each other the way you are, not projecting any defence. In this situation, we do not feel there is any misunderstanding between us, since we like ourselves the way we are, also liking the person with whom we can feel that way. In this situation, we typically feel we can 'be ourselves' with the other person.

It is the feelings that do not make us feel good that we have to understand. They are the ones that are the source of conflict. They are the ones which hold us back or lead us to attempt to deal with them by projecting or displacing them on to others where, of course, they do more damage.

Feedback: if good, tell the other person how you feel about them; if bad, how you feel about yourself.

BEHAVIOUR

All behaviour arises from an objective. Thus, we treat others in a certain way because we expect to get some benefit from the way they respond to our behaviour. Usually, we respond to the other person's behaviour as we experience it; we do not take the time to ask, 'Why are they behaving that way?' Trying to understand 'why' is an intellectual process and therefore the analysis takes time. Literally, before we can think, the emotions take over.

Our emotional response happens instantaneously, overriding our thinking. Our response is therefore likely to be based upon our emotional reaction, that is, how we are feeling, and our thoughts are likely to be distorted because they have had no time to catch up with what is going on. Hence, the heated arguments, which seem so silly afterwards, or which we seek to maintain out of not wanting to 'lose face,' even though we have to struggle hard to justify our immediate reactions to the precipitating event.

When we go even further and ask, 'What am I getting out of behaving this way?' or 'What is the other person getting out of behaving this way?' we are really getting beneath the surface. In fact, linking the behaviour to why we think or feel the way we do is the device we use to bring our beneath the surface conflict to the surface level where we can become fully aware of it.

It is impossible to relate your experience unless you connect it with its origin. You cannot change your behaviour in ways you want to unless you see what causes it. You cannot make another person understand your feeling unless you can illustrate it with an example of the behaviour which caused it.

If you can change that behaviour or change your perception of it – either will do – you put yourself in control of those feelings which arise from it. Now, you are no longer alienated or hostile. You are no longer dependent upon the other person for the way you feel but are managing your own responses in a way that works positively for you and the other person.

What we require is a method first to understand how to manage our feelings and second how to relate them to others. The objective is that we both receive positive benefits from changing the negative behaviour which previously existed between us.

We will not understand the situation unless we can relate it to the behaviour which caused it to happen; discussing feelings will seem remote and abstract unless we relate it to our concrete experience. The process therefore involves moving from acknowledging feelings, to the recognition of how our behaviour caused those feelings, to then establishing alternative behaviours which will create the feelings we would prefer to have.

Behaviour is the 'connection' and needs to be inserted between the surface level and beneath the surface level:

On the surface	For example: Withhold or avoid the issue Debate with myself or you Argue Justify Blame you Pretend
Behaviour	Identify precisely what happened
Beneath the surface	For example: Make connections Understand you Insight into myself Confront the issue

or

On the surface	For example: 'Putting you down' 'Getting back at you' 'Leaving you out' 'Pretending you don't matter' 'Being aloof to you'
What happened	Reasons
Beneath the surface	For example: Recognize what I am protecting myself from How the fear of being unprotected arose How to change my or your awareness to cope with my or your behaviour

EXAMPLE OF PROCESS

On the surface	Ask yourself, 'What feeling do I have about the other person?'
Concrete behaviour	**Ask yourself, 'What have they done, or not done, to make me feel about them the way I do?'**

or connection	Having got your feeling about them clear, link that feeling with what they have done, or you think they have done, to lead you to feel that way about them. There is always a connection to be made.
Beneath the surface	Ask yourself, 'How must they feel about me to have done what they did?'
Insight	This brings you to the source of your problem with them – how you think they must feel about you explains the way you feel about them. And then, a little deeper – it is not them that is the issue, it is the way you are feeling about yourself.
Resolution	Now, you could just say, 'It's all their fault,' and wait for them to treat you differently, or you could do something about it. Blaming them won't help. Blaming keeps you at a superficial level at which there will be justifications, excuses, and so on, but no resolution.
Initiate - reverse feedback	State your conflict. A good way to begin is, 'I think you feel I…')

If you initiate by telling them how you feel in the situation, you are more likely to get them to join you in understanding why you feel about them the way you do, and how they might have behaved, unwittingly or not, to make you feel that way. They might even assist you to become aware of how your behaviour, again unwittingly, contributed to bring the situation about. None of this would ever happen if we were aware of how our defences were being unconsciously expressed through our behaviour.

LEVELS OF EXPERIENCING

Surface level	For example: Avoiding
Projections: (about them)	Blaming Aggression Defensiveness Justification
The connection – Your behaviour:	It may be a large or very small thing they did. Sometimes the very small things are the worst

What happened to cause you to think and feel about them

because they exemplify the way you think they really feel about you

Beneath the surface level
Reflection:
(reverse feedback)

You realize:

How you think they feel about you

They may not have been aware that their behaviour had the opposite effect than they intended.

Insights:

That you may have caused them to behave the way they did because of not being aware of what you do to contribute to the situation.

How you feel about them arises from how you think they feel about you

That you both want the same thing but your behaviour is distancing you rather than getting you what you want.

How you contributed to cause their behaviour

Resolution:

You are aware of your behaviour.
You are aware of their behaviour and why you misperceive what they do and why they misperceive you.

How you can change your behaviour and theirs to enable you to bring about the feelings you both want

You are aware of how to help each other get what you want in future.

SOME EXAMPLES OF REVERSE FEEDBACK

Surface statement	'You don't know what you are talking about. I get frustrated because...'
Behaviour	'You give long, complicated explanations.'
Beneath the surface initiating	'I feel left out. You do not find what I say interesting.'

Surface statement	'You don't know how to manage anything. I'm annoyed because...'
Behaviour	'You say that I had better leave it to you.'
Beneath the surface initiating	'I feel you don't think I am capable.'

Surface statement	'You don't consider anyone's feelings. I get angry, because...'
Behaviour	'You didn't invite me to the meeting.'
Beneath the surface initiating	'I don't think you feel I'm important.'

Surface statement	'You frighten me a bit because...'
Behaviour	'You're quiet. I don't know how to take you – perhaps you have thoughts about me you are not saying.'
Beneath the surface initiating	'I think you don't like me.'

Surface statement	'You irritate me because...'
Behaviour	'Everything always has to be done your way.'
Beneath the surface initiating	'I think you feel I'm not clever enough for you.'

The surface statements are the more likely to lead to excuses, arguments or avoidance; the beneath the surface statements (reverse feedback) are reflective and are thus likely to engage both parties in an exploration to understand how the feelings arose and what can be done to change those perceptions for the better.

The thing to say to someone who makes any sort of statement including a reflective one is, 'Tell me more about why you feel that way.'

When you realize that accusations, as well as any expression of hostility or defensiveness, arise from an unaware feeling the person has, it is important not to respond at the same, surface level. Instead, respond in a way which helps the person connect his behaviour with the way he is feeling.

Crying, when used as a defence, seems to be used more often by women. Whereas women may cry, men seem more likely to become aggressive. Crying and aggression are opposite sides of the same coin. When crying is used as a defence, the person makes themselves a victim, in effect saying, 'Look at how you make me feel'. The other may 'give in', thereby appearing to justify the victim's behaviour, or may become angry – a critic – as a defence against feeling trapped.

In order to get you to the beneath the surface level where meaningful dialogue can take place, here are some suggestions for ways of responding to situations in which you find yourself. The questions are **not** demands, so should be uttered in a tone of voice which seeks, not to blame or judge, but to understand:

'Tell me why you feel that way'
'You seem to be feeling (... angry... irritated... fed up... etc). Why is that?'
'Are you feeling the way you do because of something I have done?'
'What do you suppose I feel about you?'
'Do you want to know how I feel?'

This is then likely to lead on to the next, deeper stage of the process when further insights are gained. Both persons come to understand that the other person's conflict involves them – it always does, because the psychological law of reciprocity operates (see the law of reciprocity in Chapter 4).

What happens is that both become aware of how their behaviour caused conflict in the other. They also understand the conflict in themselves that caused them to behave in that way. Awareness of how both contributed to the situation – not one, but both – makes resolution not only possible but likely.

Now, instead of justifying the way we behave to each other, our dialogue becomes reflective. Instead of non communicating with statements such as, 'You deserve it', or, 'You bring it on yourself', which is being a critic, we make contact with reflective statements such as, 'I didn't realize that when I did that. . . it made you feel that I was leaving you out. . . don't care about you', and so on.

This period of reflection will lead on to a deeper realization, such as, 'Perhaps I've been trying to do it all myself because I didn't want you to know how unsure I felt about it all', or 'Perhaps I was acting as though I didn't care because I was frightened that you may not care as much as I do – I'm frightened of showing my feelings, so I gave you the opposite impression of what I want'.

When someone says, 'I'm going to level with you,' do they talk about you or them? Only telling you about them is truthfully 'levelling'.

CASE STUDY

A surface level communication in the Middle East was an angry letter sent by King Hussein of Jordan to the Israeli leader, Mr Netanyahu, which declared: 'You are destroying the peace process and I haven't an ounce of trust in you'. In the past King Hussein was the Arab leader most sympathetic to Mr Netanyahu. The Israeli leader replied: 'There is no place for this criticism and no place for this tone.'*

The King's statement is blaming at the surface level whilst the Israeli Prime Minister's reply is a surface level justification and denial. It is interesting to speculate what might have been the consequences for peace negotiations had the King spoken at the beneath the surface level: 'I think you feel I do not matter, I feel rejected,' and if the Israeli had enquired: 'I would like to understand why you feel that way – is it something I have done?'

Maintenance of defences out of pride and fear of 'backing down' make it seem impossible that these leaders would ever gain anything from each other except from last minute compromise at the brink of conflagration. That Mr Netanyahu might be an initiator, thus pre-empting the King or any other leaders such as the Palestine leader, Mr Arafat, by anticipating potential misunderstanding at the beneath the surface level, 'I think you might feel I might let you down', is almost inconceivable. People who talk to each other this way find accord; there is no risk of war.

*Reported in *The Independent*, 12 March 1997

Gaining awareness is the major step – control of feelings and management of behaviour are impossible without it.

SUMMARY

Understanding our behaviour and that of others requires us to communicate at the beneath the surface level. It is here that insights are gained into why we use defences. Reverse feedback engages both parties in a non-threatening process which resolves conflict and creates positive feelings.

Optional exercises

The first exercise is designed to assist you in focusing upon any conflicts which prevent you and another person getting the best from your relationship. Even if you think your relationship is wonderful, it would be useful to make sure that there is nothing that either of your are avoiding. This exercise, like all those which follow, works to the extent that you trust yourselves to be open.

You are to write down your own feelings and thoughts. Making everything concrete in writing assists your focus. You project onto the page how you think the other person might feel.

If you complete the exercise by yourself, you may find you begin to perceive aspects of the other's behaviour in a different light. You may be able to resolve any of your misperceptions by yourself. And, maybe, your own behaviour to the other may change as a result of your awareness. Completing the exercise in the presence of the other could be even more valuable since you might both ensure that neither of you is colluding.

Having practised so thoroughly with the first exercise, the second allows you to gather a great deal of feedback from a number of relationships. Here, you are asked to initiate straightaway at the beneath the surface level. The exercise not only asks you to engage in reverse feedback with a number of significant others, but allows you to see if any patterns emerge.

Exercise – understanding our situation

Instructions: This can be done with a partner or you can write down what you might imagine to be the case.

You
Surface statement: Write your surface thinking or feeling about the other person:

_____
_____
_____
_____
_____
_____

(The other person)
Surface response: Write or say what the other person says or does about what you think or feel:

_____
_____
_____
_____
_____

Behaviour Write what the other person has done:

_____
_____
_____
_____
_____

Write the other person's version of what was done:

_____
_____
_____
_____
_____

Beneath the surface reflection
Write what you think the other person must feel about you to have behaved that way:

_____
_____

Beneath the surface reflection
Write what the other person says they feel about you:

_____
_____

_____

_____

_____

_____

Initiate reverse feedback: Write what you will say to the other person to get a dialogue 'beneath the surface'. It will probably start, 'I think you feel…':

Response: Write what the other person says about their 'beneath the surface' feeling:

_____

_____

_____

_____

Insight:
Write or say what fear about yourself you had that arises from the feeling you thought the other person had about you:

Insight:
Write what the other person says that changes the feeling you had about yourself:

_____

_____

_____

_____

Insight:
Write or say how you contributed to bring about the behaviour in the the other person:

Insight:
Write or say what the other person says they did, albeit unknowingly, to bring about the situation:

_____

_____

_____

_____

Resolution: Write one or more actions you will take in the future to change the behaviour you do not like or to clarify misperceptions. It is helpful here to write down the actual words you will use to bring about what you want. If you check them with the other person, this can be a 'psychological contract' between you both

Resolution: Write down the actions the other person will take in the future to change the behaviour they do not like and to clarify misperceptions. Writing down the actual words to be used helps to anticipate and rehearse the agreed behaviour and helps ensure clarity in the 'psychological contract' between you both

For me to initiate with myself:

_____
_____
_____
_____
_____

For the other person to initiate with their self:

_____
_____
_____
_____
_____

For me to initiate with the other person:

_____
_____
_____
_____
_____

For the other person to initiate with me:

_____
_____
_____
_____
_____

Who does what/when

_____
_____

Who does what/when

_____
_____

Exercise – reverse feedback

Instructions: This exercise can include all of your significant relationships. In order to resolve misperceptions it is essential not to deny, but to seek to understand how you are both involved in causing the situation.

In Part 1 write the names of the people on the left hand side of the page. Then, for each person, complete the statement for what you think they possibly feel about you. This is a statement of your conflict and is also the statement for you to initiate with them. When you have done this, have a beneath the surface dialogue with each person in turn. Decide who will initiate first.

The other person should write down your statement against your name in Part 2 of their own copy. When they invite you to 'Tell me more', you can reveal your perception of their behaviour and why it makes you think the way you do. You both may gain insights as the result of a beneath the surface discussion of your perceptions and conflicts. Having understood how the situation arose between you, establish what you will do in the future.

Then, the other person initiates their statement with you. Write it down against their name in Part 2. Have a beneath the surface dialogue about the cause of their perception. Before you go on, make sure you have a method of resolving any possible future misperceptions.

Part 1
Name   What I think you possibly feel about me:

_____   _____
_____   _____
_____   _____
_____   _____
_____   _____

Name   What you possibly think that I feel about you:

_____   _____
_____   _____
_____   _____
_____   _____
_____   _____

Other learning:
How far and in what way have you 'projected' your feelings on to the other person?
What was the nature of their 'projection' on to you?
Are there any 'common themes' emerging from your dialogues?

Notes/insights/resolutions

_____
_____
_____
_____
_____

3

Enjoyment

And our institutions, our organizations, the 'establishment' – even these we are learning to use for our own joy. Our institutions can be improved, can be used to enhance and support individual growth, can be re-examined and redesigned to achieve the fullest measure of human realization. All these things are coming. None are here, but they are closer. Closer than ever before. The future is exciting. The pursuit of Joy is exciting. The time is now. We'd better hurry.

Will Schutz, *Joy – Expanding Human Awareness*

INTRODUCTION

On his appointment as Chief Executive of UK Corrugated Ltd, Pat Barrett's opening words to his managers were, 'I intend to enjoy myself; I hope you will, too.' Reactions ranged from approval, to bemusement, to apprehension. Was this really a responsible way to behave in a business that needed such a radical 'shake up'?

It is strange how difficult we make it for ourselves to follow Pat's example. The issue of why we choose *not* to allow ourselves to have enjoyment gets to the root of why we hold ourselves back in all aspects of our lives.

What constitutes 'enjoyment' may have a deeper meaning and wider implications than is often thought. Will Schutz (1967) uses the word 'joy' to mean, 'living with one's whole being'.

The word 'wholeness' may sound somewhat spiritual, but it has exactly the same meaning as the physical notion of wellness. The absence of enjoyment in organizations is likely to be directly proportional to the amount of illness. An unwell organization is not choosing to give itself the best chance of completing its task.

It is not at all uncommon for people to feel guilty about enjoyment. For example, they feel that they should be serious or that people won't respect them, or they feel afraid in case they look stupid, especially if they fail to keep it going.

I thought of 'enjoyment' as an alternative title to this book. It is equally what this book is about. But I didn't trust you to pick up this book if you didn't think it was serious, purposeful stuff which might, like medicine, look a bit difficult to digest, but would do you good. Certainly, I do not want booksellers and librarians to place this book on the 'fun books' shelf! I want this book correctly classified where you have found it, under 'management'. Later on, I found an excellent book by Andrew Matthews (1989), who had the courage to call his book simply *Being Happy*, which I would recommend. It is about many of the same things as this chapter and provides useful advice on how to live your life.

Part 1
Living

Test every work of intellect or faith
And everything that your own hands have wrought,
And call those works extravagance of breath
That are not suited for such men as come
Proud, open-eyed and laughing to the tomb.

W B Yeats, Vacillation, from *The Winding Stair* (1933)

THE ENJOYING ORGANIZATION

Success or, to use a word which means the same thing, fulfilment, is the inevitable consequence of creating an enjoying organization. Everybody can make this happen. All you are required to do is be yourself.

Enjoying does not require you to be in the limelight, or to hold everyone's attention with entertaining jokes, although a current organizational 'fashion' is to provide special events in order to have 'fun' – as a foil and counterbalance to normal 'work'. Helen Jones (1996) noted, 'Playing games in the office is now all part of the rules.' This is in line with the idea of 'work hard, play hard'. Some organizations set aside times during the working day in designated 'play areas' so that employees can let off steam or be 'creative'.

I am not against these ideas as such, but they do not really get to the issue of enjoyment whilst at work. The implication with having purposely set aside times and places for fun is that they are a compensation for the 'hard grind' we are expected to suffer when we get back to work.

The trouble with such ideas is that enjoyment is still viewed as separate from work, that work is something that people need relief from. Work is still viewed as a drudge. Surely it is much better to incorporate enjoyment into work itself.

A popular idea is that of the 'outward bound' process. This puts employees in a novel, unrelated to work environment in which the introduction of team skills is further impressed by the natural bonding which occurs when people are in mildly dangerous physical situations together. The theory is that feelings of fellowship and the acquired skills will translate back into the workplace. Again, I am not against these approaches, but I do not think that an out of work activity fully addresses what happens at work. By taking the issues out of the work situation it may in a subtle way be avoiding the issues, whilst appearing to address them.

The issues of team building are best addressed where the team actually functions together – in the workplace.

Furthermore, the team which is together at work is together precisely because of the choices individuals have made to be in that environment. An outward bound process takes them to an environment in which they have *not* chosen to be together to work. In a significant way, the outward bound environment creates a demand for a different team, one that is designed for that particular environment, not the normal work environment.

These approaches are best described as 'halfway house' approaches; they may be amusing, a relief from work, or educational, but they are not necessary. They are 'separate from', or 'an aside', or 'bolted on to' the work environment in which we normally relate. They are not natural and integral to it. They may focus on a process and often create an appearance that 'we have done team-building' and yet have failed to deal with the core issues of why people are not enjoying work in the first place, and why everything reverts to normal upon return to the everyday setting.

Enjoyment will happen quite naturally and easily once you know how; you'll do it almost without thinking as you develop yourself. We must, of course, get the balance right. I don't mean that enjoyment should be riotous fun. I don't mean being stupid. I don't mean irresponsibility. I mean the sort of enjoyment that delights in being at work, for the company it gives and for the challenges it creates. The sort of enjoyment that is based upon an awareness of one's skills and those of others. The sort of fun that believes that difficulties are to be overcome, not endured. The sort of fun that attends to the 'here and now' – enjoying the process of living now, not deferring, denying or putting off because we fear what others expect of us and how we think we ought to behave.

Ultimately, the enjoyment we experience depends upon the degree to which we have freed ourselves from conflict.

Would you rather have the opposite of enjoyment? Do you have a fear about it? Do you think we have some responsibility to be deadly serious? Believe me, our customers and clients and all of our colleagues, including our bosses, want us to enjoy ourselves. If we do, they will want to join in. Nobody really wants to be part of the doom and gloom team unless their concept of themselves, perversely, is that they deserve to be miserable!

People trust us more when we are confident and happy. If we have no worries that burden us, they are not burdened either. They want to see us buoyant and upbeat. They begin to worry when they see us doleful and full of care. They begin to fear that we are not in control of the situation and begin to think of investing their money, their time, their energy, elsewhere with people who look as though they will be more fun.

We know when we are enjoying: it is when we are using our self completely. When there are no blocks which we impose upon ourself or are imposed by others to hold us back. When we feel that we are aware of ourself, but still discover aspects of ourself which we like. When we use our awareness and skills in ways that matter to us because they make a difference, and when we are fully involved in what we are doing, and who we are with.

When we are fully alive, that is, not dwelling upon some feeling of guilt or held back by doubt, but being ourself, then we are enjoying.

If you are not enjoying, why is this so? Don't say, 'I don't know why.' If you do say this it means you are trying to avoid becoming fully aware of your situation, in case you have to do something about it! Actually, the answer is instantly available to you if you want to hear it. Just relax for a moment and ask yourself, 'What is stopping me enjoying?'

It is often helpful just to feel in one's body and mind what it is that is making you feel uncomfortable, weighing you down or holding you back.

The answer has just popped into your mind, hasn't it? If it hasn't, don't think you can't or that you are not doing it right. Just relax. Give yourself time and ask yourself again. The answer will just come to you. Give yourself more time until you know why…

Alright, so now you are aware that something is not the way you want it to be. The next thing is to do something about it – in other words, take control. Does this begin to get frightening? Now you are confronted with the conflict. You want to do something, that is, but are afraid of doing so. What are you afraid of? Admitting to yourself what you are afraid of is the first step; it is real progress.

It is this that is stopping you from enjoying and being yourself. Ask yourself what you are getting out of not doing anything about it. Nothing at all really, you say, just the comfort of stagnation. And, of course, by avoiding all the risk, you are denying yourself all the enjoyment.

Only by doing something with your new awareness will you enjoy. Risky, yes, but exciting too! And won't you feel you have let yourself down if you just carry on as you did before? No, the process of doing what you want to do, of actualizing what you are capable of doing, will create your enjoyment.

Enjoyment is the experience of completion, having acted with awareness.

Notice that I did not say anything about 'becoming what you want' or of 'getting what you want'; I talked only of the 'process of doing'; it is principally in the 'doing' that enjoyment arises, not in the 'getting'. That will look after itself. Finding a 'reason' for putting off enjoyment until you become what you think you want is denial.

It is illusory to think you will ever arrive at where you want to go; it is the road you travel that is your reality, not the place you are going to.

And when you have done what you want to do, it wasn't so difficult in the end, was it? The doing is never as bad as the anticipation. So, get on and do the next thing. It doesn't stop there. Don't rest on your laurels. They'll fade, so go out and acquire some others. There's plenty more enjoyment to be had.

If you never meet trouble, plainly you are not sailing hard enough.
J D Sleightholme, *The Trouble with Cruising*

Part 2
Denial

Things said or done long years ago,
Or things I did not do or say
But thought that I might say or do,
Weigh me down, and not a day
But something is recalled,
My conscience or my vanity appalled
                    W B Yeats, Vacillation, from *The Winding Stair* (1933)

DENIAL

Denial is the defence mechanism in which you are a helper to yourself by avoiding the situation.

SECRETS

Suppression and containment inevitably result in disastrous outcomes. Norman F Dixon (1994), in an article entitled 'Disastrous decisions', writes, 'The more emotionally important a decision (to do or not to do) the bigger the chance of it being irrational'. Dixon graphically depicts railway and aeroplane accidents, military bungling and political policies, among other things, as being rendered more 'hazardous by the mechanisms of defence – unconsciously determined devices whereby the conscious mind is protected from anxiety and other unpleasant feelings through blocking, or neglecting, or sanitising, bad news. Repression, denial, rationalisation, perceptual defence, the resolution of cognitive dissonance and kindred other defences are in reality trading survival for peace of mind'.

COMPLETION

It is not enjoyable to be weighed down with remorse. The most awful part of dying is the regret for what we have done that we wanted to undo, or do that which we have not done. It is unlived experience that we yearn for, the chance to be fully alive with those suppressed aspects of our integrity and potential.

Integrity is a word which summarizes action based upon our awareness. We may not reach perfection, but anticipating failure is merely a justification for avoidance. No action is always a failure, because, deep down beneath the surface, we know we have the competence to resolve and complete upon conflicts. It is only the fear of initiating which prevents us.

Potential has to do with using ourself as fully as we know we are competent. Not that we want to be increasingly famous or more powerful, but to get that balance at which we feel we are fulfilled. It is not to compromise from fear of trying, but to employ ourself to bring about what we can imagine we can do, because we know we can.

To the extent we are not fulfilled, we are letting ourselves down, we are being less than the self we could be. In this case, in going to the grave, we would have plenty to regret. We are proud, going to the tomb, if we have made our life 'complete'.

'Things I said and did not mean, or things I did not do or say' all represent energy that was never used. Instead, it was 'withheld' or 'bottled up', becoming a source of regret in our lives. It is sad to witness a defence, such as a bitter, critical attitude, in people at any age, but particularly sad to witness them in the elderly – because there is less and less time to 'complete'.

Time doesn't make our conflicts go away either. The trouble with conflict is that it is timeless. It is as real, perhaps even more pressing, the longer it is avoided.

CASE STUDY

I forget which newspaper it was in which I read the report of a man in his seventies who returned the mathematics prize, which he had won at the age of 14 years, to his school, because he had cheated. He said that he had lived with the shame all his life and wanted to 'get it off his chest' before he died. It is what is perceived as necessary for us to do to forgive ourselves that is important, returning to the point of innocence before the 'sin'. Our feelings determine who we have to make our 'settlement with' and how much of this we need to do publicly. In his own case, this man wanted to 'give back' in a very public manner and was prepared to face such judgements that might be made. Those remaining who may have been affected by his original cheating may be inclined to forgive him, not just because so much time has passed in the interim, but because they may understand something of the conflict he must have been under to resort to cheating in the first place. This conflict probably had something to do with a fear that, without cheating, he would never live up to the expectations he supposed others had of him. Ultimately, it was his own expectations of himself with which he had to wrestle. And, again, it is less to do with whether others might forgive him than with his capacity to forgive himself.

It is never too late to act upon and 'complete' with the energy that one still has, even though out of fear we say, 'It's too late now'. The very fact of guilt is testimony to the presence of energy which is not being liberated, but remains suppressed.

It is normal for completion to be accompanied by crying. In this case, crying is a profound, cathartic experience.

The best thing to do with any conflict is not to let any time pass before taking action. Do it now. The longer you leave it, the worse it gets; the sooner the better. And the more time you'll have to let yourself have enjoyment!

Never think you've seen the last of anything.

Eudora Welty, *The Optimist's Daughter*

CAUSE OF CONFLICT

A conflict is a discrepancy between a thought and a feeling. For example, the thought might be that good leaders don't show any doubt when, in fact, they are paralysed by indecision. Or the thought might be that your customers need to feel that you know what you are talking about when you are terrified they'll realize you are way out of your depth. The conflict is that if you show any doubt then people won't trust you.

In fact, you are confusing the show of competence with real competence. If you tell people your conflict, the reverse of what you fear will actually happen. People feel good that you trust them enough to be open with them, that you believe in their competence enough to assist with your difficulty. Your competence in telling them your conflict is the first step in reassuring them that you really are the person who can enable them.

We are talking here about the competence with which you lead your life and relate to others; the competence that consists merely in 'looking good' is fragile indeed (see Chapter 8).

In contrast, if you say nothing about your conflict, they would pretty soon begin to get an inkling there is something on your mind you are not telling. And then they begin to worry about you, which adds to your anxiety as you begin to wonder, 'Do they realize, but are afraid to say, that they think I don't think I can manage, which is true, I can't manage, I'm only pretending, hoping it will all work out right in the end!'

Suppose you hate social events, but think that, to be a good boss, you should attend them. You may go along and everybody knows how uncomfortable you feel; they can't wait for you to leave so that they can get on with having a good time. But if you feel comfortable not attending, people will not think any the less of you for not going. The really important matter is the way people feel about the way you behave to them. If they think you don't go along because they are not significant to you, that is something you really do need to correct. But if it is because it really is the function you don't like, not them, then that's all right. The thing to do is to make sure people know they are significant to you, but this significance is not lessened by you not attending a social occasion. You can do other things, in circumstances which suit you better, to demonstrate that people are significant to you.

BURNOUT

You will burn yourself out if you lead your life in the manner which you think other people expect of you. In this case, you begin to lead the life you think makes you acceptable to them, rather than your own. It is ironic that you should want to come up to someone else's expectations of you, when they are not coming up to their own expectations of themselves. If you lack confidence in your own values, you enslave yourself by taking upon yourself the defences of others.

One of the cruellest tortures we give to ourself is feeling guilt about not coming up to the expectations that a parent or significant other person, such as a teacher, had of us. Often this arises so strongly because, although we did not know it and they did not know either, they were projecting their own feelings of failure on to us. That is, they expected us to compensate them for the way they did not feel about themselves. The implied messages which pressurize us are, 'I'll only love you... You will only be worthy... if you come up to my expectations, don't let me down', and so on.

This gets a little tortuous and analytical, but we might take this a stage further if we want. We might ask ourselves if we are being fair to our parents, or teachers, to blame them for the guilt we say they made us feel. Perhaps we are misperceiving their intentions. As a result of not coping with our own expectations of ourself, without awareness, we reverse the process and conveniently displace or project our conflict back onto them.

The first responsibility is towards yourself. How can you enable another person with their life, if you are not first of all 'leading' yours in the way that makes you feel successful? Remember, this must be success in your terms, not in someone else's.

People sometimes make a 'rod for their backs' by adopting some moral imperative. It usually comes out in the word 'should'. 'I should care more, I should do more for people, I should work harder, I should try to be nice.' Who says so? Ask yourself, 'Who am I trying to please? Who put this word "should" in my head? Why am I driving myself to do something I "should" when I really don't want to? Or perhaps I say "should" because that absolves me from taking responsibility. In other words, if I do what you say I should, it will be your fault if my life turns out to be a mess.'

Try saying the same things again, but this time putting in the words 'I want' to replace 'I should'. Does this help you take responsibility?

How does it feel when you say, 'I want'? Are you really saying 'should' because by appearing to feel guilty – 'I would, if only I could' – gives you an excuse for not doing what you say you should. The truth is that you really don't want to, or that you find an excuse for not doing what you want. Maybe you are afraid of trying...

When you read the word 'should' in this book, I suggest you ask if it enables you to enjoy. If it does not, I suggest you ask, 'in whose interest "should" I do this?'

PROTECTING OTHERS

Not delegating is an obvious way to feel stress. Actually, delegation is not the problem if you continue to worry about that which you have delegated. The fear is not being competent, because you trusted someone who, you should have known, would let you down. Therefore you had better make sure everything is done yourself 'that's the only way,' you tell yourself, 'to make sure it's done properly.'

The problem is more to do with your 'negative gain', that is, what you get out of not delegating. One thing might be that you tell yourself people like you for protecting them from extra work. Another thing might be that you avoid giving anybody the chance of refusing to help you, so you head off any anticipated rejection. Another might be that you are unconsciously thinking that, if you wear yourself out, others will come to appreciate you, or like you better. (See 'Delegation' in Chapter 10.)

FEAR

Aren't fears useful? Don't they act as useful checks which stop us getting our fingers burned and from getting into all sorts of trouble? That sort of fear protects us from the way we don't want to be, for example, burned. That is not the sort of fear that I am concerned about here.

The sort of fear that is much more damaging is the sort of fear that stops us from being the way we *do want* to be. It is only the fear itself that stops us, not the state of being we can imagine if only we had the courage to overcome the fear. This sort of fear is self limiting and serves no positive purpose. It is negative energy because it burdens us as opposed to releasing us. It shackles us to our conflicts instead of allowing us to be ourselves.

NEGATIVE ENERGY

The conflicts in an organization exactly reflect the conflicts of the leader. The organization may be a team, but could also be your own, personal organization – your mind and body.

Conflict is restless, destructive, bound up energy. To the extent negative energy prevails, control and focus are lost. It follows that our job is to enable ourself – as the leader of ourself and of others we relate to – to be aware of the conflicts. If we are clear about ourself, we enable the whole organization to be clear.

Releasing ourselves from conflict is the greatest contribution we can make to empowering the whole organization.

Possibly out of deference to their appointed leader, or due their own self doubt, subordinates are surprisingly accepting of their leader's petulance. But nobody has a 'right' to anger. Linda Clark (1974) quotes George Wilson (1963): 'We readily recognise the red face of anger, the set face of determination, but we do not always connect the outward expression with an inner, unresolved form of tension'.

All that is required to deal with these unconscious forces, so destructive to personal as well as corporate success, is to become aware of them. Linda Clark (1974) also quotes from Bayly (1958), stating that all that was necessary was the 'discovery of the power of the inner man to take charge and to choose deliberately to think and act in ways that are more constructive than the old behaviour patterns'.

It is surprising how slowly our organizations have adapted to the insights of psychology. For example, writing as long ago as 1941, F W Bailes wrote: 'Nothing kills the healing consciousness as easily as the habit of criticism. Criticism is a mild form of hate and sometimes it is not such a mild form either. It would be a wise move to refrain from criticising anyone, no matter how much the criticism would appear to be justified.' What appears to be righteous anger, even when it appears under the guise of getting subordinates motivated, is only ever a displacement.

STRESS

We have the power to choose how we want to be. It is only a question of resolving the conflicts which prevent us. It follows that we can choose whether or not to experience stress.

Of course, you might imagine extreme situations, such as a concentration camp, for example, where it would be difficult not to experience stress, but we are not talking about such extraordinary circumstances. We are discussing the stress that arises from our everyday working, social and family lives. In these situations there is nothing which prevents you from having a choice.

The stress we experience is almost entirely of our own making. Whilst it may be impossible to avoid all those external events in which stress will occur – things go wrong, people are not always perfect – how we choose to cope with the potential stressors is entirely up to us.

Suppose we are annoyed because a traffic jam makes us late for a meeting. We feel bad about letting our colleague down. He or she accepts our apology, yet we worry that they feel we couldn't be bothered to get there on time. And there may be some uncomfortable truth which we are fearful of becoming aware of: that we could have left a little earlier to get to the meeting, or that we do make a rod for our own back by cramming too much into our day or leaving things to the last minute. On the face of it, we cannot be held responsible for the traffic jam, but some part of our frustration and annoyance is an attempt to find a culprit for our anger, thus displacing it from away from ourselves.

If we deny there is anything we can do to change the situation in which we find ourself, we worry about when something is going to happen to us next. We become a helpless victim. But if we believe that there is something we can do, we immediately feel empowered; we perceive we have the power to take charge of our own destiny. Self worth increases as we see ourselves managing our lives as opposed to worrying about what will happen to us.

Feeling we are in control is incompatible with feeling stress.

Not confronting conflicts is also a major cause of stress. If you feel guilty, for example, you experience the stress of fear that someone will see what you are trying to hide. Or if you tell lies, there is the fear that someone will find out, or knows already and is waiting to get their own back.

Whether or not we experience stress depends upon an attitude of mind. It is not quantifiable. Individuals differ as to what it constitutes – why does one interpret an experience as stressful and another as a welcome challenge? It depends upon our confidence in running our lives the way we choose, that is, that we can cope, not only cope, but retain our feeling of self regard.

People who are enjoying, do not suffer stress.

ILLNESS

There are two views of illness. One is that there is nothing you can do about it – it descends upon you from somewhere outside you or it is genetically programmed, and therefore we cannot help but be victims. The second view is that sickness is a symptom of our suppressed conflicts – therefore we are choosing to be sick.

Even if you find it difficult to accept the second view totally, it is worth asking yourself, if you are sick, whether you have a conflict which is in some way connected with it. Be careful, in this situation, of any inclination to quickly make a 'denial'.

Medical practitioners know that almost all cases they deal with are at least partly, and mostly entirely, psychosomatic. For example, could the fact that you have a 'bad back' in some way suggest that there is an aspect of your life you are not in control of? Again, could the fact that you breathe so shallowly, or that your skin itches, imply that you have a doubt about whether your are acceptable, that is, whether you have significance? And, again, could your depression be connected with doubts about how much people like you?

In his book *Profound Simplicity,* Will Schutz (1979) connects different sicknesses and injuries to different areas of conflict. Thus, the management of the body, particularly the musculature and skeleton, is linked to conflicts of control. Ian Murray (1997), a medical correspondent for *The Times*, reported research from the Arthritis and Rheumatism Council: '… depression was responsible for more back pain than lifting heavy objects. The researchers discovered that *a feeling of not being in control*, and general dissatisfaction, was responsible for one in four of all new cases of lower back pain'. Quoting from research in *The Lancet*, Jeremy Lawrence (1997) reported research from the Department of Public Health at University College, London: 'Findings from one of the most comprehensive studies of the effect of work on health show that workers who have little control over what they do in their jobs are at higher risk of heart attack than their bosses'. Our skin, lungs and digestive system connect us with the world, so that conflicts of significance are experienced in these parts. Our internal organs, especially the heart, are linked with conflict of likeability, that is, how much we are loved and cared for.

Achterberg (1985) made use of Schutz's pioneering insights and brilliantly revealed, in *Imagery and Healing,* that 'Awareness of the effects of our conflicts almost always renders surgery, drugs or other external interventions irrelevant'.

In their book, *The Healing Power of Illness,* Dethlefsen & Dahlke (1990) state, 'Every infection is a conflict that has taken on physical form'. For those who are interested in the meaning of symptoms and how they can be interpreted, this book will prove a great resource, bringing together philosophical, psychological and medical views. It deals with the issue of illness in the most comprehensive way I know and, of course, much more thoroughly than I can do here.

> Illness is both humanity's great opportunity and its most precious commodity. Illness is our personal teacher and guide on the road to wholeness. Various paths to this goal are available to us, most of them difficult and complicated, yet the most obvious and personal of these for the most part goes unheeded and ignored – namely illness. This is the path that is least susceptible to the mirages of self-delusion. That, no doubt, is also why it is also so unpopular.
>
> Dethlefsen and Dahlke, *The Healing Power of Illness*

Goleman (1996) observes, 'This inattention to the emotional reality of illness neglects a growing body of evidence showing that people's emotional states can play a sometimes significant role in their vulnerability to disease and to the course of their recovery. Modern medical care often lacks emotional intelligence'.

How does the conflict come to operate in these ways? You will remember from Chapter 2, 'Resolving conflicts', and from 'Cause of conflict' in this chapter that a conflict arises when there is a discrepancy between a feeling and the thought you want to disown. Thus, 'I can't cope, but I think good leaders should not show it'.

One way of attempting to deal with conflict is to 'bury' it. But, because they are still there, not having been resolved, conflicts affect our behaviour without our being aware of it, so we begin to behave as critics, victims, helpers or demanders.

Another way for us not to deal with the conflict is to 'embody' it. In other words, the suppressed conflict takes the form of our illness. We can choose to say, 'Something has injured me or something has made me ill', or we can say, 'How am I colluding with myself to bring this about?' This question about illness corresponds exactly to how we might choose how much of our behaviour to become aware of. Thus we could choose to say, 'There's nothing we can do, it's the fault of others', or 'How do I benefit from (what am I *really* getting out of) behaving the way I do?' Is your behaviour really a negative gain when you examine it closely?

Yalom (1991) writes of the case of his patient, 'fat lady', who experienced, '... emotional flashbacks... memories... that followed a coherent pattern: as she lost weight she experienced the major traumatic or unresolved events of her life that had occurred when she was at a particular weight'.

A radical way of regarding our illness is to encounter it as an opportunity. This is not a popular way of regarding illness, but when you think about it deeply, you can see that it is the key to understanding yourself better. When you have the key you are able to walk through the door that was poisoning your being. This is the message of the book *Hug the Monster*, by Miln Smith and Leicester (1996). The idea is that our own 'monsters' – our conflicts – are our fears. To deny them is to deny ourself. To learn from them what they desperately try to tell us, converts them from monsters to allies.

In his book *Imagery and Healing,* Achterberg (1985) shows that illness is the ultimate way for us to tell ourself that we refuse to continue the way we are and, that if we do not do something about it, things could get worse. The desire to resolve conflict is so strong that the body itself initiates at the beneath the surface level in the only way it knows how. To respond with, 'Tell me more about how you feel' is the way we gain insight into the negative gain we receive from colluding with ourself in our illness.

> Death from what we do not want is the commonest of all the causes.
> Saul Bellow, *Henderson the Rain King*

WORRY

If you choose to be worried, it may be because, unconsciously, you think others may not regard you, respect you or that they might reject you. So, you look worried to show them how (dutiful, serious, hard working, caring) you are. Your negative gain is that you hope to feel better about yourself by behaving how you think others might expect. Maybe you hope they will feel guilty and like you better when they realize what you suffer on their account. Perhaps you think looking worried conveys the proper, respectful image to show… But it is all illusory; it does not suffice to enable you to feel good about yourself. Then you may begin to worry that they will see through your little 'game'. Eric Berne (1966) has described these ploys in his book, *The Games People Play* (see Chapter 8).

Perhaps you are worried about the future, or what people might think. That gives you a convenient negative gain for not taking any risks today, or for doing nothing at all!

The question to ask is: 'What is my negative gain for behaving to myself this way?' Understanding your negative gain is exactly like understanding your illness – it is necessary to be aware before you are able to make the choice to resolve your conflict.

ANXIETY

It is a strange thing, but the truth is that we choose to be anxious. Of course, this is something we unconsciously choose to do; if we did it consciously, we would be aware of how we are colluding with ourself, and, with awareness, we wouldn't do it. So, what can lead us to be so full of foreboding, so full of anticipation that something will go wrong, that things might get worse, to look on the dark side?

It is the fear we have that people might not like us if we were to be seen to be enjoying ourself. Perhaps we experience a conflict at feeling good about ourself and compensate by feeling guilty that others are less well blessed by fortune. Or, maybe, we are afraid of 'letting ourselves go' because we have been rebuked in our childhood for being silly, irresponsible or uncaring. So we adopt a mood of anxiety in order to head off potential criticism. It is saying, 'You'll like me better or respect me more, if I look suitably grave.'

If an organization loses 10 per cent of its man hours due to stress, absenteeism or sickness (not at all uncommon – some organizations lose 15 per cent or more) this is directly proportional to its lack of awareness of what it is doing to itself. No wonder such organizations appear to lack control and focus!

Part 3
The Enjoyment Process

As human beings, the polarity of our consciousness constantly places us in a situation of conflict, in the field of tension between two possibilities. All the time we have to *de-cide* (literally to 'cut away'), to reject one possibility, if we are ever to realise the other. So it is that we are always lacking something, always un-whole. Happy are those who are able to admit to this constant tension, who are aware of this conflict inherent in human nature, for most of us are inclined to assume that our unawareness of any inner conflicts means that we do not have any.

Dethlefsen & Dahlke, *The Healing Power of Illness*

There are all kinds of reasons why you may not be feeling so good about your work or other areas of your life. Here are just a few of the possible feelings you might have, though there many more: unsettled, listless, confused, bored, irritable, resentful, not understood, powerless, tired, cheated, annoyed, unimportant, silly, pathetic, uncared for.

There are millions of feelings which all of us share. They are unique to you only because of your own situation, history and personality. But because all human beings share the same potential for feeling, we are all capable of understanding each other. Sometimes you may think you are alone, but you never are; we are all participants in a web of identical emotions. When you realize this, you begin to perceive what a wonderful opportunity this shared experience gives to us to understand ourselves with and through each other.

How can you then understand yourself better and then progress with your being? Maybe you think that what has happened to you is so different from anybody else's experience that nobody will be able to help. Maybe you think something even worse: that you cannot even help yourself. Perhaps that is why, when people ask you, 'What's the matter?' you reply, 'I don't really know', or 'It's nothing important really,' or 'You wouldn't understand.' Perhaps you are having an internal debate with yourself, asking yourself the same question: 'What's the matter with me?'

What you are doing is hiding from yourself, stopping yourself from becoming aware. You deny there is a problem out of fear that being honest with yourself may bring issues to the surface that you will not be able to cope with. So you believe it's better to 'let sleeping dogs lie', or that these things are best 'swept under the carpet'. Who are you trying to convince?

Unfortunately, when issues of conflict are buried, they don't go away. We may think they are forgotten, but the reality is that they remain in the unaware part of our mind, where they continue to plague us. Until they are dealt with, they cause us to act in ways we don't like.

For example, we are not aware why we 'bite people's heads off', become so hard to please, sarcastic, judgmental or self righteously overbearing. It is defensive behaviour, designed without awareness to take attention from us and project it onto others. It never seems satisfying to resort to anger or irritation, even though we seem to score off people in the short term.

In the longer term such behaviour leaves us feeling regretful, unsatisfied, incomplete. We don't like 'acting out of character' and hate ourselves the worst for being out of control. We may curse our fate that we were 'born this way'.

There is nothing genetic in this; the truth is that our, supposedly, buried conflicts are influencing us in ways we are unaware of. We don't like being tired, irritable, powerless or any of those millions of feelings that make us unhappy. But we pretend that it has nothing to do with us. We would prefer to be able to absolve ourselves from responsibility, as though our state of mind and body is caused by something that through pure chance has just happened to descend upon us from out of the air. As long as we collude with ourself in this, we can try to convince ourself that there is nothing we can do about it, that if we remain passive our problems too will disappear. In effect, we are in the state of unawareness which is called denial. Denial is the defence we use to be a 'helper' to ourselves – helping ourselves to remain unaware.

There is an alternative way to be. And starting is simple. It is only the desire to take control of what happens to us. It is to accept that, 'If the way I feel is determined by me, then, I am the best person to do something about it'.

Determining your own life is made easier by realizing that, although unique, you share the same feelings as everybody else. And although the range of feeling is infinite, it is possible to make sense of what we experience so that we do not allow ourselves to be victims of our emotions, but to take charge of them.

All our human feelings, fears and states of mind are structured in a logical way. We can therefore understand them and, understanding them, go on to do something about them. Understanding or, if you like, awareness, must precede action, otherwise you will go heading off trying out all sorts of behaviours which may not enable you to make your bad feelings good ones. Often people who act without awareness appear to 'put their foot in it', have a 'big mouth' or behave 'like a bull in a china shop'.

Quite simply, if you are not feeling good about yourself, there is some part of your life you are not coping with successfully. You probably know what it is, although you may try to 'put it out of your mind'.

All right, the truth is that you are not coping. If you can be honest with yourself you are already making progress, because you are already taking responsibility; in effect, you are saying, '*I* am responsible', instead of trying to believe that somebody else or some circumstance is doing something to you which you have no control over. If you wait for other people to make things better, or for the situation to change, you may wait forever.

Thinking you are unable to cope must be for one or all of three areas of feeling. Will Schutz (1994) has shown that everything we feel relates to these three, so that if we understand them we can understand any aspect of the infinite range of emotion. Schutz's profound, practical work on the three dimensions of feeling shows us how to take control and alter the mechanisms which can help us to run our lives in the way we want.

Amazingly, all our experiences of not feeling good about ourselves, that is the same meaning as 'not coping', are related to the three dimensions. As there are only three – and this is the psychological structure you share with the rest of us – it makes it much easier to understand feelings than you might have ever thought possible.

COPING WITH BEING IGNORED

'I'm not significant enough.'

One way of attempting to cope is to be pushy or intrusive. That would be an 'over' compensation. The opposite of the same coin is to withdraw. That would be avoidance. To cope successfully, you decide to include yourself when *you* want to. You do not make your actions conditional upon what others might think of you. Furthermore, if you want to include people, you will include people first rather than wait for them to come to you. Instead of wondering whether you are important to people, you will ask them if they want to be with you or want to have you with them. Their answer at least lets you know where you stand; instead of fearing the worst, you can focus elsewhere on the basis of what you hear from them.

COPING WITH REJECTION

'I'm not likeable enough.'

You decide that it is up to you to initiate openness. If you don't try, you'll never know. Maybe the other person is rejecting you because they fear you are rejecting them. The irony is that you are both waiting for each other. Remember, the law of reciprocal psychology states that your conflict is also shared by them! It is up to you to explore, by revealing what is in your own heart. What is the worst that can happen? A rejection is no worse than what you are experiencing already – the fear of being rejected. And if things really are as bad as you fear, at least you have an objective basis to change your situation.

COPING WITH HUMILIATION

'I'm not capable enough.'

Act in ways which will allow you to apply yourself competently and effectively so that you change things to the way you want. What you imagine yourself capable of doing, you can do, otherwise you could not imagine it. The self you can imagine is the real you, so not choosing to be the way you know you can is letting yourself down. In short, you remain unfulfilled. You must get the right balance here. You should not attempt too much all at once because this is also incompetent if it unnecessarily causes failure. Nor should your actions be understated, for fear they appear unconvincing and not powerful enough for it to be clear what you are doing.

Sometimes we avoid demonstrating our capability because we fear others may be hurt, or because they won't like us that way. These kinds of thought are usually excuses from which we obtain only negative gains, thus copping out of doing what we really want, but are afraid of doing. If you do what is right for you, it is impossible to hurt anybody in the process. They are more likely to be pleased that you are being more yourself.

Being yourself enables them too – the clearer you are about yourself, the easier you make it for them to be clear about themselves.

Hurting anybody else is incompatible with being yourself.

THE TURNING POINT

It is easier to make the changes you want once you are aware of what you get out of being the way you are. This is called the 'negative gain'. It is what we give ourselves for unconsciously **not** choosing to be or do what we want out of fear of failing.

A negative gain provides a temporary compensation – a kind of second best – for finding an excuse **not** to do what we want to do, because our fear prevents us. Negative gains are false friends, because they seem to make us feel better in the short term, but turn out to be a sham as we realise we are failing to make things better for ourself.

We even feel worse when we keep on using the same old mechanisms of avoidance. Negative gains are different from 'rewards' where we have chosen to be or do what we want. Examining some typical negative gains should make the concept clear (see also Chapter 8).

At first it seems strange that we get any benefit from being sick or from not feeling good about ourselves, or from telling ourselves we can't cope. All these things we are choosing to be, but, of course, do not really want. That is because we are choosing them unconsciously.

A moment's thought shows us that when we are sick, people tell us they miss us for not being there with them; their concern tells us that we really are important, after all, though it is a pity we had to be sick in order to find out. If we don't feel good about ourself, then we don't feel that we are letting ourselves down when we fail. By not coping, other people begin to cope for us, which relieves us of the responsibility.

Understanding our negative gains for not being the way we really want to be brings our fears of being ourself into perspective. It is the point of awareness where we say, 'Do we go on and do something with our awareness, or do our hearts fail us and we turn back?'

At this point, if we fail to use our newly gained awareness and the energy it provides, we experience once again the feeling of letting ourselves down. For example, we reinforce our fear that we are not competent. Feeling bad about ourselves once more, we find it easier to blame others or circumstances for our predicament. Inevitably, relationships turn sour and life seems to be so much of a ramp.

On the other hand, we might use our imagination...

IMAGINATION

There is a gap between our imaginative potential and what we are achieving, therefore we do not enjoy ourselves to the fullest extent. In other words, we make ourselves miserable because we know that we have another way we could be. It is not trusting ourselves to act upon our imagination that is the problem.

The process through which conflict is resolved is a task which is, of itself, enjoyable. The growth in awareness, which is a discovery of the self, is a state described by Will Schutz (1967) in his book *Joy*.

Whatever you can imagine yourself being and doing is the real you, otherwise you could not imagine it.

Tap into your imagination. Don't underestimate its power. Allow yourself to be guided by it – you cannot go wrong! There is only one danger, and that is that you don't trust yourself fully.

Trust follows on from awareness. It would be naive to trust ourself if we have no awareness of our competence. For example, it would be silly to think we could fly when we do not yet know how! Therefore, make small steps which successfully increase your trust in your competence; too big a step may be self defeating.

Out of fear that you cannot trust yourself, you might hold back and do nothing at all. You fear you won't achieve, before even getting to the first hurdle. So, it is not surprising when you fail to make it past the first post. Lacking experience, you almost expect to fail. And if you do, you can pick up the old comforts and certainties, telling yourself, 'See, I knew I would never be able to do that, I'm not that sort of person.' But it doesn't feel comforting for very long, does it? The truth is, you *are* that sort of person you imagine – and you let yourself down.

Telling people about your conflicts will engage them and bring them close to you. It would be inappropriate (intrusive) to include those who were not affected with you in the situation or had no interest in you, but otherwise, you will overcome your fear of rejection if you simply tell people what is in your mind.

It is because we so much fear rejection that we make excuses, saying, 'They wouldn't be interested,' or, 'It would only hurt them,' when it is our own fears we are trying to protect ourselves from.

It is tempting to protect children, although this is really a way of protecting ourselves from having to deal with their reaction. Children feel more secure when they know what is going on than when you have, so you think, shielded them from the truth of what is going on.

Feelings are just the same in 'grownups'.

CONFIDENCE

Have confidence in yourself; what you can imagine being, you are; what you see yourself doing, you can. Sometimes you might feel you should hold back, and are unnecessarily hesitant because you anticipate that being yourself may have the effect of upsetting others.

Or, you fear that they may feel 'put down' by you. Actually, you are trying to avoid people not liking you by not being yourself. It is as though your negative gain is, 'I won't show them the "real" me so if they reject me it won't be me they are rejecting'. In this case, your behaviour is a 'hostage to fortune' – you are making a decision on their behalf as if you were them, anticipating rejection where there is none. You are acting 'as if...'

SUMMARY

Our aim in every aspect of our lives, at home, socially and at work, is to enjoy. This is nothing about which we are ashamed since, when enjoying, we are most effective. The process of reverse feedback expands our awareness and releases the joy which we hold back from fear of being ourselves. Enjoyment consists of being one's whole self. Wholeness means the same as wellness. To deny oneself also denies the organization. It is impossible to complete the task when there is denial. Thus, the organization is fulfilled when we are enjoying.

Optional exercises

The purpose of these exercises is to create an awareness of negative thoughts and feelings as the first, necessary, step to changing them in order to be fully yourself. Whatever negative feelings exist are the ones which hold you back. This part is thinking at the surface level. Do not evaluate your feelings at this stage as this is better done later.

Having admitted the existence of feelings you don't like, it is best to write them down in the space provided. This ensures they do not slip away if you collude with yourself to allow your attention to wander.

The next stage is to relate your negative feelings precisely to what was done to make you feel the way you do.

From here, you can gain insight into your conflict: that what has been done is incompatible with feelings of regard, respect and warmth.

Finally, you can choose to initiate your conflict at the beneath the surface level with the person with whom you share this situation. Notes to guide you follow the exercises, though if you have read about reverse feedback in Chapter 2 you will have already have had some practice.

Exercises – coping with fears and feelings

1. 'I'm not important enough.'
2. 'I'm not likeable enough.'
3. 'I'm not capable enough.'

You are asked to consider your own feelings in relation to other people and to yourself. Examples are provided for you, but there is additional space for you to add any other feelings if you want. It is useful if you are able to add your own words as these will be most meaningful for you. Try not to process out, for example, telling yourself, 'I don't really mean that,' or 'It's not suitable.' Whatever comes into your head is right.

Then, ask yourself the questions which are below. They are grouped into the three areas of feeling. Think about each statement separately and ponder upon them slowly.

Give yourself a score in relation to each statement on a scale from 0–9. 9 means you agree totally with the statement, 0 means not at all, and 5 is about average for you.

What is wanted is for you to become aware of even a slight feeling about the statement, even though you do not think it is always or generally true for you. The fact that you can identify with the statement *to some extent* is sufficient evidence. A tendency to rush on might indicate that this is an area you unconsciously want to avoid. So, this is where you really ought to stop and pay more attention.

At this point, bring to mind your own words which describe you in the way you are not as fulfilled with yourself as you would like to be.

As you do this, experience why you are not feeling so good. You will find that there is some way in which you can identify with at least one of the areas. You may have no difficulty in identifying with all of them.

1. Score each statement in a way that reflects your own feeling.

	0–9
I am feeling left out	_____
It does not matter whether I am here or not	_____
People don't want me with them	_____
People will not leave me alone	_____
I am intruding	_____
I am not regarded	_____
I am taken for granted	_____
There is no time for me	_____
I am not considered	_____
I am ignored	_____
I am not acceptable	_____

All these areas have to do with feelings of low significance and with fears that you are in some way being ignored. Think of any other ways in which you feel that you are not significant or with fears you have that you are being ignored. Use your own words that are most meaningful to you and best describe the way you feel.

_____

_____ _____

_____ _____

_____ _____

What, precisely, has happened to make you feel this way? Try to move on from the feeling to remember and experience the situation that is causing the feelings. All our feelings are the result of something that has been done to us or something we believe has been done to us. Sometimes feelings also arise because people do not do what we want them to.

Write down what you do or others do to make you feel the way you do:

_____

_____

_____

2. Score each statement in a way that reflects your own feeling

0–9

I am not cared about	_____
I am unloved	_____
People say I do not talk about myself	_____
People don't confide in me	_____
Other people are liked more than me	_____
Someone has found someone else or something else they like more than me	_____

I can't be honest with the person I most want to understand me _____

People want an affection I cannot give _____

I am afraid that the relationship may go bad if they get to know
me too well _____

I feel hurt because our relationship is not close _____

I cannot talk about what would make me happy _____

People would not be interested in the way I feel _____

People say they do not know what I am thinking _____

All these areas have to do with feelings of not being liked (feeling that you are not loved is also part of this) and the fear that you are in some way rejected. Think of any other ways in which you feel that you are being shut out or ways in which you are closed to others. Use your own words that are most meaningful to you to describe the way you feel.

_____ _____

_____ _____

_____ _____

What, precisely, has happened to make you feel this way? Try to move on from the feeling to remember and experience the situation that is causing the feelings. All our feelings are the result of something that has been done to us or something we believe has been done to us. Sometimes feelings also arise from what people do not do that we want them to.

Write down what you do or others do to make you feel the way you do:

_____

_____

_____

3. Score each statement in a way that reflects your own feeling.

0–9

Things are not happening in the way I want _____

I am too controlling _____

People do not trust me _____

I do not trust people _____

I do not feel dignified _____

Someone has 'scored a point' off me _____

People have unrealistically high expectations of me _____

I am afraid to let go _____

I am not doing what I want _____

I am not using myself effectively _____

I feel foolish _____

I am not achieving _____

I am a failure _____

I intimidate people _____

All these states are examples of feeling that you are not capable, that you are not doing a competent job with your life and fear that you might be humiliated. Think of any other ways in which your feelings are reflected in these ways. Use your own words that are most meaningful to you.

_____

_____ _____

_____ _____

_____ _____

All our feelings are the result of something that has been done to us or something we believe has been done to us. Sometimes feelings also arise from when people do not do what we want them to do. What has been done or what do you fear might be done? What are the circumstances of the people who you feel are stopping you determine your own life. Why are you allowing them to do this to you?

Write down what you do or others do to make you feel the way you do:

_____

_____

_____

_____

You might be feeling bad about yourself in one or perhaps all three of these areas. Having brought to your consciousness those things that make you feel unhappy, acknowledging that it is your responsibility to do something about it, if you want to, is the first step in taking control of your life. Without having taken any action, you will already feel stronger and more self assured from the consequence of having accepted the fact of choice, or self reliance.

With this understanding, you may not have to do anything – awareness may be sufficient. Probably, you can see ways to stop the behaviours you do that lead to situations in which you do not feel good about yourself. Reverse feedback is generally the next best step. Here are some suggestions about how you might take it from here:

Initiate with the person in the situation what I think they feel about me.

Ask the other person if they feel about themselves the way I feel about me.

Change my behaviour to them so they feel significant, likeable and capable.

Recognize my 'negative gain' for using a 'defence'.

Do for myself what I have been demanding they do.

Initiating the issues with another person who is willing to listen, whether or not they are connected with the issue, will provide you with more insight and enable you. To the extent you do not feel comfortable initiating with another person, this is itself a conflict which is worth engaging.

The thoughts and feelings that may have emerged from the exercises above may have echoes with some you may have identified already in the previous chapter. They may emerge again during later exercises as you explore further beneath the surface.

4

Winning Teams

We do not see people as they are. We see them as we are.

Corruption of a Talmudic saying

INTRODUCTION

Are you with the people you want to be with? If not, why?

These are essential questions for any member of any team, let alone the most senior person. They focus upon the significance of your relationship to them. You will have difficulties if people suspect they are not significant to you – they will begin to ask themselves if they would be more appreciated somewhere else. Unconsciously, the question is: how much do you want to bother about each other, since you may not feel significant to each other anyway?

This is also the essential question for two people who wish to marry, for job selection and team building, as well as for company mergers and acquisitions.

The best thing is if you can view your colleagues, or any person whom you are joining in any kind of endeavour, as giving you a chance to fulfil yourself with and through them. This stance immediately creates feelings of regard, respect and warmth which will be instantly reciprocated. You can tell people that you want to be with them and you should really mean what you say.

It is surprising how often we put off telling people about feelings that they are desperate to hear about. Perhaps we feel embarrassed, because of our lack of experience in expressing ourself, so we make an excuse, telling ourselves, 'I think they know they're important, they don't expect me to tell them, so I don't need to bother.'

There is no way out of this – these things have to be said; however much you think they know, they may have some doubt. Telling them certainly won't hurt, and if they know already, it is pleasant to have it confirmed, and at the very least, it prevents doubt arising, so nothing is lost. But if they have a doubt, then your silence magnifies the doubt many times. As a consequence, you may wonder why they are so bad tempered or are avoiding you. The mechanism is that because they don't think you want to be with them, they defend themselves by avoiding you back.

If you have doubts about your own significance to them or them to you, it's better to confront the issue with them. Use the method of reverse feedback to initiate your conflict, in this instance, possible conflict, described in Chapter 2.

In truth, the issue is there. Both of you are aware of it, and will probably do your best to avoid dealing with it by withholding. You might tell yourself that perhaps they are not as bad as you fear and that they'll get better. Or you'll just put up with it and you make the excuse that, 'It is unavoidable to have to work with people you don't rate'.

This chapter shows how well you can work with everybody, whatever the apparent, surface incompatibility. Therefore, how to understand and overcome the defences we use forms the major part of this chapter.

TEAM BUILDING

There are some teams, as in a marriage, where we may suppose the partner is selected as the part of a truly free choice! Organization teams seldom form in the same way unless they are 'start up' organizations. It is more likely that the people who form the team are there already – perhaps not the people you necessarily would have chosen. It is the roles that determine who works together, not necessarily the feelings of the people, although this may change over time.

Whatever your feelings about people at the outset, you must believe that they are significant to you if you are to build a productive team. As close colleagues whose job touches yours, the sooner they realize their significance to you the better. Communicating your feeling of their significance will be reflected back by them to you.

It is good to have the regard of your colleagues. You find pleasure in experiencing how pleased people are to have you included with them. And this is all because of what you started!

Regarding each other for the significant effect they are going to have in our lives, perceiving them as giving us an opportunity to increase that regard, eliminates any fears of being diminished or left out, and creates an atmosphere which motivates us to work together.

Example

Above the surface	+	'It's great to be with you' or, alternatively,
	–	'I wouldn't have chosen you and I don't think you would have chosen me.'
Behaviour	+	'You do important things. You have a presence I admire. Being with you elevates my sense of significance.' or, alternatively,
	–	'In the past, you have indicated you do not want to be with me.' 'You indicate that you should be above me.' 'You don't talk to me unless you have to because it is a business matter.'
Beneath the surface (using reverse feedback)	+	'I think you feel the same way I do – I couldn't have chosen anyone better to be with.' or, alternatively,
	–	'I think you feel you would rather not be with me.' 'I think you might feel that I have got in your way.' 'I think you feel I'm not important to you.'

It is essential for there to be a common perception of the feelings people have about each other. Any misperception causes conflict, so that neither achieves what they want from the situation.

To the extent that people are in a group where there are members who feel they are being tolerated or feel they have to tolerate others, the group is lifeless, lacking dynamism. The energy that is contained produces lacklustre performance. In this situation, energy is wasted upon dealing with the conflicts which arise from self doubt. Energy is better released for exploration and creativity, and to building a powerful, motivated team.

The psychological issue is: if you do not feel significant, it is difficult to perceive your impact and develop your self regard.

If you are not seen as significant, you may never get to be known better; people will never find out how competent you can be or how likeable you really are. It is as though the window through which you are perceived is too small so that your greater potential remains out of sight.

If your competence is in doubt, why should you be trusted? Trust is impossible without the assurance that, first, people feel you are significant to them, and, second, that people feel that you will be competent in your treatment of them. We are not talking about technical competence here, we are talking about how competently you relate to others and enable them to deal with their feelings which arise in your relationship with them.

The objective is to communicate that the other person is going to make you feel you are in the best team!

TEAM MAINTENANCE

Maintenance involves the confrontation of any doubt as and when it arises. Even better, confronting it as a possibility before it arises.

No matter is too small. Though it may be distorted or be less strong than their own perception, what thoughts and feelings are yours are in some way a reflection of theirs. If a thought or feeling enters your head as a doubt, conflict or issue with someone, and you are telling yourself it is not worth bothering with, it is the very thing you *should* bother with. The fact that you are asking yourself whether you should be bothering is proof that you are attempting to find a negative gain for avoiding. You ignore the impulse to initiate at your peril. This almost always means being open with the other person about your conflict.

It is as well to remember that psychology is reciprocal: if a doubt has entered your head, it has entered theirs as well.

At such moments, it is all too easy to do nothing, to find excuses: 'Oh, it's not important,' or 'I'm being silly,' or 'This is going to be too blunt, he or she might be hurt.' These only lead to negative gains, because the conflict remains unresolved.

These are all defences manufactured instantly and, sadly, almost predictably, to help you to avoid doing something that it is difficult – difficult for you, not necessarily difficult for the other person.

But remember what is happening at this moment – other people are also aware, even if it is only partly aware, of the same issue that is on your mind. Unless you deal with it, the issue will be passed by and ignored, but it won't go away. It continues to exist in the unconscious. Festering, it causes resentments and fears that manifest themselves later. It is a matter that has not been addressed and not completed upon. The best time to confront issues is at the time; completing frees up energy to get on with the next task.

This is the most essential task of the total leader. How do you do it? You say something along the lines of, 'Please, can you stop? I cannot attend fully to what is happening because I have something on my mind that bothers me. It's a conflict because I don't want to hold you up and waste your time, but I do not feel I am being effective.'

When people know that there is something that is so important to you that you want to communicate to them before anything else, you have their attention. Now, you will undersell yourself and lose them unless you tell them what the conflict is.

Initiating beneath the surface is the most exciting behaviour you can do. It gets people present with you immediately.

Establishing the conflict is the important thing. Conflict arises between a thought and feeling, such as, 'I think that the fact that I'm here means I should be adding something, but I don't feel I am.'

Engaging colleagues with the conflict is the quickest and easiest way (a) to resolve it and (b) to show yourself how you can contribute in a way that is motivating for you and for others. Note the use of the word engage – it means that you are dealing with each other because of your mutual significance.

Remember, your responsibility to yourself and to them is to contribute. The task is to discover the extent to which the situation is not fulfilling you. At this moment, your conflict is inhibiting the progress of the task. Therefore, this is the most important matter to be addressed. It might be put like this:

Example

In relation to feeling ignored

Above the surface	What you might think but 'withhold' 'You only want to listen to yourself.' 'You take advantage of people.' 'You never support me, I always support you.' 'You irritate me.' 'You infuriate me.' because …
Behaviour	'When I began to tell you about something that was important to me, you changed the subject and talked about yourself.' 'You dump your problems onto me.' 'You want to be included in my meetings, you don't tell me about yours.'

	'You leave me out.'
	'You keep me waiting.'
Beneath the surface	What I initiate
	'I think you feel I'm not significant,' or, 'I feel ignored.'

In relation to feeling rejected

Above the surface	What you might think but 'withhold'
	'You are too businesslike.'
	'You have no feelings.'
	'I hate you.'
	because…
Behaviour	'When I ask you about yourself, you lead the conversation to what you have done, or where you have been. You don't answer my question.'
	'You never ask me how I feel about what you do.'
	'When I try to tell you about something that is on my mind you say that you'll find time later on or that you're too tired.'
Beneath the surface	What I inititate
	'I think you don't like me.'
	'I think you feel I don't like you.'
	'I feel you want to shut me out,' or, 'I feel rejected.'

In relation to the feeling of humiliation

Above the surface	What you might think but 'withhold'
	'You are off the point.'
	'You are talking above my head.'
	'You annoy me.'
	because…
Behaviour	'You did not listen to my suggestion.'
	'Your use of technical language leaves me out.'
	'You assume I don't understand.'
Beneath the surface	What I initiate
	'I feel I'm not being effective.'
	'I think you feel I cannot make a contribution.'
	'I think you feel I am incompetent,' or, 'I'm feeling humiliated.'

By this time, you'll have nods of agreement to carry on. Note that you are in total control. Instead of feeling weak and vulnerable, you are absolutely in charge.

When you say what is on your mind, saying what your own experience is, notice how others attend. The atmosphere is alive. Everyone is present. Some will say, 'I was thinking the same thing,' or 'That's right, we've got to clear this up before we go on.'

What you have done by your behaviour is to indicate to everyone that they are important enough to you for you to want to include them in something that really matters to you, that they have the competence to help you find a solution, and that you like them enough to be open with something that is difficult and risky for yourself. You have engaged them in all three areas of feeling. They cannot fail to be motivated by someone who is making them feel the way they want to feel about their self.

That is total leadership. You have confronted the block that the group was prepared to ignore. It is the most *real* of all of the issues that the group has to deal with. They come closer as a result. A feeling emerges that we as a group can deal with any issue. We trust each other to help each other out, even with matters that are risky and personally difficult. What a great group to be in!

THE LAW OF RECIPROCITY

The nature of our psychology is that it is reciprocal. We talk about individual psychology as though we were islands, but we are not. We are all enmeshed in an emotional web, much closer than we ever thought.

The law of reciprocity states that my perception of you is also, in some way, a reflection of me. The only addendum to this law is that my perception of you is either true or its opposite is true. That everything is itself or its opposite is also a psychological law. I'm not sure yet that it's a universal one. For example, and to leave psychology and enter philosophy for a moment, if I maintain that no such thing as God exists, am I saying that this means that God does exist. It may be that if I can imagine that God exists, I have the power to make him exist (if that is not blasphemous) otherwise I could not imagine him.

We make a mistake in supposing that imagination is different from reality, or that our emotional experience is different from someone else's. This polarization of our thinking is the way in which we attempt to make sense of our world. But no one thing exists by itself; it can only exist as the other half of an opposite: one thing is only ever the 'opposite side of the same coin'. When we reconcile apparent differences or opposites, within ourselves or within our relationships, we experience the triumph of our endeavour in unity.

Human beings have always found that what they imagine turns out to be true. It is because it has always been there already, it only needed to be found! However, metaphysics is not the subject of this book. It is enough to understand that the law of reciprocity works, unfailingly.

What homo sapiens imagines, he may slowly convert himself to.

Saul Bellow, *Henderson the Rain King*

It works this way. As you can understand others only to the extent that you understand yourself, your perception of others must include a part of you that is true, whether you are consciously aware of it or not. Thus, if you say someone is a fool, it is because you recognize the other in the part of yourself that is also capable of being foolish.

You are revolted by the murderer or the psychopath because such people actualize the destructive thoughts you also have, but do not act upon. It is having acted upon those thoughts that makes those people different from ourself. We lock such people away because they have no control between the thought and the deed. Their punishment may also serve to remind us that the 'id', that dark, uncontrolled energy, must be guided and monitored by the civilizing effect of the 'super ego'. We would want ourselves to be locked up too, in order to prevent ourself doing those things we might fear doing if we were out of control.

Our day to day conflicts are less extreme in that they do not lead to physical expression, but nevertheless are destructive of the quality of our lives and our capacity to deal with our situation.

The law of reciprocity means that what I perceive you to have done to have created my conflict is in some way a reflection of a defence I am employing. Your perception of me also contains your defence. Thus, if I make you aware of my conflict, I shall also make you aware of yours. This is why the listener discovers that he has as much to learn from the exchange at the beneath the surface level as the initiator.

The roles become reversed as the listener and the initiator become aware that what they thought was dividing them is revealing what they have in common. What they thought to be their differences is really what they share, but were not aware that they did.

When you deal with your conflict, you also deal with the other person's. This is what brings people closer and builds a feeling of identification and empathy. An example is given below when discussing projection.

PROJECTION

Can you be certain that what you are thinking and feeling is also what others are thinking and feeling? It sounds a risky assumption to make!

Suppose they say that what I think is on their mind isn't? Maybe it is, but they deny it, or maybe, not being aware, they don't know it is on their mind yet. Or maybe, it is you who are not aware. In which case you are projecting a feeling onto them that is all you, but nothing of them. This is something that happens very rarely, and may not ever have happened. Usually there is some shared experience, even if it is in the ratio 95 per cent you and five per cent them.

This is a bit 'by the way', but the only situations where I can see there are entirely 'false' projections are in cases of abnormal, clinical psychology – for example, the schizophrenic who imagines that someone is trying to kill him, the rapist who thinks that someone really wants to be raped, the child abductor who feels that they are doing what is best for the child. These are interpretations of a desire to be loved, which is natural to everyone, into a hideously distorted defence mechanism in which the abuse of another person is insanely justified. In clinical situations in which feelings are so aberrant, the normal boundaries in which we check out our perception of what others want from us have been overruled; the murderer does not ask us if that is what we want, nor does the rapist, they assume that what they want is what another person wants too. Their belief in their omniscience is madness. We recognize these instances as gross projections and deal with them accordingly, protecting ourselves from them with therapy or internment.

But, in our normal day to day lives we are not dealing with these issues and the law of reciprocity implies no disadvantage or exploitation of anyone – it just 'is'. How we use that awareness determines the extent to which we discover the situation that exists between us.

The law of reciprocity leads us to question how much of ourself we are projecting on to others. In other words, to what extent is what you think or feel about another person a reflection of what you think and feel about yourself. If it is a projection it is a part of you that you would rather think was the other person than yourself. So, to some extent, you may be trying to blame the other person for feelings you do not want to be aware are also within yourself.

The safest assumption to make is that, in some way, you are perceiving the other person as a reflection of yourself. If both want to become aware of why and how this happens, reverse feedback enables you to resolve misperceptions that have been causing you to doubt yourselves and each other.

A note on how we reflect the feelings of others – remember that a projection is an aspect of yourself you dislike on to someone else. You perceive them as unlikeable? They will perceive in you something that is unlikeable. They will think that you do not like them. You will realise that they do not like what they perceive in you. You think they do not like you. This all starts because you do not like yourself. Therefore, as you are an emotional mirror, you had better start reflecting the aspects of yourself you do like!

In the meantime, your job is with your awareness. To become more aware of yourself, that is, to become aware of the defences you may be using, it is helpful to start off with how you feel about the other person. Then to proceed deeper until you discover how your feeling about the other person is really about yourself. Then, you may try to resolve the doubt you have with yourself, by asking the other person to give you feedback in order that you can be clearer about yourself.

Perhaps it may be that you can be clear about yourself, without the other person's assistance, once you have become aware. In this case, you will have become aware that what you attributed to the other person was entirely you. However, since it is extremely unlikely to have been entirely you – be careful you do not collude with yourself to avoid the issue. It is wise to complete a discussion at the beneath the surface level with the other person, if only to make sure.

The following examples are derivations of a diagram by Will Schutz (1994) called perceptual accuracy. A full explanation is to be found on page 91 of *The Human Element* (Schutz, 1994).

Example

(Note: whenever 'projection' is used, it is equally possible to use the other defences)

Your perception

You _____Other person

1 per cent   100 per cent

How much is the other person, how much a projection?

Naturally, it is impossible to quantify in terms of exact percentages how much is me and how much is you. The point is made only to show that even if our feelings did represent widely different proportions, the power of the perception still includes us. Also, it is often the case that someone in this relationship who feels they are involved very slightly discovers they are much more involved than they ever thought, once they become aware. In other words, denial can be a very powerful mechanism, hiding much more beneath the surface.

How much is projection? How much are you seeing the other person clearly? Even if only one per cent of your perception of them is a projection, that is, a reflection or distortion of you on to them, it is the only part you can deal with. It is no good saying, 'You are mostly to blame.' Although that may be true, there is no possible way to quantitatively judge such matters. In any case, they may not want to deal with the unaware part of them that you perceive.

Suppose you perceive they are confused and the truth is that they are hopelessly confused almost always, whereas you are rarely confused. In this case, you are perceiving in them the very small part of yourself that is also you. Thus, your perception of them reveals to you a part of yourself you are rarely aware of, perhaps because you do not like it. This may explain why you feel anger, because they remind you of an aspect of yourself you would prefer not to be aware of. Because you do not like to feel confused, you may want to deny that you are confused at all, and that, therefore, it is all 100 per cent their fault. Saying it is mostly their fault, even though it may be true, is also a defence. In this instance, the defence is displacement or being a 'critic'.

Example

Your perception: 'You are confused.' (displacement)

You _____... (truth)... _____Other person
1 per cent   100 per cent

Then, use the model for resolving conflict – reverse feedback – in which you initiate beneath the surface level:

The route to awareness

You	The other person
Surface level	
What you think about them	'You are confused.'
What you feel about them	Example: 'Irritated'… because…
Behaviour	
What you do to make me feel this way	'You lose things of mine.'
Beneath the surface	
What you must feel about me	'I don't think you care.' (If you cared, you'd take care of things which are important to me.)
Insight: What I fear about myself	'I do not like to feel I may be unimportant, it does not make me feel good about myself, it makes me doubt my significance and self worth.'
Insight: How I unknowingly bring the situation about	'I am blaming you for the way you make me feel. It is the way I feel that is important, not the fact that you are confused – you may like being confused!'

The next stage is either to organize your life so that you are not affected by their confusion – you stop lending them things or in other ways do not prevent your own desire to be efficient by allowing yourself to be dependent upon them. You recognize that the two of you have goals which are different, and you get nowhere by blaming the other because their goals are not yours.

Maybe you also have to be aware that the reason you lend the other person things is because you fear that they won't like you if you don't. This gives you another issue with yourself to become aware of, otherwise you may continue with behaving in a way to them, in this example lending things, which ultimately makes you irritated with them.

The truth is that you lend things to them because you want to be liked and you experience rejection when the fact that they lose the things you lend communicates to you that they don't place as much significance on what you do for them as you do. That is, they don't care for you as much as you care for them. You can stop allowing yourself to be a victim, by being aware why you might want to be (see 'Rewards and negative gains', Chapter 8).

Small, apparently trivial incidents often release large emotions. It's not just a pencil of yours they lost, it's not just that their appointment with you slipped their mind – it's symbolic about how you feel about each other. The power of such minute incidents or gestures is to threaten everything else there is in the relationship. Unfortunately, as the result of a small word uttered without awareness, people never talk to each other again, walking out on their relationship. Cabinet members resign for similarly trivial incidents. And, unconsciously, we go to war.

Example

'Beneath the surface' dialogue

Initiator	Listener
You	The other person
Beneath the surface	
My conflict: 'I feel that I am unimportant to you.'	'Don't be silly, of course, you're important.'
Don't be diverted, stick to your feelings: 'You may say that, but the things you do make me feel that I'm not important, really.'	'Is it something I've done? I'm sure I didn't mean to do anything to hurt you. Tell me more.'
'You lose and mislay things that are essential to me, but you don't seem to care.'	'I should have told you how grateful I am that you let me share things.'
'I suppose that when you lose things of mine, I think you don't care. I've taken the trouble to lend you something and it's irritating when it's not returned.'	'I do care. The fact that you go out of your way, I suppose it makes me feel I'm important to you.'
'I think I care about you because I take trouble, but you don't. You don't even apologize.'	'I suppose I hope that if I say nothing you may not notice. That's a strange thought – maybe I lose things deliberately. Perhaps I'm trying to pretend it doesn't matter.'
'Tell me more about why you would want to "deliberately" forget?'	'Perhaps I see it as a way of getting from you an acknowledgement that I matter.'
'So, what you're saying is, that I matter more than I thought; what	'I should learn to know you value me without expecting tokens of it. I

I thought was not caring for me, was actually caring about me.'

'Also maybe I use gifts as a way of getting affection. From the time I was a child, I always doubted people cared about me. I used to take sweets into school and give them to friends – emotional bribery, probably. I suppose I also realize that I have to care for myself, not do things to others which I think will prove that I am worth caring for. Deep down, I've never been sure that I am likeable person.'

suppose being confused and losing things is a way of not taking responsibility. I want to be able to say "I care" without making a test of it.'

'If I do lose something of yours, I should recognize the significance it has. But I don't think I will be losing anything of yours in future!
It's strange what you say about yourself, because nobody gave me anything when I was a child. My feelings are really the same, I should learn that I am worthy of affection, not expect other people to make me feel good about myself.'

It may be thought that this dialogue is somewhat 'ideal'. What happens in a 'real, live' situation where the other person may not be so willing? If you do not allow yourself to be diverted and stick to your feelings, it very rare indeed for the other person not to respond. Remember that reciprocal psychology states that they are responding to the part of you that they perceive in themselves. So, in engaging your issue, they engage their own. However, if the other person does not want to engage with you, that is also their choice. You may have become aware that you are not, in the end, as significant to them as you would want to be. More likely, it may mean that you have opened up an area that they want to avoid. Pushing them too far may make them feel they are losing control. By raising their awareness of the situation, but not pressing the point, you create an atmosphere in which they are more likely to make the choice to engage with you at the beneath the surface level.

Resolution: in the above example, what do we do about it from here on? The behaviour may not change, the initiator still may enjoy lending, the listener may remain just as confused. Perhaps not, perhaps the behaviours will change. But even if not, the feelings which now accompany those behaviours have definitely changed. Both parties have a deeper understanding of what the other person wants in the relationship. It draws them closer together and prevents a potentially disastrous schism.

The question is, are you responsible for what you do not let yourself know you are doing?

Marilyn French, *The Women's Room*

DISTORTIONS OF PERCEPTION OR DEFENCE MECHANISMS

The first thing to get straight about defence mechanisms is that we all use them. They are perfectly natural. We could not get by without them. They are our 'human' behaviour.

It is only when we use them excessively, without knowing we are doing so, becoming dependent upon them, that they are a problem. When defence mechanisms are employed to oil the wheels of our relationship we find them mutually useful; in this case they are not, strictly speaking, defences. When they begin to interfere and destroy our personal sense of adequacy and our relationships, then they are doing nobody any good.

It is when we become dependent upon the defence rather than self reliant that we need to become aware of what we are doing to ourself. For example, if you are unsure of yourself and seek reassurance from someone else, you are using a defence (compensation, see below), but it is a very human thing to do – we can sympathize and tolerate your need to know. We have to be careful here, however, because if we tell you that you have no need to feel unsure, but we really feel that you are unsure, we are colluding in your defence. Colluding means that we are really helping ourselves help you not confront the situation. It would be much more useful to both of us if we enabled you to perceive the situation because then, instead of being dependent upon us, you could make better choices for yourself.

Obviously, keeping you unaware of the defence you are using does not enable you to perceive your situation. So, you are given feedback in which we aim to enable you to see yourself, so at least you know. With that insight, you can decide to take control of your own life. But if you keep returning for reassurance, we begin to get bored or irritated by your dependency. We begin to feel exploited because you are stretching our initial desire to enable you into a full time job. Indeed, the danger is that we become helpers rather than enablers. In this situation we help you because we identify in you a convenient way to use our own defence, that is, to sort out your problems rather than deal with our own. (The defence we use here is identification, see below.)

These mechanisms become defences when they are used without awareness. Since their effect is always personally or interpersonally destructive, it serves no purpose to tolerate them.

Usually, making ourself or the other person aware of the mechanism they are using is sufficient to break the habit. Thus we might say, sensibly, 'Being dependent upon us, you will never learn to cope for yourself,' or 'I am frightened I may become dependent upon you if I allow you to help me all the time.' It is rather more brutal to say, 'You've got to learn to stand on your own feet,' but probably true.

Being a 'victim'

If you make yourself a victim, it appears that your concept of yourself is that you deserve to suffer. You put yourself in a position of waiting for other people to recognize you. You seem to be making up for feelings of guilt that can never be assuaged no matter how hard you try. You take a lot upon yourself and others take advantage of you.

The mechanism you use is called projection. The aim is to get people to like you by doing what you think they want. It is as though you feel you can only define yourself in the eyes of others, that you have no right to be yourself, but to be as others want you to be. Your fear is that, if you were to be yourself, people would withdraw their liking from you.

Not being aware of yourself you distort the messages people give you. You think that you deserve it when you feel people are dissatisfied with you. You feel you have let them down, that you should have tried harder. In this case, the message they give you is distorted. Your self doubt leads you to distrust the message. Thus, when people say, 'You're great!' you turn it into, 'He's just saying that, he doesn't mean it.'

Fear of believing in yourself makes you look to others to believe in you. What do you get out of (what is your negative gain) being a victim? Well, you don't risk rejection and you don't ever confront your deepest fear – that the self you might turn out to be if you weren't a victim might be unlikeable.

> Surface behaviour of the victim:
> 'You don't include me.'
> 'You ignore me.'
> 'You don't think I'm competent.'
> 'You make me look stupid.'
> 'You don't like me.'
> 'You reject me.'

Being a 'critic'

If you make yourself a critic, you are judgmental. There are many things wrong with the world and many people who are wrong too. But they don't see things your way, so everything is their fault. Everything would be all right if only the world and people would change; you see no cause to change yourself.

The mechanism is called, technically, displacement. The aim is to get to like yourself by getting people to change so that they think and feel the way you do. This proves that they were wrong and you were right all along. It is as though you cannot confront any fears, doubts or uncertainties you have about yourself, so you look for those things elsewhere. You find them easily enough, by spotting elements of the self you fear you might be, in others

Not being aware of yourself, you distort the message you give people. Because you do nothing to sort out yourself, you are a hard taskmaster as far as others are concerned. Your underlying self doubt leads you to distort the message you get from people. You turn, 'You're great!' into, 'I know I'm right, but I don't trust you; you're only saying that to win me over or trying to buy me off.'

Fear of believing in yourself makes you disbelieve others. What do you get out of (what is your negative gain) being a critic? Well, you get people trying hard to please you and avoid your criticism, and you don't have to risk confronting your deepest fear – that the person you would be if you were not a critic may not be likeable. This would mean you wouldn't be able to blame others anymore, wouldn't it?

> Surface behaviour of the critic:
> 'You are not important.'
> 'You are not worth acknowledging.'
> 'You are incapable.'
> 'You are stupid.'
> 'You cannot be trusted.'
> 'You are not likeable.'

Being a 'helper'

If you make yourself a helper, you are good at sorting out people's problems for them. There is plenty for you to do and people are only too willing to let you help. You are quick to see what the matter is and can be relied upon to give good advice. The question is, who are you actually helping? Perhaps you should start with yourself first. It is worth also considering how far you are helping others who may be better off learning to help themselves.

Technically, the mechanism is called identification. The aim is to like yourself vicariously by seeing others overcome their difficulties. You identify with their difficulties, so that their success establishes a feeling of success in you, that you are frightened of directly experiencing yourself. The fear is of failing, so it is safer to deal with others' perceived needs rather than your own difficulties.

Not being aware of yourself, you distort the messages you see in people by thinking they are the same as you. You think your way of seeing the world is the way the world sees it. It is not uncommon for you to become a representative of what others feel and think: 'People in this country do not want... People do not know what is best for them. I know what your problem is...The trouble with you is...'

Fear of believing in yourself makes you certain that others should believe in themselves. What do you get out of (what is your negative gain) not dealing with your own problems? Well, you get lots of people to tell you how wonderful you are and you don't have to face your worst fear, which is 'Perhaps I am not likeable myself, I have to put on an act and pretend people are more important than I am; they wouldn't like me if I didn't help them.'

Surface behaviour of the helper:
'You don't believe in your own significance.'
'Your trouble is that you don't put yourself forward.'
'You should learn to rely on your own capability.'
'You need to realize that you are not silly.'
'You should learn to trust yourself.'
'You will never become aware while you are so closed.'

Being a 'demander'

If you make yourself a demander, your needy behaviour puts people in a spot. It makes them think it is their fault or perhaps they owe you something. Often, you start by giving people a chance to feel good about themselves by helping you. It is a device which can bring you a quick satisfaction, but doesn't last very long – asking people to make you feel good about yourself is ultimately never satisfying: it is you feeling good about yourself which really counts.

Technically, the mechanism you use is called compensation. The mechanism enables you to get people to compensate for the lack which you fear you have in yourself. Of course, people know you do not lack anything, that is why they hastily reassure you. There was once a young woman about whom everybody agreed upon her exceptional beauty, but, strangely, she mentioned several times that she thought she was unattractive. People were amazed by her admission, but after a while her continual seeking for compliments got rather boring, and her behaviour tended to make her appear somewhat lifeless and, indeed, unattractive.

As a demander you communicate, 'You have the power to make my life better. I want to leave it all to you so that you make everything perfect for me. You can help me best by protecting me, by not letting me take responsibility for myself. I could not survive without your help.'

Not being aware of yourself, you distort the way you feel about yourself, telling yourself that you are nothing unless other people make you whole. You distort the way you feel about others because you see in them what they can do for you that you fear you cannot do for yourself. In the end, the fundamental lack of trust in yourself leads you inevitably to lose your trust in them too. In this way, people never come up to your expectations. And if people give up on you, you find someone who is more sympathetic, who is prepared to allow themselves to be roped in in order to help get you over your difficulties.

Demanders sometimes appear pathetic and helpless, but are as often highly successful. You may think of your own examples of those who combine riches and fame with a childlike innocence and vulnerability. Not surprisingly, those who have fallen into the demander's trap often feel exploited. This manipulative quality is not apparent at the outset.

You do not believe in yourself and you do not believe in others either. What do you get out of (the negative gain) being this way? Well, you get lots of temporary support which means you do not have to do anything for yourself, and you avoid confronting the worst fear of all, which is that if people saw you clearly as the way you fear you really are, they wouldn't like you, which would prove that you are right about yourself.

> Surface behaviour of the 'demander':
> 'Am I important to you?'
> 'I want you to include me.'
> 'You must not ignore me.'
> 'Am I capable?'
> 'I want you to take control of me.'
> 'You must not laugh at me.'
> 'Am I likeable?'
> 'You must be open with me.'
> 'You must not reject me.'

Character 'flaws'

Defences are means of protecting ourself from our fears: that we are not significant, competent or likeable – those three dimensions of feeling that we have discussed earlier. In the above examples I have said that we use them because of our fear that, deep down at the core of our being, we really are not significant, competent and likeable.

You may ask, 'Well, aren't we sensible to protect ourself if we really are unlikeable, incompetent or insignificant?' Actually, it is only the fear of not being those things. Fear is not the thing itself. Always, when we get down to the core of a person's being, we find not the absence, but the very substance of significance, competence and love.

It is worth repeating that we all use defences. We must do, because we all possess flaws or, more accurately, think we have flaws in our character. So we use defences to try to cover and manage our flaws in our attempt to 'live with ourselves'. We cannot blame ourselves for using defences; if we were perfect, of course, we would not need to. But we have to try to forgive ourself for being less than a saint.

We are often attracted by people because of their flaws. It may be because they make us feel less bad about ourself (compensation). Ask yourself why you might be attracted to someone who was judgmental (a critic) or someone who was deferential (a victim) or someone who thinks exactly the same way about things as you do (a helper).

Perceiving another person's flaws makes them rather easier to live with, as long, of course, as the flaws are not over excessive and demanding of us. Conversely, people with no apparent flaws, 'super humans', are often very difficult to live with. Perhaps it is because they seem to set standards that make us feel inadequate. We like heroes who are modest because they imply that they are just like us; we could do what they do, if we wanted to enough. We do not like heroes who display an air of contempt or superiority; we take a perverse pleasure in witnessing their downfall and getting their 'come uppance'. Strangely, they might lose their significance and the respect we pay them, but we may like them more when their humanity is revealed.

CASE STUDY

Humanity is something we can understand and empathize with; heroism and sanctity are very difficult for us to comprehend. An example would be Ffyona Campbell, the round the world walker, whose prickly defensiveness is made understandable when she revealed that she was this way to defend her guilty secret. Jojo Moyes, writing in the *Independent*, (4 November 1996), made the conflict clear – 'No wonder Ffyona proved a difficult heroine: her spikiness was an understandable reaction to the knowledge that she hadn't done the very thing for which she was being lauded. Few people have not experienced that blinding relief at having confessed – whether it is the errant husband or the exam cheat. And yet, somehow, Ffyona Campbell has suddenly become a more interesting and sympathetic figure'. We might come to respect her in a way she would never have guessed – for

her courage in doing what was the most difficult thing, telling the truth –
and like her more for it. It also looks as though she might be turning into
a person we would like to be with, in fact, someone not too dissimilar from
ourselves.

TELEPATHY

Whether or not it can be proved, something is communicated between us;
we may as well act as though telepathy is real, because we are aware of
each other as though it is. Everybody has the same feelings and thoughts
that you do. You are not alone. If you say what is on your mind, someone
else will say, 'I was thinking the same thing.'

This is not the kind of telepathy that transfers precise information, but
the type which combines us together in our emotions. It is called 'emotional telepathy' or 'affective intelligence'. It is well established that what
is observed is changed by the observer. There is accruing evidence for this
in biology as well. Rupert Sheldrake (1997) claims that people have an
innate ability to tell when they are being watched, even when blindfolded
and separated by a window.

I do not know whether researchers will ever define all those small signs we
use, particularly with our facial muscles, to be able to say that it is really all
sign language, or that there is some as yet undiscovered electrical force, not
telepathy at all. But it doesn't matter, the transfer of feeling between us is so
rapid we cannot witness how we do it. It happens – let's call it telepathy.

Compassion (co-feeling) signifies the maximal capacity for affective imagination, the
art of emotional telepathy.

Milan Kundera, *The Unbearable Lightness of Being*

The best teams consist of individuals.

The failure of a single person to be their self diminishes us all.

THE BEST GROUP

Organizations rarely consist of ad hoc groups, that is, groups who simply
come together because of their common interest, although this is the best
way to come together, and when it is done properly can become a concor-

dance group. What defines concordance is that the group makes a decision taking account of the feelings of everybody involved (see 'Making decisions', Chapter 11).

Most organizations start off with some sort of imposed structure in which there are appointed leaders. In an ad hoc group, leaders emerge naturally, depending upon what the group wants to achieve. The law of the situation holds in such groups.

The characteristic of ad hoc groups is that they arise from what members want, they are not there as a result of people having to join. Almost always, the ad hoc group is formed by people with a similar motivation to bring about change. When an ad hoc group is institutionalized, that is, given power within the structure of the organization, keeping its spirit and motivation, it ceases to be a 'rebel' or 'pressure' group, but has a unity which characterizes a concordance group.

TAKING TIME WITH 'THE BAD THINGS'

The good things take care of themselves. The bad things are the ones that hold us back. They only go away if we deal with them. Paradoxically, dealing with the 'bad things' does not make us feel bad, though we might have expected it would. Dealing with them, that is, initiating at the beneath the surface level and resolving them, is a liberating, joyful experience.

ENTHUSIASM

Enthusiasm is present in a team in which participants see a way of being that is in line with their vision of themselves. The happiness that is generated is contagious and gives everybody confidence.

If others get the impression you are unhappy, they will fear that they are the cause of it – that, in some way, you are not happy with them. Their way of coping may be to avoid you, for example, which may make you wonder what is wrong with you that they are too frightened to tell you. Then, before you know it, you really will have become dispirited!

Maybe your team begins to feel that you are only happy when you are doing all the work yourself. The implication here is that they cannot be trusted. Showing delight with the contribution that others make in their work makes them feel good about themselves, and they'll do more of the same thing. Failures will be gradually eliminated in this way.

It depends which way you choose to go – to be delighted by their success or dispirited by their failures. It is nothing more than whether you see a glass of water as half full or half empty; do you look on the bright side or the dark side? Only one way gives you an opportunity. When you have delegated or are in any way relying upon others, don't examine what they do, don't find fault, don't critically evaluate, don't check the details and don't say, or even faintly imply, 'I wouldn't have done it that way'. Whilst a few people might improve, just to show you, the majority feel nervous and undermined by such behaviour and begin to think, 'Why do I bother?'

Actually, you should not have handed over control (empowered someone) if you are going to take it back. It is a mistake to empower someone if this disempowers you. It may mean that you have empowered someone who cannot use that power appropriately, which is irresponsible leadership on your part.

Of course, allowing people to make small mistakes may be a responsible part of their training, it depends whether empowerment is under control or abandoned. When someone is empowered, make sure that small mistakes aren't going to be significant and the potentially serious issues which might be damaging have already been addressed.

If you feel that failures have to be mentioned, then make sure you handle it the way that is going to increase the person's self esteem, not diminish it. First, you comment positively on those things that have gone well. Then you initiate at the beneath the surface level the conflict you have with their behaviour. If they deny your conflict has anything to do with them, that is, they don't choose to engage with you, there's not much you can do about it. This kind of impasse rarely, if ever, happens with beneath the surface initiating. By contrast, if you insist that they have a 'problem', they will see you as unfair and 'picking upon' them unnecessarily. In other words, they will play victim to your critic.

The way it works is that small faults disappear as the result of positive feedback. Potential large faults are eliminated by the process of conflict resolution (see Chapter 2). If new threats arise which may change the basis of your previous psychological contract, then these issues have to be renegotiated. Almost always, the problem is one of fearing that the other person's lack of competence is going to make you look or feel incompetent.

You should not empower others if you remain fearful that you may feel or look incompetent as the result of what they do. If you have such fears, you will interfere, look at details, be distrustful, check up upon them, and so on. Get to the stage where you are able to show enthusiasm with the result of what they are empowered to do.

ALLOW OTHERS TO TAKE THE TILLER

Using a nautical metaphor may help to illustrate a point about control and being over controlling. Do not remain in charge because you feel others expect you to do so. Let others take responsibility whenever you feel you can. Take small risks, not big ones. Taking small risks eventually whittles away the size of the big risks.

Be alert if people think that what you want from them is stretching their competence too far. At the same time, make it clear that you know they are competent, as and when they feel themselves ready. In an atmosphere that has allowed you to be aware of your own fears, and aware of how competent the team is at any time, you will be alerted to any big storms that blow up. People will know their limits, they won't try to manage by themselves because they feel they'll be letting you down, or because they have something to prove to themselves. Do not take over at the first sign of a squall. Otherwise, how will the crew ever learn how to become captains?

CREATIVITY

If I have a better idea than my boss, will he take my idea in preference to his own? Furthermore, will he promote my idea *as if it were his own*? (The issue is about defensiveness, empowerment and creativity. It is about recognising others and delighting in being part of an energy that is larger than oneself.)

How are ideas fertilized, nourished and disseminated? Why would someone want to ignore a good idea? If it comes from oneself, it would be out of fear about how to deal with that idea; in particular, what would others think, and the consequent excuses that are made to oneself.

The negative gain for not communicating a good idea is that you avoid the risk of humiliation. If it is for not welcoming another person's idea, it is out of fear that admitting the value of another person's idea is in some way diminishing oneself. It is out of fear that you won't look good unless people see that it is invented by you.

Not admitting the value of the idea is a put down – to yourself and to others. It is a deliberate withholding of the truth. It creates doubts in the other person as to what you think of them. Literally, you are not giving them truthful feedback. They will experience a sense of rejection. Next time they have an idea they will keep it to themself. They won't trust you with it.

WITHHOLDING

Does what is on your mind concern the other person? Why then are you keeping things to yourself? Is your silence a form of lying or withholding? How do justify your behaviour? What are you not saying that, maybe, you think you should?

At the same time, beware of thinking that you 'ought' to feel guilty when you don't. For example, just knowing something about another person (as long as it does not affect their lives) is no reason for you to experience guilt or conflict.

I don't know whether you've ever gone in for lying yourself. But I can tell you it leaves one with such a horrible feeling later. Lying, I think, must be the ultimate sin. It's treachery. And treachery is the worst of all.

Henrietta Garnett, *Family Skeletons*

Suppose you know that a person is to lose their job and they are happily talking to you about how much they are enjoying it? Does guilt arise because they are unaware and you are aware? Or is it because you are exploiting them because you fear that if you tell them the truth they will stop working or might make you feel that you have a responsibility to them? You ought to tell them this information as soon as you know it, because withholding it is preventing them from taking control of their lives.

CASE STUDY

Suppose you feel guilty because you know you have a job, but you do not know yet whether they have or not. You are frightened to tell them you have a job because of your fear they will feel bad about themselves because they are rated less highly than you. Psychologically, you tell yourself that you are 'helping them by not telling them the truth'. Another danger is that you fear that later on they will recall the conversation and feel badly about you because you did not think they were important enough to you for you to tell them something that was related to what the conversation was about. Even though they are not affected by the information, you have diminished their feeling of significance to you.

The issue is with keeping a secret. What purpose does it serve? Go back and deal with your feeling of guilt. Telling them about your feeling actually engages them with you because they perceive your behaviour accurately as they become aware of your conflict. It gives them a perception of where you are and where they are. It might actually help reduce some of the confusion they have about their own position, that, if things are being worked out for you, things may be in process for them. By telling them, you will have indicated that they are important enough for you to do your best for them, that is tell them about any conflicts you have in your own relations with them.

The fear is that you will lose respect and trust. What happens is the opposite – you gain respect and trust. That does not mean that you have to advertise your success to everybody. That may well be seen as a sign of arrogance. But dealing with a conflict that you may have in a manner which relieves the conflict for you is the only way to preserve your integrity. Also, in doing so you are creating the atmosphere for the new teams and the new organization. The other thing is, that these people whom you are trying to help by not disclosing your good fortune, will actually be pleased for you. If you are not open, they may attempt to protect themselves afterwards by denying that you had any choice but not to tell them, though a gulf will have been created. And it is difficult to recover, once lost. Indeed, a team building opportunity has definitely been lost.

Your first, defensive thought might be, 'Well, what is happening to me has nothing to do with them, I shouldn't feel guilty'. But your second, aware, thought might be, 'In this situation, they would actually expect me to say something about my position, the psychological situation makes that obvious. And I have a conflict I am not dealing with (suppressing). Can I deal with it by myself? If I do, there is a risk I lose something in the relationship. Or, I could choose to tell them. There is still a risk, but I get rid of my conflict which is good for me, and I put them in control of information which may be important to them, which is good for them. In the latter situation, if they choose to feel hurt, if they try to make me feel bad, having telepathically recognized my feelings of guilt, then that is up to them. I can only tell them my awareness, how they choose to deal with it, perhaps by being critical or choosing to be a victim, is up to them. They, in the end, have to deal with their own feelings.'

These issues nearly always arise out of fear of how we will be viewed. Mostly, when we tell people of what is good for us, they will be pleased for us. It may not completely resolve their own fears, but it creates no new ones and goes a long way to resolving some that are 'under the surface' and may appear later on. Is it so bad for people to know that you will be offered a job even though they will not? If you say what you know, they will learn that you will tell them what you know on other issues.

You may hesitate, making an excuse for yourself: 'If I tell them this, they may push me for more details that I don't yet know.' Tell them you'd feel incompetent in discussing things you don't know about, that there are vague plans, there always are possibilities, but nothing that is in any way firm. If there is a matter that concerns them, you will certainly tell them. Also, if it is a matter which affects them, they should definitely be included.

Do not make a promise to anybody not to say something about a matter that will involve you in a conflict. Better not to know. If you have made such a promise, you must be open with those people who say they are relying on you not to tell the secret. Doing so will help them resolve their own sense of guilt which led to them to ask you to keep a secret in the first place.

I have never yet found a situation which might be called a candidate for justifiable secrecy. People suspect something is going on anyway. It is never the truth, but invariably the secret which causes the trouble.

OPENNESS

Being open does not mean that you are obliged to tell your work colleagues all about what is going on in your private life. Much of it may not affect them and will therefore largely be boring. But it is necessary to tell them about any aspects which may affect them. And don't assume you can keep your private life separate from work; any conflict which you suppress may well come out at work in ways you are not aware of and therefore in ways you may not be able to control.

For example, suppose you grumble at somebody at work for doing a half hearted job when, unconsciously, you are feeling defensive because you think you are not giving enough time to your children. These things happen – the psychological mechanism is that we tend to blame people for behaving in ways that we don't like in ourself – as you know, it's called displacement. In this case, doing a half-hearted job must contain subliminal echoes of feeling half-hearted about one's children. Even though the person may, in fact, have been doing a half-hearted job, you will not be confronting the situation if, without awareness, you are being driven by your own unconscious feelings of guilt.

Being open does not mean that you have to tell all the salacious details either. Suppose someone says, 'You are looking a bit down,' or 'You don't seem able to concentrate,' or any remark which indicates concern. Saying, 'I had a problem at home,' if that is the truth, immediately tells the other person that it has nothing to do with them.

That gets rid of their main concern: that your quietness, annoyance, irritation, detachment has something to do with them. Once they learn it has not, the matter is largely resolved from their point of view.

Their secondary concern may be whether they would be letting themselves down by not offering to help, expressed as asking if you are able to deal with the problem. Also, they may not want to be let down by you, however much they may sympathize; their own competence may be compromised by your behaviour, if you are detracting from the team's performance. Saying, 'If you have noticed something, I'm afraid you might think it is affecting my work,' gives both of you a chance to draw up a plan of action together, and, if it isn't, makes the situation clear for both of you. He is satisfied that he is not being excluded from something that may be significant, you have got it out in the open without having to talk about matters which might well involve other people who are emotionally close to you but not present.

Of course, there are also times when you need to talk more fully to someone who is willing and able to give advice, but that is different because the issue is about the situation you find yourself in and is, therefore, detached from the counsellor.

POWER

Power which is based upon authority is based upon 'power over' because it does not integrate the experience and expectations of those who are in the situation. The only effective authority flows from the integration and co-ordination of those who are involved and affected. Clearly, if people are not involved, they will not feel themselves responsible. The result is of your making, not of their incapacity for understanding or lack of willingness to take responsibility as you may wish, defensively, to believe.

The people who love you are the least willing to acknowledge your deceit.

John Irving, *The Cider House Rules*

SUMMARY

How to understand and resolve our defences has formed the largest part of this chapter. Through understanding our negative gains for using a defence, we liberate ourselves from them, perceiving a process by which we create a team, which consists of individuals, yet has unity.

It may seem as though this chapter has been as much about pairs as about teams. However, all teams consist of pairs and each relationship is vital to the fulfilment of the whole. When teams obtain the unity of understanding and purpose it is called concordance. How teams can reach this state of excellence in their performance is described in Chapter 11.

Optional exercise

The exercise assists resolution of misperception with each team member. To do this, you are asked to explore at the beneath the surface level those defences you might unconsciously be relying upon. Gaining insight into why this happens is the way to create regard, respect and warmth in your relationships. The more you initiate upon your feelings, the more your team will be motivated by each other – being a winning team. (There is much more about Teamwork in Chapter 10.)

Exercise – beneath the surface issues

The following exercise has space for up to four people to complete the exercise with you, but there is nothing to prevent you gathering more feedback from more people.

On a scale of 0 to 9, where 9 means totally, 0 means not at all and 5 is average, score each statement (a) for the way you perceive your relationship. When you have written down your own scores for them (under I see you and you see me) you can write down the scores, under (b), for their perceptions of your relationship. You can then have a beneath the surface discussion about your perceptions.

In our relationship:	I see you	You see me	I see you	You see me	I see you	You see me	I see you	You see me
(a) You or I prevent us relating better	——	——	——	——	——	——	——	——
(b) Your scores	——	——	——	——	——	——	——	——
(a) You or I become a 'victim'	——	——	——	——	——	——	——	——
(b) Your scores	——	——	——	——	——	——	——	——
(a) You or I become a 'critic'	——	——	——	——	——	——	——	——
(b) Your scores	——	——	——	——	——	——	——	——
(a) You become too much of a 'helper'	——	——	——	——	——	——	——	——

(b) Your scores   __ __   __ __   __ __   __ __

(a) You are too much   __ __   __ __   __ __   __ __
     of a 'demander'
(b) Your scores   __ __   __ __   __ __   __ __

(a) You 'withhold'   __ __   __ __   __ __   __ __

(b) Your scores   __ __   __ __   __ __   __ __

(a) You do not deal
     with 'here and   __ __   __ __   __ __   __ __
     now' issues
(b) Your scores   __ __   __ __   __ __   __ __

(a) You feel tense   __ __   __ __   __ __   __ __
     or uncomfortable
(b) Your scores   __ __   __ __   __ __   __ __

(a) You do not feel   __ __   __ __   __ __   __ __
     equal
(b) Your scores   __ __   __ __   __ __   __ __

(a) We do not have   __ __   __ __   __ __   __ __
     deep discussions
(b) Your scores   __ __   __ __   __ __   __ __

5

Total Motivation

There is only one single standard by which one can form an estimate of a human being – 'his or her movement when confronted with the problems of humanity'. These problems are the attitude adopted towards fellow men and women, one's vocation, and love.

Alfred Adler, 'Social Interest: A Challenge to Mankind', from Patrick Mullahy, *Oedipus Myth & Complex*

INTRODUCTION

Management theorists have long debated whether people are more motivated by the promise of 'carrots' or by the threat of the 'stick'. Recently, the 'carrot' method has been favoured, quite rightly, because the 'stick' is so uncertain – workers react against it in unpredictable ways. The 'carrot' method, sometimes known as 'positive reinforcement', always works in the direction that is being reinforced.

For example, if a teacher finds something in a student's essay to praise, the student will be motivated to continue to produce praiseworthy essays. If the teacher denigrates the essay, the student might be motivated to do better next time, but might also go and throw a brick though the window of the teacher's car.

It depends what the student feels as a result of the teacher's comment – clever or stupid. Clever is positive, stupid is negative. Positive feelings always work in the direction that is reinforced, as a result of removing any threat to the ego. Having experienced a behaviour that makes it feel good about itself, the ego seeks to enhance itself still further by undertaking more of the same thing. That is behaviour which is energized.

In contrast, negative feelings demand a restoration of the ego, perhaps by adopting a defiant attitude of 'I'll show you'. The energy is the same, but it is wasteful or destructive, not positive. Unfortunately, the motivation is 'to get back at you for the way you have made me feel'. In this case, the student may be spurred on to demonstrate to the teacher that they really are deserving of praise or they may cease to bother, drop out or react in other ways which are destructive. Even if they work harder to prove themselves, the relationship between teacher and student remains shaky – there is a real possibility that at some stage the student will find a way of 'getting back at' the teacher as a way of compensating for the way he felt years earlier, and even though he may have been a successful student, ostensibly as a result of the teacher's style and, therefore, might 'logically' be expected to be grateful. It will happen subconsciously, perhaps with the student snubbing his teacher at a reunion, feeling that he 'never liked' his teacher. In fact, I have known students who later came to be promoted above their former teachers and who then gave their teachers a 'hard time'. I have seen the same thing happen many times in organizations as subordinates have been promoted over their former bosses.

This chapter presents a process for understanding what motivates others and what motivates you. (The model upon which it is based comes from Will Schutz (1994.) As is always the case, the essential task is to resolve those situations which are demotivating. Although it may be too much to expect to be enjoying all of the time, it is always attainable through the process, if we choose to engage in it.

UNITY

The very act of perception splits our consciousness in two. The 'I' becomes differentiated from 'you' or what is 'out there'. We polarize everything into its opposites and then force ourselves into the conflict of deciding what is right or wrong, good or bad. We forget that our perception contains the thing as a whole, it is only the act of perception which creates an apparent differentiation.

It is a paradox that without this differentiation reason would be impossible, but that to experience the unity, in which differences are resolved, is the aim of humankind. In the same way that we seek to make whole splits within ourself, so do we seek to resolve splits between us.

In reality, all human endeavour serves but one aim: to learn to see the connections more clearly – become more aware.

Dethlefsen and Dahlke (1990)

THE HUMAN CONDITION

There are two things of which we can be sure. First: we spend our lives in pursuit of being ourself. In those moments we are, we experience fulfilment, joy or unity. Second: in a very short time, situations arise which cause us to doubt ourself. Life moves on.

It is useful to be sure what self fulfilment consists of, how to get it and make sure we have a way of coping with difficulties.

Fortunately, what makes us fulfilled is easy to understand, particularly as it means the same to each one of us. We may go about it in different ways, but what constitutes happiness is a state of mind which is the same for you, me and everyone. And, of course, we will want to avoid anything which causes us not to be happy. These are the same things for all of us as well.

What, then, is motivating or, alternatively, demotivating? For me, the words being, fulfilment, happiness, success, joy and unity are all the same state to which motivation draws us. Religious thinkers have used synonymous words such as heaven or nirvana.

We respond positively as we experience feelings which make us feel good and we respond negatively to feelings which make us feel bad. Even the fear that we may experience the bad feelings is enough to make us react immediately and violently away from any real or imagined threat. It is a biological mechanism which aims to protect any threat to the integrity of the entire organism. Physically, the mechanism alerts us to the possibility of any predator. Psychologically, we are alerted to any threat to our ego.

You will have had experiences in which most people might have thought you were excellent when you did something, but one solitary individual thinks you weren't so good. Who do you attend to? The single one who represents the only threat, however minor, to your existence. Imagine yourself talking to a large audience. It is a wonderful speech. As you finish, everybody claps apart from one person who look annoyed and bored, who makes a remark to his neighbour. You are probably attending more to this one individual than to the hundred others.

In a very real way, wounding of the ego threatens our emotional existence, and, indeed, if our ego has been knocked badly enough, may well affect our ability to take our place in the world. Where the ego cannot cope, social withdrawal, anti social behaviour and even damage to the self may arise as a result of avoiding rather than confronting what appear to be intractable problems.

The ideal state is to be both happy in the present and yet see ways of becoming happy in the future. This is important because we are only ever on the cusp of a present happiness. It is a rolling ball on which we stand. We think we have got where we want to be, but unless we keep moving, where we were ceases to be where we want to be.

The analogy can be applied to all our endeavours at whatever level we function. It certainly holds at the personal level. It also holds at the organizational level and is the reason Robert Kriegel exhorts us, 'If it ain't broke ... break it!' Success is illusory, we will want something else tomorrow. It is as well to recognize this and act upon it rather than be caught out. So, we have to have had the experience of success. Now it is necessary to move on while that experience is strong enough to remind us that we have been and can be again, before the experience fades and we forget how to achieve it or before we feel we are risking too much to go on being so ambitious for ourself.

Our lives must contain both a present and possible state of happiness. If it is not possible then, naturally, we give up. Absence of a present state of happiness is bearable, as long as a possible state of happiness exists. However, denial or 'deferred gratification' is not fun for very long. The trouble with extended denial is the danger that it becomes distorted into some kind of 'holy crusade' which sees the denial as an end in itself, rather than the state of well being it replaces.

Happiness is only ever temporary – unless we take action to constantly regenerate it anew. We are easily dissatisfied. Sometimes organizations try to motivate employees through deferred gratification. Workers may be motivated in the short term, once or even twice, but become cynical as yet further long-term grand schemes are rolled out which will come to fruition at some long-term future date. People are motivated by what they can get now. Whilst long term plans are important, of course they are, what we do today also has to be personally rewarding, otherwise ways will be found to avoid doing it.

This is why it is a nonsense to have corporate objectives which do not immediately motivate us by creating an environment in which positive energy can be experienced. The long term objectives are never reached. We never get there. They are an illusion. Whatever we are, whatever we achieve, wherever we get to, we want to be, or do, something else.

Chasing rainbows or hoping to find the pot of gold raises our hopes but is not ultimately satisfying. The moral is that we never get there – it is the way we spend our time that is critical, not where we get to but how we go about getting there.

Will Schutz (1964, 1967) has defined the process that gets us where we want to go and gives us what we all want. It is not, as we all always knew, material success, although our actions seemed to indicate otherwise, but how we feel about ourselves that is the key to our happiness – success, motivation, feeling of well being or fulfilment of our self concept.

How we feel about each other depends upon how we behave towards each other; the way we behave to each other depends upon our feelings about each other. Feelings are very rapidly established, possibly after a few seconds, but some behaviour must have taken place in that time to start it off. It quickly becomes an academic issue: after a very short time, behaviour and feelings have an impact upon each other. If you can remember the model which follows, you will have all the knowledge of psychology necessary to understand what is happening to you and to everybody else.

Motivated

⇑

Positive feeling	Significant	Competent	Likeable (warm)

| | ⇑ | ⇑ | ⇑ |

Behaviour	Include	Control (influence)	Open

| | ⇓ | ⇓ | ⇓ |

Negative feeling and fear	Insignificant	Incompetent	Unlikeable
	Ignored	Humiliated	Rejected

⇓

Demotivated

Figure 1   Model of psychology (after Will Schutz – 1994)

(Note: I have added the words influence and warm, in brackets, to the model. They are also Will Schutz's words. I find these words enable my personal understanding and I have found them more useful than control and likeable when communicating the concepts.)

INTERPERSONAL BEHAVIOUR

Include

The first decision we take is who we are going to be with. Do we want to be included in this organization? Do we want to be with this person? Do we want to have this person as a partner? The social level is the most superficial level of inclusion. It has to do with whether your name is down as belonging to this organization: are we on the register or on the company payroll?

There is a deeper meaning to being included – the psychological one. It arises after a while as we participate or when some significant event happens which makes us feel that we are not only there, but also accepted and involved. It is a feeling that we are no longer on the outside, physically, socially or mentally, but that we belong and are really 'in'.

For me, the word 'involve' touches not just the social levels but the deeper, psychological ones as well.

Examples of words and phrases related to this behaviour are: in, belonging, engaged, as well as opposites: out, excluded, uninvolved.

Influence (or control)

This is the behaviour which describes the way in which we take on and direct our authority. To whom do we report and who reports to us? What influence, power and responsibility do we have? At a superficial level, we might see our name in the organogram, which is generally represented hierarchically – those who have most influence being at the top and those with least influence at the bottom.

At a deeper level, influence is not a matter of reporting structure or of authority, but of who is respected. People influence by subtle means. The managing director's opinion on an issue may be shaped more by someone outside the board than by those on it.

Influence may range by degrees from autocracy, the most gentle form of coaching. The reason I like the word influence is because people I have worked with have appeared to find it more acceptable than control, which seems to many to be 'black and white', 'all or nothing', 'on or off'. But being entirely controlling or having all the influence means the same thing, as does having only a little control or only a little influence.

Examples of words and phrases related to this behaviour are: dominate, insist, persuade, suborn, as well as opposite words, such as abdicate, submit, powerless, weak.

Open

In this area of behaviour we discover the nature of the relationship we are going to have with each other. How open are we going to be with each other about what is going on? Are we going to be factual and businesslike or how much can we talk about our feelings? At a superficial level, organizations may make information available through dissemination of accounts or through company newsletters.

At a deeper, psychological level, are questions of whether or not we know what is really going on. Are there secrets, and how much is confided? Are people open about their difficulties, doubts or fears, or is there a pretence that everything is OK?

Such have been the misconceptions about openness since it has emerged as a popular concept that we need to be clear what sort of openness Will Schutz is referring to. It is not necessarily about everything that has happened to you. It is not about your secret life or those things you feel guilty about. It is those things you are thinking and feeling which are significant to your relationship. If it is personal, but is affecting your relationship, it is best to regard it as interpersonal.

To the extent you have thoughts and feelings about someone else which you do not confide, they experience rejection. They may sense you are withholding or lying to them even though they pretend you are not, as a way of protecting themselves. For example, they make themself a victim by pretending, 'I don't deserve to know', or a demander, and telepathically communicate, 'Don't tell me. Show me you care by not being open.'

This quality of openness requires that we take the initiative in reflecting the conflict back to the other person with whom it arises. As has been said before in Chapter 2, some amount of trust is required to take this initiative.

Examples of words and phrases related to this behaviour are truth, honesty, warmth and confiding, as well as opposites, such as lying, deceit, closed, factual, businesslike and withholding.

INTERPERSONAL FEELINGS AND FEARS

Significance

If you include someone, you indicate they are important. You can do this by recognizing them or acknowledging them. It depends what is called for in the circumstances in which you find you are involved together. Some are more superficial than others, but all have the potential to send crashing signals which impact upon us. It may be as slight as spotting somebody in the distance. Will they acknowledge you or not? Should you acknowledge them? What happens if you acknowledge them and they do not recognize you or make out they haven't seen you? Not wanting to be ignored, you may ignore them first! The trouble is, you may worry that they know you have ignored them, and they probably do. They may ignore you first the next time, unless you can make the situation better by telling them that you think they may feel that you ignored them, but you didn't mean to, but that you were frightened of making a fool of yourself, and so on.

The same sort of behaviour is leaving someone out of a meeting, which may have immediate consequences to your relationship and to organization effectiveness.

To the extent we do not make people feel significant, but make them feel they are not important enough to bother with, or ignore them, which is deliberately making them unimportant, we set up difficulties between us whose ramifications are difficult to predict, except that we can be sure that they are likely to be negative.

We have to ask in every situation we find ourself: 'Am I including people? If I am unsure about whether to include somebody or not, then I will?' The debate you have about whether you should or not is really you trying to avoid doing something you are frightened of doing. So, you will help yourself and your colleague best by doing what you have been trying to avoid doing. Another way of putting this is to say that you have been a 'helper' to yourself by denying what is significant.

If in doubt, it is better to over include than under include. People can decide they don't want to be included, but at least their fear of being ignored has not been touched.

We are motivated by people who make us feel significant. If they feel we are significant, we feel they are.

Ensure that people can decide for themselves whether to be included with you or not. Denying them the chance may not be inclusive so much as intrusive. Just inviting yourself in ignores them just as much as you might feel if you were left out. Over inclusion will communicate their significance and also make them feel assured that whenever there may be a time when they might fear that they will not be included, you will make sure that they get the chance to be. (And if you sometimes forget (?) to include them, they may have enough of a reservoir of strength in their ego not to feel negative.) They will feel that you would be a good person to be with, if they want to be. As a result of feeling good about themselves, they feel good about you.

Examples of words and phrases related to this feeling are: regard, status, priority, importance, seniority, preference, as well as to opposites, lowly, humble and negligible, and to fears of being left out, passed by and ignored.

Inclusion, significance and defences:
Victim: 'I don't deserve to be included.'
Critic: 'You don't deserve to be included.'
Helper: 'People don't include you.'
Demander: 'You must include me. You must let me include you.'

Competent

You convey to others you feel they are competent to the extent you allow them to have influence and to take control. It would be foolish to rely upon people's competence, if they are not. On the other hand, recognition of competence makes us feel good. We tend to feel others are capable when we feel capable ourselves.

If we do not allow someone to take responsibility, use their skills and do for themselves or for us those things which they are competent to do, they may stop trying. They may never learn that they are competent because they never get the chance to practise and take risks. They may never get a chance to learn from their mistakes. Then, when we want them to be competent, they may fear that they cannot be.

Finding out what one's capabilities are always carries with it the risk of failure. It is a failure to feel that one is competent when there is no evidence for it yet. That is like letting oneself down. It also carries the risk of looking stupid if one fails. Extending one's competence always carries an element of pride, that we think we are better at something than we are demonstrating at present. And the sin of pride can so often result in a fall. Being sneered or scoffed at does nothing for the ego and may stop us from trying in the future.

I knew a managing director who, for reasons you can guess (yes, he must have been fearful of his own possible lack of competence), poured scorn on any of his directors' ideas when they did not agree with his, with the result that he got a board that never had any ideas. Humiliation is a particularly strong fear in organizations where skills are so essential, but the skill of our competence in handling a relationship is core in all our relationships, in formal organizations and otherwise.

Just as in significance, how much competence requires just the right balance. Allow too much influence and you may not have the competence necessary to guard against failure. And if they fail, you will feel a failure too. In fact, it will be your failure because you should have been competent enough to know they weren't competent enough in the first place. Too much influence and you stunt their growth. They give up trying or think they cannot, when they can.

Here again you've failed because their failure is really yours. You should have been competent enough to recognize that they could demonstrate more skill. To get the balance right, do not confer it because you think you should, but because you and they have 'levelled' with each other and ironed out any accompanying fears you both have.

When people think that you feel they are competent, they think that you are competent too. When we think that someone is not competent, when we want to reduce the influence they have over us, we should ask we are trying to protect ourselves from, what are we afraid of, what do we get out of thinking about them that way? (See 'Rewards and negative gains', Chapter 8.)

Examples of words and phrases related to this feeling are: respect, competent, clever, trust, efficient, proficient, and to opposites, such as weak, inadequate, inept, incompetent, and to fears of seeming stupid, making a fool of oneself, appearing ridiculous, humiliated.

We are motivated by people who make us feel competent. We tend to treat them the way they treat us.

Control, competence and defences:

Victim: 'I'm not capable. I shouldn't have any influence. I know I'm stupid.'

Critic: 'You are not capable. You should not have any influence. You're stupid.'

Helper: 'You should not feel you are not capable and should not feel you shouldn't have influence. You should not feel you are stupid.'

Demander: 'Make me feel competent by doing it for me. Make me feel capable by letting me do it for you. Tell me I'm not stupid by letting me do it. Tell me I am stupid so I won't have to do it.'

Warm (or likeable)

It would be silly to be open with someone you hate. It seems that they might well take advantage of you. If we are at war, the relation is cold, not warm, so it is inadvisable to signal what my plans are. The opposite is true.

If you are open with another person, they suppose that they must be likeable. This is because it would be unnatural to be open with someone whom you did not care for, in case they harmed you. Liking someone implicitly conveys that we care for each other and that neither of us have anything to fear. They feel good about being likeable. It abolishes the fear they have that they may not be.

People who feel likeable in the presence of the other person feel that the other person is likeable.

It is worth remembering that whether the other person is likeable or not has nothing directly to do with them, it is whether you feel likeable when you are with them. If you do, then, as a result of this, you will feel that they are likeable.

The same is true of the feelings of competence and significance. When you think about it, this gives you tremendous power to influence the way a person responds to you. If you can somehow make them feel significant, competent or likeable when they are with you, they will feel that you are too.

People want to be liked. It enables them to like themselves. Or, if you prefer, it eliminates the fear that they are not likeable. In the same way, trusting people enables them to feel trustworthy. If other people trust them, perhaps they can have the courage to trust themselves.

We are open with each other to the extent we feel we can trust each other. Someone has to start the ball rolling and go first. It is confronting the beneath the surface issues that is important. When we have some awareness that the other person has 'something on their mind' which they are not telling, we may think they feel we cannot be trusted. And so, as a way of protecting ourself, we keep our secrets from them too. For example, we are a critic and think, 'I don't want you to confide in me,' or a victim, and think, 'You never confide in me.'

Sometimes it is necessary to initiate the conflict you have about not thinking the other person can be trusted, although you feel you want to. Perhaps it is because you are afraid that they will not receive and deal with the matter as seriously and respectfully as you feel it deserves. When you trust a little bit and experience trust in return it is easier to trust a little more.

The feeling of rejection which accompanies a breach of trust is powerful and poignant. Once broken, it may be impossible to repair. People who have had their trust abused may never trust again. To be precise, their experience is that they cannot trust themself to give of their trust wisely, so they won't give their trust at all. Or they may spend their lives hopelessly trying to destroy trust in others, in order to get back at whoever abused their trust in the first place. They might attempt to compensate by thinking that other people are just like them, being fools to give of their trust. Such a syndrome may describe a succession of failed relationships, and explains much about so-called 'anti-social behaviour'.

Examples of words and phrases related to this feeling are: care, honest, love, appreciate, enjoy, hold dear, and to opposites, such as hate, loathe, despise, and of fears of being spurned, dumped, exploited, shunned, scorned.

We like people with whom we feel we are likeable.

Openness, likeability and defences:

Victim:	'You don't like me. I deserve to be rejected.'
Critic:	'I don't like you. You deserve it.'
Helper:	'You should be open with people. You should like people. You should not feel rejected.'
Demander:	'Tell me you like me. Don't reject me.'

SUMMARY OF DEFENCES

Critic:	'I am not nice to you and you deserve it.'
Victim:	'You are not nice to me but I deserve it.'
Helper:	'You are not nice to yourself and you don't deserve it.'
Demander:	'Tell me I am nice.'

PERSONALITY

All the richness and diversity of human behaviour and emotional response can be placed in one of the three dimensions: inclusion, control and openness. Whilst our circumstances are different, our feelings and our behaviour are the same. We respond differently, not because our feelings are different, but because we have learned to cope with our circumstances that way. In other circumstances we may have coped differently.

Sometimes we think our personality or character is fixed, that we were 'born the way we are', whilst the truth is that that is only the way we have learned to cope. We can unlearn and learn to cope differently, if we want, by understanding the circumstances that led us to cope the way we did, and then trying out other ways of coping which may be more appropriate for us now than the old ways which may be familiar, but no longer useful.

Suppose we learned to cope with our parents by being quiet and getting out of their way. It becomes the way we are. But years later we may hate ourself for being so quiet, or so loud, so passive, so aggressive, and so on. Why were we born this way? The truth is that we weren't. We found it useful to be that way at the time. As it worked in those circumstances we continued to use it. We used what we became familiar with and did not give ourselves a chance to learn to be any other way.

We might have chosen to cope with our parents by being loud and demanding. Now, since we hate ourself the way we are, we want to be different, but are unsure how to be. Being 'born that way' becomes an excuse for not trying to do what is now difficult for us, although we are dimly aware that we can do it, otherwise the thought would not have occurred to us.

Not doing what we want to do and know we can do leaves us unfulfilled; because we are letting ourselves down our self esteem suffers; we don't like ourself as much as we want. We may react by unconsciously blaming people who are loud and extroverted because, secretly, we want to be like them. Or we demand that they be like us in order that they do not remind us of our failings; if they change, we won't have to.

If we really cannot be as we want, the thought that we can be would not have occurred to us.

Sharing the feelings is what enables us to comprehend another person's unique identity and similarity to ourselves. Everything we do, say or feel – all our experience – fits into Will Schutz's Model. Using this structure we can understand, process and resolve doubts and difficulties as they arise.

We are motivated by people and them by us, by the way we behave towards each other. We can change both our feelings and our behaviour by understanding what we contributed to bring that behaviour about and what we get out of behaving towards each other the way we do.

How much a person is motivated by you is not only the product of how you behave towards them, but also their feelings about themselves. As we have seen, you can enormously affect the way people feel about themselves when they are with you and, hence, the way they feel about you and behave towards you.

SUMMARY

All of us have feelings about ourself which are the product of many experiences of relating to others. Feeling good about one's significance, competence and likeability creates a kind of fund or reservoir. It can easily be depleted by the most trivial setback, but to the degree it is strong rather than fragile, it is possible to perceive defensive behaviour in others for what it is. Then we are able to cope with awareness of those doubts about oneself that inevitably arise.

This chapter has focused mainly upon motivation from the interpersonal perspective. How to look further into your personal motivation can be found in Chapter 9, Personal agenda setting.

Optional exercises

The three questionnaires which follow are designed for you to make concrete those thoughts and feelings you have about people and you think they have about you. Writing them down helps to clarify and to define useful initiatives for you to take to become motivated by people in the way you want. Take a present or a past example, a big or apparently trivial matter. Do not begin to process or justify, the objective is to understand how your perceptions arise. Use your imagination to put down what you feel.

Having done the exercise, you should gain insight into your own and others' behaviour that forms your feelings. The next step would be to initiate with the other person at the beneath the surface level. This should lead to an awareness in which you experience increased regard, respect and warmth for each other.

Instructions:

Do not allow yourself to be limited by the page. You can write down as many people as are relevant.

Exercise – understanding motivation

Surface	Behaviour
Names of people who make me feel significant:	What they have done to make me feel that way:

1 _____   _____

2 _____   _____

                                    _____

3 _____   _____

How I feel about the people who   1 _____
make me feel that way
                                    2 _____

                                    3 _____

Beneath the surface   Behaviour
People I think ignored me or made   What they have done to make me
me feel insignificant: (maybe some feel this way:
of the same people)

1 _____   _____

                                    _____

                                    _____

2 _____   _____

                                    _____

                                    _____

3 _____   _____

What defences are we both using?

Insight: What are they getting out   _____
of treating me that way?   _____

                                    _____

Insight: How do I collude to bring   _____
about their behaviour?   _____

                                    _____
Resolution: What words do I use   _____
to take the initiative in order to be _____
significant?
                                    _____

                                    _____

                                    _____

Motivation and people – competence

Surface   Behaviour

Names of people who make me   What they have done to make me
feel competent: feel that way:

1 _____   _____

                              _____

2 _____   _____

                              _____

3 _____   _____

How I feel about the people who   1 _____
make me feel that way

                              2 _____

                              3 _____

Beneath the surface   Behaviour
People I think humiliated me or   What they have done to make me
made me feel incapable: (maybe   feel this way:
some of the same people)

1 _____   _____

                              _____

                              _____

2 _____   _____

                              _____

                              _____

3 _____   _____

What defences are we both using?

Insight: What are they getting out   _____
of treating me that way?   _____

                              _____

                              _____

Insight: How do I collude to bring about their behaviour?

_____
_____
_____

Resolution: What words do I use to take the initiative in order to be competent?

_____
_____
_____
_____
_____
_____

Motivation and people – likeability

Surface

Names of people who make me feel likeable:

1 _____

2 _____

3 _____

How I feel about the people who make me feel that way

Behaviour

What they have done to make me feel that way:

_____
_____
_____
_____

1 _____

2 _____

3 _____

Beneath the surface
People I think rejected me or made me feel unlikeable: (maybe some of the same people)

Behaviour
What they have done to make me feel this way:

1 _____   _____
                               _____

2 _____   _____
                                  _____
                                  _____
3 _____   _____
                                  _____

What defences are we both using?

Insight: What are they getting out   _____
of treating me that way?   _____

                                          _____

Insight: How do I collude to bring   _____
about their behaviour?   _____

Resolution: What words do I use to   _____
take the initiative in order to be   _____
likeable?   _____

                                          _____
                                          _____
                                          _____
                                          _____

6

Values and Vision

Missions are stupid. I have no mission. No-one has. And it's a terrific release to realise you're free, free of all missions.

Milan Kundera, *The Unbearable Lightness of Being*

INTRODUCTION

What you want most in your organization is a climate where everyone can feel self fulfilled. Therefore, there must be a process which allows you to deal with any doubts that might hinder you from becoming yourself.

An atmosphere in which self fulfilment is not only desirable, but made possible, is one in which you are aware that you are significant to the organization, that you can use your competence in the way that allows you to have influence and that you can be open about any matter which you fear may be blocking you from being yourself.

The vision and values must contain the intent and a method to resolve any issues which prevent you feeling good about yourself – anything less than that will not allow the organization to function optimally. Vision and values are therefore connected to the process by which we relate together.

THE VALUE OF OPENNESS

Values need to enshrine openness. First, be open with yourself about your feelings and, second, be open with others about any conflicts that include them. Particularly be open within those situations where you are tempted to avoid that conflict.

Many organizational theorists, such as Jaques and Clement (1994), view openness as a value which allows freedom 'to express true opinion and allow opportunities for participation in context setting and policy making'. This is a very limited, superficial definition of openness, because it covers only the inclusion and control criteria, and, even then, not in the depth practised in total leadership. This kind of definition is really only about information exchange; it comes nowhere near the quality of openness required to resolve misperception. As I said earlier (in Chapter 1) failure to deal with conflicts inhibits performance.

The correct definition of openness is reverse feedback. Anything that is not openness – deceit, lying, pretence, avoidance, withholding, little white lies – prevents us from knowing where we are, what is expected of us or what feelings people have about us. In these circumstances, doubts about ourselves arise, and we may feel negative as a consequence of you employing defence mechanisms to displace your doubts on to us.

If we spend our time defending ourselves against each other we may never be as productive as we could be, and are motivated to be. Openness is the tool with which we overcome our defences so that we are able to complete the task.

THE VALUE OF RESPONSIBILITY

Each person is responsible for the way he is leading his life. Instead of blaming your boss, a colleague or the organization, do something about it yourself. Change is unlikely to arise as the result of doing nothing. Doing nothing is also a choice. The value, therefore, is that, if things are not the way you want, you are the one who is responsible for changing them.

If you *care* it is a sure indication that you feel responsible. The best person to do something is yourself. It is no good saying that someone else is more responsible or that someone else should be responsible. The buck stops with you.

Responsibility means doing something about the situation you find yourself in. Extrication from the situation can only be achieved by you taking responsibility for initiating your conflict at the beneath the surface level with the person whom you feel is included in it.

Do not compromise in what you expect of yourself. Treat yourself in the way you would like other people to treat you. Then, you are likely to treat them in the same way. Thus, the values of people who work together become increasingly congruent.

Conversely, if you 'put up with' a situation which you hate, you begin to despise yourself for not being strong enough to do something about it. Hatred of oneself poisons relationships. To the extent you feel you are 'letting yourself down,' you will blame others for the situation you find yourself in. Or, you may encourage them to be critical, because your suppressed guilt makes you feel you deserve to be blamed. These, as you will have recognized, are projections from you on to them – you would really like to see them do something you would like to do yourself – getting back at the organization for the way you think it is making you feel.

CASE STUDY

The formulation of responsibility in total leadership goes some way further than that put forward by Jaques and Clement (1994), who make a distinction between 'accountability' and 'responsibility'. The former relates to what we are appraised upon as having done well or badly. The latter relates to our social conscience and our personal sense of what we should do. Jaques and Clement propose that:

> Subordinates must strive to take 'responsibility' toward their managers whenever they consider it to be for everyone's good for them to do so. That is to say, they must take initiative in bringing forward their arguments as strongly as possible where they think their manager is taking a wrong direction, dropping the matter, of course, if the manager does not in the end agree.

This begs so many questions, for example, how can an individual make a judgement about 'what is for everyone's good?' and why should he 'drop the matter, of course'? For me, there is too much room for error in these sorts of behaviours, too many opportunities to perpetuate the old rigidities and the old defences.

My answer to these examples is, first, that the subordinate *does what is for his good*, anything else is likely to be a 'projection' of his fears onto others. Second, that he *does not drop the matter until both he and his manager agree*. Thus, his 'accountability' includes the resolution of any real or potential conflict in order to find the law of the situation. In total leadership *there is no distinction between 'accountability' and 'responsibility'*.

VISION

As we have seen, the values are simple and straightforward; the vision simply enshrines the values. This always follows. For example, what sort of vision follows from organizations whose values are secret or who create dependency? Probably there is something happening in that organization that it is ashamed of or embarrassed about.

Also, if you get the vision right it is easily translatable into operational values. This is often difficult with so called 'mission statements'. I am not talking about objectives, as they are different from mission statements; objectives relate to the attainment of the task and arise, practically, from our understanding of the law of the situation. Mission statements, on the other hand, are like aspirations or expectations, unless they do meaningfully connect with a way we have to go about getting what we want. Mission statements too often seem like dogma – commandments which have little to do with our everyday experience of what is actually happening.

A vision fails if it is of a type that espies the 'promised land'. Organizations which attempt to develop such a vision will always find it elusive. It is much more satisfying to lead our lives on earth the way we want to today! Our vision has to do with the way we conduct ourselves in the support of our values. If we do this, we will inevitably get to where we want to go. In following 'the yellow brick road' the first thing to do is to take the first step.

As Robert Kriegel (1991) says, 'Many of us have had a similar experience of living for a goal and, upon reaching it, feeling let down.' Goals become 'yesterday's news'. He recommends that, 'goals should follow dreams'.

> Goals create limitations on the imagination and inhibit innovation.
> Robert J Kriegel, *If it ain't broke ... BREAK IT!*

When the individual's and the organization's goals are congruent there is a vision; values are the enabling process by which the vision is realized.

CARRYING OUT THE VISION

If, as Kriegel recommends, 'Leadership should follow vision', let us have a vision which is immediate and renewable, now and always. Like Kriegel, I believe that the only way is 'to have a personal vision or dream to fuel the fire in our hearts'.

Now that we are agreed upon enjoyment and understand total motivation, we know the way to go.

Think of something you could do that would make you feel good about yourself. Careful! If this implies getting one up on someone, getting back at them, your feeling of goodness will not last very long. You may experience guilt or worry that they'll get back at you in turn.

So, has something you would like to do or be come into your mind? It's likely to be something you're a little afraid of doing, otherwise you would have done it before. If you are not experiencing a little trepidation, try taking a little more risk with your imagination and 'live a little closer to the edge'. You might be afraid, because you are unsure that people will like you if you do what you want. You may even tell yourself that it's better to do nothing, then you won't make others feel uncomfortable or risk making yourself look silly.

But the vision also consists of responsibility to ourselves. How can we be responsible for others unless we start from a position of self responsibility? Failing ourselves means failing them. It follows, as the night the day, if we do something to take ourselves further, we also create opportunity for others.

The more immediate the 'vision' the better. It should connect where we are now with the next step which arises from the situation we find ourselves in. The law of our present situation determines the next step. It follows inexorably, one from the other.

A vision that is many steps away fails, because we cannot see any 'law' in the connection. It is not likely to be a compelling vision if too far away from our present experience. How can we be sure, from such a long way off, that this will in fact be where we will want to be when we get there? The best vision sets us out on the road, but it is getting right each step on the road that is important. If we do that the vision will reveal itself in the process. We will always keep the vision in sight if we practise the values.

Each step makes sure that everyone involved wants to take it. If you make a step without involving the other person who is part of your team you risk going separate roads. Out of fear that their vision may not be the same as yours, you may tell yourself they would not understand and that your paths differ, but how do you know if you do not give them a choice?

Keeping people informed of conflicts you have with your situation and with your next step gives them a choice of whether to join you or not. Assuming they cannot or will not want to is a choice you make not to include them. Effectively, you deprive them of the choice to take responsibility for themselves.

Also, do not feel you have to take responsibility for the choices that people have made to be with you. The fact that they are in the situation with you is a result of their choice – blaming you for persuading them to join you is to deny that they had a choice. That is unawareness. They always had a choice, whether they admit it to themselves or not. Saying they did not is a ploy to avoid taking responsibility for their lives and to attempt to make you responsible instead. It is demanding that you compensate for their fear.

Her pattern was to avoid decisions until decisions made themselves – until she became aware that the avoidance had been the decision.

Anne Redmon, *The Genius of the Sea*

You only can lead *your* life. First, by making sure that you are open with yourself about why you are making your choices. Secondly, by enabling others to be clear about the choices they are making which involve you.

This vision acknowledges the law of reciprocal psychology: that individuals are much closer to each other than they might sometimes care to imagine. Your conflict is almost never your conflict alone. Your conflict arises in part because of your perception of what you imagine another does to you to make you feel the way you do. When you tell the other about your conflict, you give them the choice of becoming aware and of sharing the conflict which they have which includes you. You both find that what has the potential to drive you apart, if you are not open about it, is the very thing that draws you together when you initiate openness.

The vision includes the premise that when you tell the other person how you feel about your conflict, they will help you understand it better by telling you how they feel. The reciprocal nature of this process brings about the essential 'vision'.

Suppose you do not know what the vision of your organization is or you are confused by it, as in the following example:

Surface level	'You don't know where you are with this company.'
Beneath the surface level	'I don't seem to matter.'

Maybe the surface statement arises in a company which has a vision to do with getting there in the end, one way or another. Maybe the vision is to do with it not mattering whether employees are aware what is going on or not. Whatever the case, the statement is a grumble. It is about the organization. It may be responded to, but it doesn't invite response. It is certainly not as intriguing to the listener as the deeper feeling. This is more likely to get attention. Of course, it is always possible that, upon hearing the projected surface level statement, a total leader may say, 'Tell me more about what you are feeling? What makes you feel that way?'

For the moment, at the surface level, any vision there may be is not shared by the speaker. Notice that the statement is a projection in which the speaker is a victim. The company is blamed for where the speaker finds himself. The deeper issue is not with the company, although it is being blamed, but what the person is feeling about himself in this situation.

The task for the individual is to take the initiative in finding out where he stands with the organization. The vision for the organization is in recognizing that individuals want to know where they are with the company because, knowing enables them to take responsibility for themselves. They are denied a choice, in other words, except, perhaps, the choice of resigning.

Assuming all individuals are responsible for what happens to them is the most empowering value for the organization to adopt. Anything less denies its human resources to itself. So, the vision is to do with creating a climate in which any conflict about this can be resolved.

The principal part of the vision in total leadership is to assume that what matters to me also matters to you. In fact, make the assumption that what matters to me is extremely likely to matter to you. The vision of the organization should be to find out how much of our imagined differences we have in common.

The vision contains the initiator's assumptions that conflict can be resolved, and that overcoming personal conflict will benefit both him and the organization. Therefore, he practises both openness and responsibility.

In the example of beneath the surface dialogue which follows, note that the listener perceives that he is going to benefit himself from hearing the initiator's conflict and that the interests of the organization are preserved by both initiator and receiver taking the issues 'personally'.

Note also how apparent division leads eventually to mutual understanding. What drove people apart, now brings them together. As the result of the initiator initiating his conflict, the receiver becomes aware of his own. The receiver is not drawn in or forced – he would probably be hostile if he felt compelled or driven – but is given a choice whether or not to be involved. In the beginning, he chooses to participate because he feels significant, competent and likeable, as the inevitable consequence of the initiator's openness. Later on, he feels rewarded as a consequence of becoming aware and resolving his own conflict.

Example of 'beneath the surface' dialogue

If the 'beneath the surface' feeling is expressed, the discussion may go this way:

Initiator You		Receiver Your colleague, boss, partner, etc
	to:	
'I don't seem to matter.'		'You shouldn't feel that way, of course you matter.'

'Thank you, but telling me I shouldn't feel that way doesn't seem to help.'

'Sorry. Tell me more about why you feel you don't matter.'

'It's like being left out, or just brushed aside, talking is avoided.'

'Do I make you feel that way?'

'Well, you often seem very busy.'

'Well, I am very busy.'

'You seem to not want to hear what I'm saying. I was just saying I feel that when there is no time for me, I feel I'm being avoided.'

'You're right. I'm being defensive. I don't mean to avoid you. I suppose I feel I'm not coping. I wish I had the time to do everything the way I'd like.'

'I didn't realize you felt that way. I just thought that you felt I wasn't important enough to bother with. Maybe I could do more to help you cope.'

'I suppose I was frightened of imposing on you, just trying to cope by myself. I felt you might resent it if I asked you to help. What a pathetic boss!'

'That's not pathetic. You seem to do everything on your own, that's all. It's good you are able to share things like this. Don't feel frightened about including me. I want to get more involved. That's great.'

'I'm really glad you stopped me. I should have brought this up myself. You're really helping me get things sorted out.'

THE PROCESS

Organizational effectiveness is determined by internal functioning and external application. Applying ourselves to a task, such as making money in the market place, developing a new product or, indeed, to any venture we undertake, has little chance of success unless we have taken stock of our resources. Are we fit, that is, healthy and well, psychologically as well as physically?

We start off by wanting to achieve. And the mere evidence of wanting indicates that we probably can, otherwise it would not have occurred to us. But have we got the skills? Therefore, before taking action it is wise to make sure we are aware how to do it. If we are not aware, we must have a vision which enables us to become so.

Awareness is the first step. Without awareness our efforts may well seem to be based upon hope and guesswork rather than control of what we are doing.

Awareness allows us to perceive our strengths, but also our weaknesses. There may be technical, experiential or personal weaknesses. The most important of these is the personal, because if these are not addressed they will inevitably undermine the others. The process of 'stock taking' or awareness raising also enables our understanding of other organizations we are working with or relating to, including our customers or other organizations who are affected by what we do. For example, we might ask our customers how they perceive us. Even better is to ask other organizations to be open with us about the conflicts we might create in them.

Awareness of our resources gives us control. Now we can begin to focus effectively. We use our motivation and our knowledge efficiently to bring our awareness of our resources to bear in just the way we want. We know what we are and can do. We are in control of what we are doing.

Without control, there can be no proper focus for our efforts. Without control, we miss the mark, we are too late, too early or appear either erratic or inflexible. Just the right balance in our control allows us to appear and behave in the way we want.

The process may be represented thus:

⇒	Awareness	⇒	Control	⇒	Focus

This is a complete representation of what happens in all organizations which learn and adapt. It describes not only what happens in all organizations, but also what happens in teams, in partnerships, in our nation and in our own, personal, organization.

In pointing out that any organism dies if it cannot adapt at a greater rate than the environmental changes around it, Hawkins and Miller (1994) also make the point that, 'Organizational learning is clearly dependent on the continuous learning of all its members'. Jeanetta Betsch-Cole (1997) made a similar statement, 'If you stop learning, you stop living.'

Thus, to focus, that is relate to the world in just the way you want, you must first become aware of yourself. Manifestly, individuals without awareness have little control of what they are doing. We stay out of their way or are cautious about dealing with them.

The same is true of organizations. They exist as a 'personality' and go through the same process of integration as individuals. At whatever level you care to take it, personalities which are well integrated are well focused, well in control and well aware.

The values and the vision must bring about this integration to be fully effective. To the extent that the values and the vision do not facilitate this integration the organization is failing its customers, but most of all it fails itself.

CASE STUDY

The process can be viewed as a wheel in which each condition – awareness, control and focus – are three spokes. As the wheel rotates, the point at which the spoke touches the ground is where an exchange takes place. This is the point of feedback as to the effectiveness of behaviour under this condition. Awareness is the point at which the individual or the organization is open about their situation. As the wheel revolves, the next spoke, control, addresses action plans and musters resources. This provides the basis for decision making which is carried out as the third spoke receives its turn. As the wheel moves on, the spoke of awareness comes to the ground again. Everything has 'had its turn', but now things are different. The process is the same, but the wheel has travelled on to a new place. Indeed, the situation is new. The individual or the organization has a matured experience, and the scenery is unfamiliar. As the wheel rotates and moves through time and space it retains its psychological integrity and adaptiveness.

In an organization which is failing itself, again, at whatever level of organization you care to take, will be found defensive and aggressive behaviours externally and internally. Success arises from confronting the behaviours which are causing failure and replacing them with behaviours which integrate awareness, control and focus.

ENSURING THE VISION

1. The quality of our relationships determines the success of our organization

You will know of organizations in which the expression of our feelings is regarded as a sign of weakness. The 'macho' image purports to be businesslike – 'We haven't got the time to discuss our feelings with each other'.

'Politicking' is a word often used in organizations to describe subterfuge and deceit. It is often mistaken for cleverness. The reality is that it spawns further evasion and duplicity. Its effects are worsened to the degree that more senior executives conspire with each other, because they have more influence in determining the organizational 'culture'. Company politics is just another way to describe negative energy.

It is true that many 'macho' organizations have been successful historically, but it is increasingly recognized that this style is unsuited to modern, effective organizations. The truth is that just about all the problems that arise in organizations are problems arising from unresolved difficulties in relationships.

In my experience of working with individuals, teams and many international 'blue chip' companies, I have yet to meet an organizational problem that did not, at its root, arise from a misperception.

If it is true that organizations can be successful in spite of unresolved interpersonal difficulties think of how much more successful they would be if they were resolved!

Thinking that, **'It's just business'**, in a film such as 'The Godfather', is an extreme representation of an organization which denies the value of feelings.

2. Openness is the way to resolve issues

Decisions can seem to take more time when people want time to discuss their doubts. That is why it sometimes seems preferable to have a leader who just 'tells us what to do' – which is fine, so long as we feel he or she is doing what we want. Openness about what *we want*, or what it is that is stopping us getting what we want, makes sure that we are contributing. Holding back on our personal doubts or difficulties with each other is not, ultimately, effective. Moreover, keeping things to oneself violates the principle of reciprocal psychology – that your difficulties are unlikely to be entirely your own, someone else is also responsible with you.

It also follows that the other person's difficulties are unlikely to be entirely their own. In an organization which has a 'power' culture, it will be usual to distance oneself from another person's failure. Finding a 'scapegoat' temporarily relieves us of the fear that the blame might be turned upon us. Rather, we should be asking ourselves what we did or did not do to contribute to that person's failure. What fixes failure on a permanent basis is beneath the surface relating so that the situation is understood. Then, what emerges is the natural law of what to do about it. Since it is agreed by all the parties involved, there is no question of blame.

It was a habit with Paul to lift what lay in his heart to a shelf in his mind so that he was safe from whatever he felt.

Anne Redmon, *The Genius of the Sea*

'Pretending everything is OK' shuts others out of your situation. It avoids engaging the real task. Similar phrases are: 'I didn't think it was important enough to mention', when the truth is that is the most important thing of all. The consequences might be that your silence is perceived as signifying that you don't like them, or don't think they are good enough for you. The truth is that you are not coping. It's simpler to tell the truth. It's going to come out in the end, so, the sooner you tell it the better!

3. Individuals take responsibility for themselves

It is desperate to fear you cannot cope, so you tend to suppress the feeling rather than bring it into your awareness. It is easier to blame someone else, so you project or displace your fear of failure onto them. The more vehement the denial that it could be you who contributed to the problem, the more unaware of the truth you really are! Taking responsibility for yourself is the only sure way to take responsibility for others. If you are clear about your difficulties and resolve them, you cannot but enable others to become clear about themselves and what they are doing.

Not only does this enhance teamwork between individuals, it has the same facilitating effect between departments where it is just as essential to break down the barriers!

To appear to be helpful, by bringing up what was on your mind later on when it is too late, enables nobody. To say, **'I could have told them'** might be intended to make you look good, but reveals your betrayal, most of all, to yourself for what you could have contributed for the benefit of all, if only you had had the courage. Confronting the beneath the surface issue is empowering yourself or, if you like, putting yourself totally in control.

CASE STUDY

Players on the international stage are affected by their feelings, just like everybody else. An example is Chris Patten, last Governor of Hong Kong who, 'No longer governor, could speak openly about the men he believes let the colony down. In his final days as governor, Chris Patten gave vent to anger at the way in which ... (various people) ... appear to have colluded with China to subvert the will of the Hong Kong people and, in the process, made his own task incomparably more difficult.'

This revelation, after the event, serves little purpose, since the time for action that would have enabled the citizens of Hong Kong has passed. Now the truth will be distorted by recriminations, cover ups and denials. Patten's anger, just or not, also reveals, through reciprocal psychology, the evidence of his own betrayal.

Obviously, Patten himself had a **conflict**, withholding what he saw as the truth, because of his duty to his superiors, but he rightly assesses the situation in which all parties were involved: 'As ever with some of these too clever-by-half decisions – "not the right time" and so on – you build up more political problems by not facing up to things'.

Quotes from Jonathan Dimbleby, A Sense of Betrayal, *The Sunday Times*, 6 July 1997

4. Raising awareness is the route to effectiveness

Appearing good on the outside is unlikely to feel satisfying unless it is also accompanied by feelings of well being on the inside. Looking good or being smart, if a cover up for inner insecurities, may confuse others as to who you really are and how much 'depth' there is to you. It is like wearing a mask and, quite rightly, people don't trust it. Unless we allow ourself to become aware of what is going on, how can we expect to take control and focus in a way which is not merely spurious, but will have real meaning for us?

'Keeping up appearances' flagrantly ignores the law of the situation – that everything, particularly our feelings, needs to be involved if we are to be successful and accomplish the task. To make our lives what we want involves us in confronting the conflicts we have, not ignoring them.

The vision is that personal aims and organizational aims are congruent; the values are the process through which the vision is realized.

AIM OF THE ORGANIZATION

I am going to offer a suggestion for a simple, single touchstone which encompasses all of the foregoing. What is simple is often the best, and my stricture is so simple that you will be aware of any departure from it without having to analyse why – you will just know that you are not living up to your aim. It is this:

The aim of this organization is that is shall esteem itself.

Self esteem possesses all those aspects of feeling that are the essence of motivation and fulfilment. Self esteem cannot exist where there is unresolved conflict or fear. Self esteem is impossible without adherence to the values of responsibility and openness. To the extent that the organization does not experience self esteem, then duplicity, compromise and 'politicking' inevitably hold sway and it fails in its task.

Moreover, it is self esteem which makes each individual's vision congruent with that of the organization. The individual contributes most to the organization when they are motivated by their personal vision. Any organization is unfulfilled so long as any individual within it, or any part within an individual's organization, is not fulfilled. Ultimately, the only vision that has value to any organization is self esteem.

SUMMARY

The following principles lead to the most productive corporate vision:

- That conflict in the organization exactly mirrors the conflict of the leaders.
- That understanding oneself is the surest way to help others understand themselves.
- That to eliminate any blocks to understanding is the goal of everyone who works together.
- That mutual understanding leads inevitably to increased performance.
- That in an organization which is totally productive, everybody is a leader.

The process required to achieve the vision is as follows:

1. *Raise awareness*
   Resolve any issues or areas which are experienced as less than ideal.
   Understand any areas of low level or misdirected energy, to understand the situation that has caused these to arise.
2. *Take control*
   Identify negative feelings which are limiting. Deal with these (a) by changing personal behaviour or, (b) by developing influencing skills.
   Confront issues that it is tempting to 'turn one's back upon'. Determine success enhancing behaviours.
3. *Focus*
   Implement and build upon the personal agenda. Create a winning team.

Monitor thoughts, feelings and behaviour. Focus again upon personal awareness and take responsibility. Initiate reverse feedback.
Enjoy the vision now!

Optional exercises

The following exercises focus your thoughts and feelings upon some of the assumptions outlined in this chapter. They are designed to establish how well you and your colleagues are living your vision.

It is surprising how much we hold back from living our vision because we do not think others perceive the situation the way we do. Engaging others in our perceptions may well reveal that they want to tread the same path we do.

As always with the exercises, the most important action is to initiate fears about doing what we would like. Overcoming the fears of practising our values creates a new unity in the way we relate. As this happens, the vision becomes real and attainable now.

Personal assessment against assumption 1

The quality of our relationships determines the success of our organization

On a scale of 0–9 where 0 means not at all, 9 means totally and 5 means about average, score the following, and anyone else you want, on how much they agree with the statement: The quality of our relationships determines the success of our organization.

Score
0–9

Write names below:

Me, _____ _____

My boss, _____ _____

My colleague, _____ _____

Team member, _____ _____

My partner, _____ _____

Any score that is less than 9 might represent a projection (or another defence) on your part, but of course would also contain some percentage of the truth.

How did the others rate you? You now have a beneath the surface dialogue to resolve the basis of your perception.

Insights _____

_____

_____

_____

_____

_____

_____

Personal assessment against assumption 2

Openness is the way to resolve issues

On a scale of 0–9 where 0 means not at all, 9 means totally and 5 means about average, score the following, and anyone else you want, on how much they agree with the statement: **Openness is the way to resolve issues.**

		Score 0–9
Me,	_____	_____
My boss,	_____	_____
My colleague,	_____	_____
Team member,	_____	_____

My partner, _____ _____

Any score that is less than 9 might represent a projection of you on to them, unless you are colluding to avoid taking this initiative. Have a beneath the surface discussion to resolve the basis of your perception.

Insights _____

_____

_____

_____

_____

_____

_____

Personal assessment against assumption 3

Individuals take responsibility for themselves

On a scale of 0–9 where 0 means not at all, 9 means totally and 5 means about average, score the following, and anyone else you want, on how much they agree with the statement: **Individuals take responsibility for themselves.**

Score
0–9

Me, _____ _____

My boss, _____ _____

My colleague, _____ _____

Team member, _____   _____

My partner,   _____   _____

Your scores might indicate a defence. Do you perceive the others the same way they perceive you? You now have a beneath the surface dialogue to understand why your scores are what they are.

Insights _____

_____

_____

_____

_____

_____

_____

Personal assessment against assumption 4

Raising awareness is the route to effectiveness

On a scale of 0–9 where 0 means not at all, 9 means totally and 5 means about average, score the following, and anyone else you want, on how much they agree with the statement: **Raising awareness is the route to effectiveness.**

Score
0–9

Me,   _____   _____

My boss,   _____   _____

My colleague,   _____   _____

Team member, _____ _____

My partner, _____ _____

You now use reverse feedback to resolve the basis of your perception
_____

Insights _____

_____

_____

_____

_____

_____

_____

_____

Exercise – establishing vision

The exercises which follow are for you to write down the conflict you have in situations. Making them manifest in black and white helps with focusing. It may be helpful to remind yourself of the dynamics of what goes on between you by referring back to the model of psychology in Chapter 5.

You might find it worth checking out your perceptions with these people!

About your boss

Name: _____

Beneath the surface statement	Behaviour What is done to make you feel that way
'I think you feel I _____	_____
_____	_____
_____	_____
_____	_____

Insight
What might your boss be feeling
about himself or herself to make
them treat you that way?

_____

_____

_____

Insight
What might you have done to
create the situation?

_____

_____

_____

Resolution
Write down what you do. Do
you initiate the statement above,
modify that statement in the light of
insights or take some other action?

_____

_____

_____

_____

About a colleague

Beneath the surface statement

'I think you feel I _____

_____

Behaviour
What is done to make you feel
that way _____

_____

Insight
What might he or she be feeling
about himself or herself to make
them treat you that way?

_____

_____

_____

Insight
What might you have done to
create the situation?

_____

_____

_____

Resolution
Write down what you do. Do
you initiate the statement above,
modify that statement in the light of
insights or take some other action?

_____

_____

_____

About a subordinate

Beneath the surface statement

'I think you feel I _____

Behaviour
What is done to make you feel
that way_____

_____

_____

Insight
What might he or she be feeling
about himself or herself to make
them treat you that way?

_____

_____

_____

Insight
What might you have done to
create the situation?

_____

_____

_____

Resolution
Write down what you do. Do
you initiate the statement above,
modify that statement in the light of
insights or take some other action?

_____

_____

_____

_____

About your partner/or other human being

Beneath the surface statement

'I think you feel I _____

Behaviour
What is done to make you feel
that way_____

_____

Insight
What might he or she be feeling
about himself or herself to make
them treat you that way?

_____

_____

_____

Insight
What might you have done to
create the situation?

_____

_____

Resolution
Write down what you do. Do
you initiate the statement above,   _____
modify that statement in the light of   _____
insights or take some other action?   _____
                                           _____

_____

Exercise – establishing vision with reverse feedback

The exercises which follow are for you to write down the conflicts you have
in situations. Making them manifest in black and white helps with focusing.
Check out your perceptions using reverse feedback to resolve the conflicts.

About the other person
                    Name: _____

Your beneath the surface statement   Their behaviour
                                      What is done to make you feel
'I think you feel I _____   that way_____

_____   _____

Insight
What might they be feeling   _____
about himself or herself to make   _____
them treat you that way?   _____

Insight
What might you have done to   _____
create the situation?   _____
                                      _____

Resolution
Write down what you do. Do   _____
you initiate the statement above,   _____
modify that statement in the light of _____
insights or take some other action?   _____

The other person about you
                    Name: _____

Beneath the surface statement   Their behaviour
                                     What you do to make you feel
'They think you feel they _____   that way_____

_____   _____

Insight
What you think he or she might be   _____
feeling about yourself to treat them
that way: _____

                                     _____

Insight
What might they have done to   _____
help to create the situation?
                                     _____

                                     _____

Resolution
Write down what they do. Do   _____
they initiate the statement above,
modify that statement in the light of _____
insights or take some other action? _____

                                     _____

7

Situation and Task

Dad once defined leadership as the art of persuading people to do what they would have done in the first place.

M Truman, *Harry S Truman*

INTRODUCTION

In jobs where success depends to some extent upon how well people work together, the job always contains two tasks. The first is more easily despatched. It is with those aspects of the job in which people's interaction largely depends upon technical skills and knowledge, such as signing cheques, creating a drawing, handling a product, operating a machine, adding figures, and so on.

The second task is not necessarily what we were hired for; it is much more important, yet demands skills for which we may have had little formal training. This is an amazing omission from the educational curriculum, considering its profound importance to our lives on a continuing, daily basis. **It is the 'psychological task' upon which our effectiveness ultimately rests**. This task is affected by the way we behave to others and the way they behave to us.

How successful we are in our behaviour is without doubt the most vital task we have before us.

This chapter looks at aspects of situations which you may encounter whilst completing the task.

CHARISMA

It is often thought, mistakenly, that leadership resides in a 'figurehead', for example, the 'chief' executive or, in politics, the 'leader' of the party. It is a dream that there can ever be anyone who, by themselves, can be so consistently motivating and inspirational that we will want to do nothing else but follow them. Jaques and Clement (1994) comment that 'people follow the charismatic leader for all the wrong reasons,' because they are following behind, rather than with.

Charisma is a quality only relevant to cult leadership.

Jaques and Clement (1994)

CASE STUDY

Opposing political leaders criticise each other for prevarication, sitting on the fence and for weak leadership. In the run up to the election in Britain in 1997, the New Labour Leader, Tony Blair, spoke of the Conservative Leader, John Major, as ' A weak leader leading a weak government'. In contrast, he attempted to project himself as a strong leader, someone with clear views about how to resolve the country's problems. An electorate is, rightly, sceptical of such 'new dawns'. They are sophisticated enough to ask or wonder whether the entire political party shares the Labour Leader's views as firmly as he says he does – are his lieutenants just being tactical, pretending conformity, avoiding 'rocking the boat' for political reasons? Of course, though we we may think that this is just politics, Mr Blair was also making a point which is psychologically accurate: what he said of John Major had some truth, even though it is true of himself as well. The appointed leader's appearance of indecision may well indicate lack of uniformity in the other ranks. In Mr Blair's case, his assertion of uniformity also may well hide disunity. But, for the moment, putting Mr Major's credibility under the spotlight, he temporarily displaces attention from his own. In politics, it is usual to be the accuser (psychologically a 'critic') so that the state of one's own affairs is not questioned. It is an old ploy – displace attention away from yourself by pointing your finger at somebody else.

Leadership can never reside for very long with a single person. If there is a strong figurehead, and the leader of a political party as well as the head of any organization may appear strong, it is only because those involved with the leader are also intimately included in the leadership. That is, they show unity as a result of their own agendas being met within the relationship.

The figurehead is only ever as strong as his own agenda is indivisible with the agenda of his team. How is this brought about? Only by confronting those beneath the surface issues which are preventing them from discovering the law of the situation (see Chapter 11).

Our politics are adversarial. They prevent us from problem solving the underlying issues that are necessary to make progress. Political debate is an endless round of point scoring. It may be clever, but it is not enabling the best in people who should be working together in the interests of all of us.

An adversarial system does not get to the real issue because debate is always about superficial perceptions rather than about the feelings that really determine what needs to get done.

One of the reasons there are so few women in politics may be that women are less prepared to play the political game. Paradoxically, they are more prepared to encounter the deeper issues which are the key to dealing with issues of administration which concern us. To generalize, men seem to exist more at the intellectual, surface level, women are more able to deal with the conflict resolution levels beneath the surface.

Dealing intellectually with problems is always the long way round, it is a process of avoidance, blaming, misinformation and defensiveness, which runs and runs. Dealing with the emotional issues is ultimately the much shorter and stronger way to ensure that things are carried out in the way we want them.

GROUP CONFLICT

The conflict in any group exactly mirrors the conflict of the leaders.

Since it is possible that the leader or, for that matter, anyone else, may not be aware of his own conflicts, it is the job of individuals in the group to make him aware of them. In other words, the danger is that: to the degree the leader is unaware, the group is unaware also. The principle task of the total leader is to create an atmosphere in which the group can give him feedback of those things about himself of which he might be unaware.

THE LAW OF THE SITUATION (SEE ALSO CHAPTER 1)

The leader's job is *not* to give orders, but to facilitate resolution of misperception between whoever is involved. This leads to an understanding of the situation, whilst the law – what to do about it – is an outcome which follows naturally from it.

The leader's control extends only so far as he can integrate the feelings and behaviour of others with his own. Furthermore, he is only effective as a leader up to the time he last achieved this integration. As circumstances change, a new situation evolves and he must be alert to potentially disruptive conflicts. This is made easier, the more there is a 'culture' in which people are able to be proactive and initiate with their conflict, gaining confidence from the success that inevitably arises from beneath the surface relating.

Giving orders will almost always create some kind of conflict, however much the receiver of such orders may try to suppress this. When orders are taken from the law of the situation, the 'orders' form a natural, acceptable outcome from the resolution of the conflict. This is called the law of the situation – any potentially destructive emotion has been nullified by depersonalizing the orders. In this case, no orders are 'given' from one person to another. The 'ego' defences are not threatened because the process is one of unity. In the situation, no individual's personal will reigns, rather the opportunity for self fulfilment is present for all the individuals.

Mary Parker Follett (1941) put it thus: 'Our job is not how to get people to obey orders, but how we can devise methods by which we can best *discover* the order integral to a particular situation. When that is found, the employee can issue it to the employer, as well as employer to employee.'

BRINGING ABOUT CHANGE

Change is not good or even necessary to have 'for its own sake'. It is too risky, especially when the livelihood and well being of others might be involved. It is perverse to walk into a situation without knowing anything about it. It is an abandonment of control that verges on the reckless. Certainly, any change involves some amount of risk, but the risks need also to be managed rather than ignored. Even the author of 'Break It' philosophy, Robert Kriegel (1991) advised, 'Take risks, not chances'.

Total leadership is adopting the process by which we arrive at an awareness of whether we should change and what we might be afraid of that would stop us doing so. This process involves us in discovering the law of the situation. Being open with each other at the beneath the surface level will provide the correct answer as to what ways we should change, if at all.

Not changing is not a problem, provided we have ascertained that we shouldn't, having resolved our personal doubts and fears about whether or not to change. For example, are you merely consolidating or maintaining out of fear of dealing with possible conflicts? What are you avoiding by telling yourself there is no need to change? What are you withholding from yourself and from others? These are the issues to encounter before you can truthfully say there is no need to change. More often than not, we find that there is something to change, something we might have wanted to ignore, but now that we have examined it, we can see no reason why we should not make some change for the better. No compromise!

COMMUNICATION

It does not matter how effective you are at speaking or how extroverted you are, so long as you are communicating what really matters. All of us need to communicate more than we normally do. The critical thing is to communicate those things that make people feel that they are included. If you have plans which connect with others, you need to tell them those plans. If you have no plans, but suspect that they may think you have, ask them first of all if what you suspect is true, and then tell them you have no plans.

Sometimes we do not include people out of fear that, if we include ourself too much, they may see us as a threat. Or we fear that we are intruding in a way which is uncomfortable for others to deal with. But the danger is that others interpret our holding back as a rejection of them! It is a 'Mexican stand-off'; both parties are distant to each other; we don't think they want to include us, whilst they fear we think they are not good enough for us. The situation is quickly resolved when one of the parties makes it clear that they are committed and that they want the other to be significant. But it is surprising how long such situations can drag on; years later, when someone leaves, they say, 'He never really became one of us.'

The truth is that both parties want to feel that they belong. Belonging has to do with how significantly you are regarded. If you don't make people feel they belong, they will keep a distance as a way of protecting their ego. Another way of looking at this is to realize that if they are doing all the inviting and you are not joining, they will feel that you do not want to bother with them. Frightened of being ignored, they'll stop inviting you; after all, why would they want to behave in a way which demeans rather than enhances them?

If you have taken on a new job with people who are going to report to you, do not fear that they may resent you for blocking their chances of career development. If they do, that's their problem; in fact, they are being defensive as a way of protecting themselves from a truth they find unpalatable. It will not enable them if you collude with them, by conveying the appearance of guilt, that they have some justification for feeling the way they do. You do not have to apologize for the fact that they were not considered competent enough to be promoted in your place. Do not fear that you will be seen as blocking their career development or future chances of promotion. The task dictates that you should be **in** with your new group. Your total commitment is much more motivating than demotivating. Whatever the past circumstances, convey that you are now fully involved with them, convey that you are fully on their side, including being open with them in order to enable them.

DEALING WITH THE 'HERE AND NOW'

You ought not to make an excuse of having so much on your plate that you are unable to deal with what requires to be confronted now. Issues between people are best tackled at the time they arise. Are you removing yourself from a situation you may fear you are unable to cope with, one that makes you defensive?

Not dealing with issues that are beneath the surface is not being present with what is happening. You are ignoring the situation. You are shutting yourself away and excluding others. Subconsciously, it communicates to others that they are not exciting enough for you, or that you have something on your mind about them which you are reluctant to disclose, that perhaps you don't feel they can be trusted. They will, in turn, find their own defence mechanisms to protect themselves from what they imagine you think about them; with some justification they may call you closed, dour, begrudging, condescending or remote.

In contrast, if you make yourself fully 'present' with people who are with you, the situation becomes exciting and oriented towards action. When we are fully included together we are best prepared to focus our energies upon whatever needs to be done. It may be a business or technical matter. It may also be to resolve any issues between us that are preventing us from being present with each other. (See Presence in Personal Agenda Setting, Chapter 9.)

BENEATH THE SURFACE

Avoidance of what is happening beneath the surface of the situation is a block to organizational effectiveness. The task is probably never achieved if the blocks are not cleared out of the way first. The leader's job is taking the initiative in showing others how to encounter and resolve the blocks.

When the initiator says, 'I think you feel that I...,' the statement expresses his conflict, simultaneously containing his admission of his lack of awareness – 'I think' – and his fear of what the other person is unaware of – 'you feel'. The focus is upon his lack of understanding and the other person is invited to enable him to resolve the conflict. As the conflict is not displaced onto him, the other is not threatened, but can choose to engage in the situation. Because he is not being accused, but, rather, asked to enable, he is likely to do so, the more so as he begins to realize he has an opportunity, *en passant*, to resolve his own conflict.

SPAN OF CONTROL

This should always extend to those people who are involved in the situation. People should not want to be included if they are duplicates of others present or if they are already represented by those present. Probably, they have better things to do with their time. A lot depends upon the experience those involved have of trusting each other not to engage in matters which affect members who are not present.

It is a mistake to base decisions upon authority, rather than upon knowledge. Yet this is what often happens in organizations. One of the reasons that leaders experience so much stress is because they think they should know everything, including their subordinate's job as well as their own. In total leadership, decisions are made by people who know about the issue. Level of authority becomes irrelevant. In this case, the law of the situation, not the organization chart, determines the span of control. The end product is that decisions are made by those who know and are interested, not by those who have the status. Span of control is therefore limited to the smallest number of people who are affected and have the expertise to carry out the task.

There is a matter of who does the limiting of numbers. There is a danger of excluding someone who feels they are being ignored if left out. The best thing is to let them decide for themselves where their time is best spent. If you feel they are wasting their time in this particular group, then this is another issue to raise at the beneath the surface level.

These issues are discussed at more length in Chapter 11.

WALK THE TALK

Or, this could be about explaining the philosophy. You may not think that an empowering philosophy needs to explained at all, it seems so obvious, natural and practical. But people who are not used to it are often baffled what to do next. Do not assume that the one time slave knows how to live like a free man – and what the responsibilities of a free man are. Of course, total leadership cannot be imposed. And it is best acquired by you demonstrating by doing what you would like others to do to you.

As a leader, it is well to remember the psychological law of reciprocity – what occupies your mind, is what occupies the minds of others – you are therefore never alone!

'BORN' LEADERS

Investigation of the relationship between personality traits and leadership behaviour… have failed to reveal any consistent patterns.

Journal of Social Psychology, **LXXXVI**, 29 (1979)

In spite of the research finding above, my assertion is that: yes, you are a born leader. In the sense that you were born with the same feelings and fears as everybody else, it is what you do with them that counts. For me, we all become leaders when we take the initiative and encounter each other at the beneath the surface level in order to discover the law of the situation. I might disagree with what the *Journal of Social Psychology* actually means by 'leadership behaviour' – I suspect we mean something different – but I agree absolutely that we all start from the same base and therefore with the same opportunity.

The point was well made by Thomas Gordon (1977) in his book, *Leadership Effectiveness Training*, saying how rapidly ideas of leadership had moved from the notion of 'inherited' characteristics, then to 'personality' traits and latterly to the 'interaction' between leaders and followers. 'In the last analysis,' Gordon says, 'it is the follower who either accepts or rejects the influence of the leader.' He goes on to observe that leaders have to 'understand the needs all human beings possess' and 'hold out the promise that they will get their needs met'. Now we have a process in total leadership in which the individual does not start with what others may need, but what he wants for him- or herself.

Sometimes people doubt they are capable of being a leader. The very fact that you can imagine yourself being a total leader means that you are denying yourself by not being one now. If you couldn't, the thought would never have entered your head. (See 'Holding yourself back', in Chapter 8.)

All we are required to do as 'born leaders' as we go about our lives at home and at work is to attend to the following.

YOUR JOB

Your job is, first, to yourself. Many people react against this statement. But, after a reflection, they come to understand that it is the only practical way to lead. It is conventional wisdom that the leader should be 'looking after others' or 'putting the needs of others before his own', but consider what happens in such a situation. The danger is that in thinking you know what is best for others, you take responsibility for them and deny their capability to look after themselves.

Making an assumption that they need your help is bound to be a projection onto them of your need to appear to be a 'good leader'. It is really your needs that are being met, not theirs, since you are demanding that they allow you to lead them. You might even create a situation, for example, unconsciously keeping information to yourself, so they cannot do without you. Of course, your negative gain is that you get to be the leader; the downside is that you are doing all the work yourself whilst they remain bored and resentful that they are not allowed to use their own capabilities.

This is not to say you should look after yourself and ignore others. People *may* want your help; your job is only to ask if they *do* want help. If they do and you want to give it, then you do. If they do and you don't want to, perhaps because you think they are more capable than they think they are, you talk to each other at the beneath the surface level about your misperception. If they don't want help and you think they do, you again talk at the beneath the surface level.

If you are being a helper, you are not being a total leader: the danger of helping is that it is a collusion of defences between a helper and a demander. If you resolve any conflict about what you may be giving and taking from each other, you will become an enabler. As such, you facilitate an atmosphere in which self fulfilment takes place. Enabler is another name for total leader.

Enabling is being a helper with Awareness.

Your first job is to get yourself right and that is asking, 'Am I feeling good about myself in what I am doing or is there anything about my behaviour that is making me feel uncomfortable?' If there is anything, you will probably experience it readily enough. It will be connected in some way to the absence of feeling significant, competent or likeable, in which case you are in some way unconsciously using one of the defence mechanisms, perhaps in one of the ways which follow.

As you are no doubt aware, 'job' is just another word for task.

DEFENCES

Critic

Are you thinking, 'People ought to be able to cope by themselves'? In which case, you might be using the defence of being a *critic*. Being stern and judgmental might well indicate that you are not coping yourself in this situation. Maybe you fear that they might reject your help or demand too much from you so that they will prevent you from being able to cope.

The way to resolve the issue for yourself is to initiate a discussion at the beneath the surface level about the conflict you have about helping them: perhaps you *think* you shouldn't help them, but *feel* you should. You might find out that if you enable them to cope, they will enable you to cope. Or you might find out that they really can cope by themselves, as you can, so that it was only your fear that they might not be able to cope that you were displacing on to them.

Victim

Are you thinking, 'People are right in expecting me to cope'? If so, you might be allowing yourself to be a *victim*. Sometimes this is referred to as being a 'martyr'. It suggests you are not coping in this situation. Although you are helping others, perhaps you want people to help you, but are afraid to ask. Maybe you feel that you shouldn't need to ask, that they should guess what's on your mind. If they took the initiative, it would mean that you would be relieved of doing what you fear doing.

The way to resolve the issue is to talk to them at the beneath the surface level about the conflict you have about being helped to cope: that you think you shouldn't be helped, but feel you need to be. You might find out that they were unaware you wanted to be helped or were afraid to ask, but now want to help you cope. Or you might find out that they make you aware that your fear of not coping was only a fear, since you really can cope by yourself, so that your fear was only a projection onto them that they expected so much of you. At this point, you have resolved the conflict by enabling each other to perceive your situation clearly.

Helper

Are you thinking, 'People need help'? You might be making yourself a too willing *helper*. Your over concerned caring for others might suggest that you are not fully coping with your own concerns. You might well be right about what people might need, but to be fully effective you must be clear what negative gain you are 'getting out of' any situation in which you might be 'taking over'. Typically, you would be relieved of dealing with your fear by tackling those of others.

The way to resolve the issue is to initiate at the beneath the surface level about any conflict you have about helping them to cope: that you think they need help, but may help too much. The danger is that you and the other person only talk about your thoughts, but not about your feelings – helpers typically talk about what 'should' or 'ought' to be done, rather than how they feel, which does not help themselves become aware. This is the tricky part, since the task is to become aware of how much you are identifying with the other person in this situation, thereby coping with their problem on their behalf, rather than your own. Again, the danger is that neither one of you is actually enabled to cope.

Demander

You might be thinking something along the lines of one of these two: 'We must help each other', or 'We have all got to learn to let everybody cope on their own'. You might be a *demander*, wanting others to share your fears so that you can feel better about yourself if others think the same way. When this happens, everyone gets distracted from the real task because they are all involved in making you feel better about your fears rather than coping with their own issue and enabling you to cope with yours. Often, a demander readily obtains the assistance of a helper. As you never learn to sort out the source of your fear, you go on demanding.

To resolve the conflict, initiate at the beneath the surface level about not being able to cope: that you think the other person copes better than you feel you do, or that you can only cope if the other person helps. Typically, demanders deceive themselves and others because they say they are talking about what they are 'feeling' when it is really only what they are 'thinking'. In other words, they have not connected their thinking to their feeling, and, consequently, have great trouble in dealing with their conflict – precisely why they want somebody else to cope with it for them! – by compensating for what they fear they lack in themselves.

A beneath the surface checking out of any possibility can simply address your doubt – ask, 'Am I demanding too much?... too little? Am I helping too much?... enough? Am I being critical? Am I making myself a victim?' You will know the best words to use. Getting the answer to how well the other person sees you coping helps you to cope, first with yourself and then with them, if that is what they want.

YOUR LIFE'S WORK

Your life's work consists of confronting all situations in which you become aware that you or the other person are using defences. Freeing yourself from defences enables you to get on with doing what you want to do and being the person you want to be. Here is a practical guide for you to use in every relationship.

MY LIFE'S WORK

For out of work relationships, substitute 'at home' for 'in my job' and substitute the person's name, for example, wife, husband, father, son, partner, as appropriate.

Boss (leading upwards)
My job is to check with my boss my fears I am doing something which prevents them from being how they want to be in their job, and, to create awareness in my boss of feelings I have about them arising from their treatment of me which prevent me being myself in my job.

Colleagues (leading sidewards)
My job is to check with my colleagues my fears that I am doing something which is preventing them from being how they want in their job, and, to create awareness in them of feelings I have about them arising from their treatment of me which prevent me from being myself in my job.

Myself (leading myself)
My job is take responsibility for my own feelings of self worth in my job, and inspire myself by confronting my fears and changing what I do not like so that I am being myself in my job. In short, constantly check my awareness with myself and with everybody I work with.

Subordinates (leading downwards)
My job is to check with subordinates my fears that I am doing something which prevents them from being how they want in their job, and, to create awareness in them of feelings I have which arise from their treatment of me which prevent me from being myself in my job.

How far do I believe I am doing the above, how much do they? To be clear about each other – to discover the law of the situation which exists between us – we have to initiate our perceptions at the beneath the surface level. Understanding the basis of our perception allows us to resolve it.

SHORT ANSWERS TO QUICK QUESTIONS

If I am not the 'appointed' leader, why should I be expected to lead?

Because in the situation you may be aware of more than the 'appointed' leader. If you do not take the initiative, you have 'withheld' from everybody who would have benefited from your awareness. Most of all, you let down yourself because you have made the fact that you are not the 'appointed' leader an excuse not to do something that you could do, wanted to do, everyone wanted, but you were ultimately afraid to do. Your negative gain is that you do not fail because you haven't taken a risk.

Do I have to lead?

If you say 'have to' you are attempting to make somebody else responsible. It is like being a 'victim'. You are an unwilling hero; when things go wrong you can say it wasn't your fault as you were forced to take responsibility you really didn't want. If you don't want to, don't – but don't then become a 'critic' of those who do.

Suppose I really don't want to lead?

Don't feel obliged to take on responsibility just because you are asked. In the end, it is what you want. Taking something on because you are frightened people won't like you otherwise is no good reason for doing something. That is the equivalent of being a 'helper' to their 'demander'. Are you aware of why you are being leant upon and what their objectives are? Are you clear about what you really want or is there some fear which is making you say you don't want something when, deep down, you really do?

How do I get the best from people?

People give of their best when they are fulfilling some vision they have for themselves. Simply, they are behaving in ways which make them feel significant, competent and likeable. Put another way, do they have any conflict which is making them doubt themselves in any of these three areas? Ask them if there is anything you are doing which does not enable them to be themselves.

How do I get support from people?

Tell them at the beneath the surface level of any conflict which involves them. Confiding what is 'on your mind' communicates that they are significant to you, that you feel they are competent, and that you like them, because you would not confide in someone you did not like. The feelings communicated to them are feelings they will enjoy and reciprocate. Thus, they will support you because supporting you makes them feel good about themselves. Do not confide anything that is not a 'real' issue with you, because if you use this behaviour to exploit people, they will find out, and never trust you again.

Everyone enjoys being an enabler.

How do I bring in the 'quiet' members of the team?

You tell them that you are feeling left out! This may seem strange, because conventional wisdom suggests that is they who are being left out. Leaders usually feel it is their duty to bring others in. But pointing out that they have not said anything draws attention to them in a way they have no control over. The truth is, that the fact they are not contributing is worrying you, so it's your problem. Yes, they may be worried about it too, but you can enable them best with their problem by enabling yourself to be clear about your problem first.

Psychologically, the issue is on your mind because, to the extent they are quiet, you are feeling ignored. There must be something occupying their mind which they are not sharing with you. Unconsciously, what is happening in your mind is all sorts of self doubt which you want to resolve: are they bored with me, am I running this meeting competently, do they know something they are withholding from me? This is why it is better to get right to the nub of the issue – yours: it may be theirs too, but don't assume so by accusing them of being quiet or drawing attention to their shyness.

So, say what is really on your mind by initiating at the beneath the surface level – 'I feel left out – maybe you know something I should also know about.' This is not sarcasm, you must make that clear. It is trying to under-

stand what is going on that is holding you back. Remember, clearing away
what is holding you back is the surest way to clear the path for them.

What happens if I think my boss is no good?

You ask yourself what is making *you* feel 'no good' in relation to your boss.
It is really your problem, not your boss's. What you want is to feel good
about yourself. Maybe you are projecting something that doesn't make you
feel good about your boss on to him or her. Or maybe you are identifying
with something they do that makes you think you wouldn't feel good if it
were you doing it that way. Tell your boss at the beneath the surface level
that you think you are not doing enough to enable them. Maybe they like
being the way they are, but maybe they will recognize an element of truth in
what you say, responding to the total leadership you are initiating, recognizing it gives them a chance to learn how to feel good about themselves.

To do this effectively they must be as sure as you are that you are not
seeking to undermine them or put one over on them, but that you see your
own fulfilment as being met by the opportunity to see them fulfilled.

What happens if I think my subordinate or colleague is no good?

The same comments apply as to your boss. Additionally, you might also
consider that any negative thoughts you have about others ultimately
rebound against you. Therefore it never does any good to keep them in.
Organizations in which people do not feel good about each other are not
pleasant to work in and success is precarious.

Ask yourself what you feel about yourself when they do or don't do the
things that you think are no good. You then have the issue with which to
encounter them at the beneath the surface level. Your telling them about
your conflict is bound to lead to an examination of the behaviour they do
that causes the conflict in you. For example, you feel left out by what they
do, or they don't tell you what they are thinking. Telling them of your conflict will bring out their own. Remember, they want to feel good about
themselves as much as you do – are you giving them every chance?

Should I have a plan?

A total leader does not need to have a plan. In fact, a plan is the last thing a
total leader wants! The plan you want to have is the same plan as everybody
else. Plans start as ideas, and the idea may have come from you or anybody.

Probably, the 'appointed' leader has fewer ideas than anybody else, simply because more of his time may be spent in making sure that the ideas of everybody else are not being withheld or blocked in some way. The plan is a dangerous one if it is the 'leader's' plan because it allows everybody else not to take responsibility. Any plan must be the plan of the team, including the 'leader': then, no member has the slightest reservation that it is the plan they want for themself; each individual feels about it the way they would if the plan were their own, individual plan (see Chapter 11).

Shouldn't I have the answers?

Notice the use of the 'should' word. Who is saying that you 'should'; where does it come from? We can pillory ourself on others' expectations of what we think they think we 'should' do. Not wanting to let others down, we maintain an image of adequacy we suppose is necessary to our position.

In any situation you may have the answers, but you may not. Don't hold back if you think you do, but check out with others any conflict you feel about forcing your own views upon them. If others have the answers, that is even better. Your job is only to ensure that the answers that others may have are not blocked by their own fears of putting them forward. Answers which are agreed with everybody who is involved are always much more creative and motivating that those that are produced by just one person, even if that person is the 'appointed' leader.

Should I admit I don't know what to do?

Notice the use of the moral imperative 'should' once again. Keeping up appearances and trying to look good is an example of negative energy. Your efforts are spent on covering up rather than getting on with the job. Then, there is always the fear that your pretence will be discovered. The chances are that people sense that there is something going on that you are not being open about, anyway. The best thing is to tell it like it is. The first step in finding out what to do is to confront what you don't know. Not only that, your openness will draw others towards you.

Firstly, you are being open with them, not keeping back something even though it is difficult to admit that you feel lost. Your own conflict makes the situation everybody is in very clear. If you don't know, then perhaps they know something which can enable you. Suddenly, instead of appearing weak, you are decisively tackling the issue. You, with others, are in control of the situation. Having been open about your conflict, 'I think I'm expected to know what to do, but I don't', you have signalled your trust by sharing your conflict with them: that they have the competence to work on the conflict with you, and that your inclusion of them on something which is important to you means that they, also, must be important. You have gone from a state in which you were trying to do everything on your own to one in which the team is involved.

Should I tell people when I'm bored?

Again, the use of the word 'should' indicates that you are processing what is 'right and proper' in an intellectual way. You are concerned, perhaps, not to hurt people's feelings or not to appear arrogant. Perhaps you have 'switched off' because you don't understand.

On the other hand, the fact that you are bored shows that you are not attending to what is going on, that the group is missing out on your contribution and even that your time might be better spent elsewhere. The danger here is that you are blaming others for your feeling of boredom; you are waiting for them to do something to interest you. The truth is that if you are bored, it's you who is responsible, nobody else. Unless you do something about it, you might go on being bored.

Total leadership consists in your taking responsibility and being open. It may be that someone else will take the initiative and point out that someone in the group isn't present, and that this awareness will improve the quality of the meeting. But can you afford to wait on the off chance that someone will step in and do for you what you would be better off doing for yourself?

It is better to tell people what your conflict is. This won't blame them, because it will put you under the spotlight, not them. Furthermore, it will address the situation which exists at the moment – the fact that you are not involved. When that situation is addressed, the group can get on with the other situation it is together to deal with.

So, you will want to say something like, 'You may think I should be contributing, but I feel I cannot add anything useful,' or, 'I think you might feel I'm letting you down.' These are different approaches from telling people that they are wasting your time, or that they are boring you.

Speaking to others at the beneath the surface level enables them to discover the law of the situation: are you actually required at the meeting, is it the meeting that has run out of steam, is it they who are losing the point, what do people want to do to make it an exciting meeting, and how can everybody be involved who wants to be?

When should I praise people?

If you feel like giving praise, you do it. Trust your heart. If you are not sure whether you should give praise or not, you definitely do it.

Holding back on giving praise may be completely misinterpreted by the other person, in fact, it almost always is. You may think they know what's in your mind, so there's no need to tell them. Because of self doubt, of which you are unaware, they interpret your silence as some sort of criticism. Perhaps they feel they might have done a good job, but are uncertain that you think it really was as good as you would have expected. All of a sudden, they fear they are not fully coming up to your standards, that they are less competent than they think they should be. They may even get apprehensive and start to make mistakes. There's nothing like a lack of confidence to create mistakes. And it's all unnecessary.

Praise people when you want to tell them where they stand. Praise is a coin that never runs out as long as you don't devalue it by giving it away spuriously, that is, saying something which you don't really feel as a device to try to motivate people. That coin has little value. There are two ways of praising. Saying, 'You did that well', is about the other person and from this they might infer your praise. Saying, 'I felt good about you doing that', is about you at the beneath the surface level. It is praise indeed.

When should I criticise people?

Never. Instead, seek with them to discover what is happening in the situation. The temptation to criticise is a displacement of your own feeling of inadequacy on to them. If someone is failing, the first question to ask yourself is, 'What am I doing or not doing that is enabling this to be a success?' Although it is highly likely that they are failing in some way as well, your best route to dealing with what is happening is to discover how your own behaviour is also helping to bring it about. In the end, it will be your own competence that is important to you rather than someone else's.

If you feel critical, it is because you are in some way feeling let down, passed by or not trusted. Confronting the person at the beneath the surface level with how you feel will lead to an examination of what they are doing to make you feel the way you do. Remember it is your problem and, therefore, your leadership consists in taking the initiative. The listener will discover how they are contributing to the situation. Perhaps they were afraid of your displeasure, so didn't inform you when things began to go wrong. Perhaps they were never clear about what you expected of them and, although they thought there was something the matter, thought you didn't want to talk about it. So, perhaps your behaviour which makes them fearful of you partly led them to withhold; their own self doubt contributed the other part.

What happens if you have done everything you possibly could? You no longer feel critical and the other person doesn't feel criticised. But, you agree, there is no competence, neither of you is enjoying the situation. In this case you have discovered that the person cannot do what you both hoped for. It is worthless to pretend that they can do something they cannot. This is not blaming. It is understanding the situation in which blame might arise if the situation is not recognized. Potential blame can be headed off by finding a way to cope so that the person can be fulfilled: different experience, a training course or arranging the task in a different way are all possible ways forward.

When should I tell my boss what I think of them?

If it is something positive, tell them all the time. If it is something negative, telling them what you think of them is likely to provoke a defensive reaction, quite understandably, which is unlikely to make either of you feel better and may harm your relationship. Instead, tell your boss how you think they feel about you. It will be more productive initiating this way at the beneath the surface level.

How do I avoid upsetting people?

Are you sure that your question is not an excuse – 'I had better not tell people in case they are upset' – for avoiding the truth. You might be giving yourself a negative gain, saying, 'I'm helping people not to feel upset.'

If it is something you are doing or are about to do, ask yourself if they have been fully included. If they are affected by what you are doing, they will want to feel as much a party to it as you do (see Chapter 11).

If it is something you are saying or are about to say, ask yourself if you are using any of the defences. In other words, is there a sense in which you might appear to be a critic, a victim, a helper or a demander?

Talking about other people will not upset them if what you are saying is positive (unless hearing positive things about themselves is a threat!). If what you want to talk to them about is negative, then you are likely to upset them. Instead, talk about yourself and what you experience when you are with them. This allows them to retain control of the situation and will prevent defensiveness; in responding to your initiative to deal with your issue, they also begin to involve themself on their own, thus dealing with their issue because *they* want to deal with it not because *you* want to.

How can I find enjoyment?

By eliminating those doubts and fears that are preventing you. Overcoming the doubts and fears is all part of it – because of the joyful release experienced in the process. That is what 'living' in the present is all about.

How can I avoid stress?

Stress arises as the result of withholding a conflict. Conflicts prevent you from feeling good about yourself. If you don't feel good about yourself you don't behave in ways in which you like yourself behaving. Dealing with the conflict at the beneath the surface level is a behaviour you will like in yourself. It will prepare the ways for other behaviours which will make you feel significant, competent and likeable. Then you won't experience any stress (see 'Stress' in Chapter 3).

How can I be good at making 'small talk'?

Not feeling comfortable in situations requiring 'small talk' usually arises from a lack of confidence in your significance. What can you possibly say that will be of interest to anybody? The truth is that you are good at making 'small talk' – it is just that you fear you are not. The fears themselves will originate in earlier experiences you have had which may have caused you to doubt that what you might have wanted to say would have any significance. It is no longer appropriate for the life you want to lead today. But how to break the mould?

Remember that what is happening to you and what you are thinking about are as important to you as others' thoughts are to them. You make the mistake of processing: 'Is this important enough, how will it be received, will anybody be the slightest bit interested?' Try simply saying what you experience. You will find that people bring their own experience to what you say. This is a social situation, one in which inclusion is the object, but where competence, apart from social competence, and openness are not expected. 'Small talk' may be an aspect of social competence you may find it useful to be better at. Rather than being bored or embarrassed in the situation, behave in a way that you do not normally do and take some pleasure from pushing back some of your barriers. For example, deliberately include yourself more than you usually do by simply saying what comes off the 'top of your head'. You may get a few things wrong, but never mind, you are teaching yourself to behave in ways that are you, but which you haven't had much practice in yet.

How can I be sure what motivates people?

People are motivated when they feel they will be as significant, competent and likeable as they want to be when they are with you. To produce those feelings in them, behave in ways which include them, give them influence with you and be open with them about any conflicts you experience in your relationship. They are motivated as you create opportunities to be more themselves (see Chapter 5).

When should I tell people the truth?

Now. It is essential that you do not put this off. The longer you put it off the worse it gets. There will never be a better time than when you have the experience. If you are not fully aware at the time, that is, withholding or avoiding, make it as soon as you are aware.

The best thing is to confront any conflict at the time it arises. In a 'one to one' situation, say it now. Even in a group situation when you begin to process the matter and find excuses, such as 'this isn't relevant to everybody', do it now. The fact that the conflict arose in this situation means that everybody in this situation is in some way connected with it.

How do I avoid hurting people's feelings?

Let other people decide for themselves whether their feelings will be hurt. The truth is that it is fearing that you cannot cope with their response that makes you want to convince yourself that you are not telling them for *their* sake, as opposed to *yours*. You are being a 'helper' to yourself by using others to protect yourself from your own issue. Cunningly, you also make yourself a victim by telling yourself that you had no choice in this situation – that you will avoid hurting people's feelings by allowing them to remain in control.

If you tell them at the beneath the surface level that you think they may not want to know what you are feeling, it allows them to invite you to 'Tell me more'. Then, if it really is their feelings, rather than your feelings, which are the issue, be alert that they are not being a demander of you by insisting that you deal with their feelings for them. In the end, you have to take responsibility for your feelings, and they for theirs.

Suppose I don't care whether telling people the truth hurts?

It sounds as though you intend to be a helper because, 'It's good for them, whether they want it, or not'.

In his book, *Why Am I Afraid to Tell You Who I Am*, John Powell (1995) warns, 'We must be careful, extremely careful in fact, that we do not assume the vocation of acquainting others with their delusions. We are all tempted to unmask others, to smash their defences, to leave them naked and blinking in the light of the illumination provided by our expose.'

Though I advocate telling the truth, it is the truth about *me*, not the truth, as I see it, about *you*.

> As Powell (1995) says,
> Nothing justifies me in becoming a judge of others. I can tell you who I am, report my emotions to you with truth and honesty, and this is the greatest kindness I can extend to myself and to you. It is another thing to set myself up as judge of your delusions. This is playing God. I must not try to be the guarantor of your integrity and honesty: that is your work. I can only hope that my honesty with and about myself will empower you to be honest with and about yourself.

I think the true believer who is convinced that she or he has all the truth is really a dangerous person, a trouble making person.

Carl Rogers, Changes, Vol. IV, No. IV

When are people ready to hear the truth?

Only when they choose. If they are not ready, they will avoid or get back at you for the way you are making them feel. They are only ready when they feel you are on their side – call it trust, or empathy, if you like. They are only ready when they feel your interest is to enable them to be more themselves and not intended to do them down in any way.

> Don't you know what fanaticism is? It is over compensation for doubt.
> Robertson Davies, The Manticore

How do I avoid alienating people?

The worst thing is to hold back. Denying them of yourself communicates a denial of them. Draw people to you by being open about your situation.

One person's failure is a failure of the whole organization, particularly of the leader.

SUMMARY

In pursuing the task through which we are able to fulfil ourselves, situations inevitably arise which hold us back. This chapter has focused upon the dynamics of the defences we employ in situations and gives some guidance on how to resolve some of the conflicts which commonly arise. More about how to deal with situations can be found in Chapter 10.

Optional exercises

These exercises are to assist you in ensuring that you are carrying out your job. The intention is that you increase your awareness of any collusion with others not to deal with any situation which may arise between you. In the second exercise, any possible collusion would be with yourself.

In both exercises you are asked to encounter whoever is involved in the situation, by taking responsibility and being open about what you perceive. The process by which you resolve the conflict you find in the situation enables you to complete the task.

Exercise – leading others

Instructions:
I check with you,——————————, my boss, colleague, subordinate or any other significant person, my fears that I am doing something which prevents you from being yourself. I think of the way we behave to each other and the feelings I experience in our relationship.

STEP 1: Copy this questionnaire and give to the other person so that you can each complete it for each other.
STEP 2: On a scale of 0–9, where 0 means not at all, 9 means totally and 5 means about average, score the other person on the way you see your relationship – 1 to 8.
STEP 3: When they have done the same for themselves, you put their scores in the appropriate boxes.

STEP 4: You then have a beneath the surface discussion to gain insight and to resolve the discrepancies. Where there are no discrepancies, you have a below the surface discussion about why you see your situation the same way. If you are scoring a person who is not with you, you can put in the score that you would think they might have given.

STEP 5: In order to assist with remembering, you write down your insights and what you resolve to do in order to be more fulfilled in your job. 'Insight' might be:

1. Awareness of what you and the other person are 'getting out of' behaving like you do (the rewards or the negative gains).
2. Awareness of how your behaviour contributes to the behaviour of others (the defences)

Leading others

Significant person:_____

		Score 0–9
(1)	I think I am a critic of you	_____
	You think I am a critic of you (their 5)	_____
(2)	I think I allow myself to be a victim of you	_____
	You think I allow myself to be a victim of you (their 6)	_____
(3)	I think I am a too much of a helper to you	_____
	You think I am too much of a helper to you (their 7)	_____
(4)	I think I am a demander of you	_____
	You think I am a demander of you (their 8)	_____
(5)	I think you are a critic of me	_____
	You think you are a critic of me (their 1)	_____
(6)	I think you allow yourself to be a victim of me	_____
	You think you allow yourself to a victim of me (their 2)	_____
(7)	I think you are too much of a helper to me	_____
	You think you are too much of a helper to me (their 3)	_____
(8)	I think you are a demander of me	_____
	You think you are a demander of me (their 4)	_____

Insights: _____

_____

_____

_____

_____

_____

Resolution: _____

_____

_____

_____

_____

_____

Optional exercise – leading yourself

Instructions:
I check with myself my fears I am doing something which prevents me from being myself. I think of the way I behave to myself and the feelings I experience in what I do.

STEP 1:   Copy the following questionnaire and give to a significant person(s) to complete boxes 5 to 8 for how they perceive you.

STEP 1:   On a scale of 0–9, where 0 means not at all, 9 means totally and 5 means about average, score yourself on the way you see yourself – statements 1 to 4. Score boxes 5 to 8 for them.

STEP 2:   You then have a beneath the surface discussion to understand the basis of the discrepancies. Where there are no discrepancies, you have below the surface discussions about why you don't or how you might be colluding.

STEP 3:   In order to assist with remembering, you write down your insights and what you resolve to do in order to be more fulfilled in your life. 'Insight' might be:

1. Awareness of what you are 'getting out of' behaving like you do (especially the negative gains).
2. Awareness of how your behaviour to yourself contributes to the behaviour of others (the defences).

Leading yourself

Significant person: _____

		Score 0–9
(1)	I am a critic of myself	____
(5)	You are a critic of yourself	____
(2)	I am a victim of myself	____
(6)	You are a victim of yourself	____
(3)	I am a helper to myself	____
(7)	You are a helper to yourself	____
(4)	I am a demander of myself	____
(8)	You are a demander of yourself	____

Insights: _____

_____

_____

_____

_____

_____

Resolution: _____

_____

_____

_____

_____

8

Rewards and Negative Gains

The secret motive of the absent minded is to be innocent while guilty
Saul Bellow, *More Die of Heartbreak*

INTRODUCTION

All behaviour arises from the anticipated benefits of its consequences.
Doing nothing is also a behaviour. Not doing what you want to do is a
behaviour as well. It follows that you receive some benefit, albeit temporary or incomplete, for what you don't do, even though it may seem to you
that you do not benefit from it.

No action is ever lost – nothing we do is without result.
Robertson Davies, *World of Wonders*

Benefits from behaving the way we want, we can call 'rewards'. Benefits
from behaving the way we do not want, we can term 'negative gains'. The
latter are more difficult to understand. They are like receiving 30 pieces of
silver, which might seem like a lot of money at the time, but only provide a
temporary comfort, not an enduring satisfaction, because they miss obtain-
ing what is really important. Negative gains never last for very long
because the behaviour for which they are intended to compensate always
returns to haunt us.

An example which might clarify the difference between the two concepts might be: choosing to be well is a reward, choosing to be unwell in
order to obtain sympathy is a negative gain.

We have already looked at negative gains in Chapter 3 when discussing
denial. Now we investigate their illusory nature in more detail. It attempts
to explain how and why we choose to collude with ourselves, and it shows
how to turn negative gains into rewards.

NEGATIVE GAINS

Negative gains are like bribes we give ourselves; temporarily, the bribe looks worth more than the real thing. We choose a negative gain because we have a fear of behaving in the way we want. Every time we give ourself a negative gain, we might feel smug but, later on, we experience the same familiar, stale emptiness. Negative gains never provide us with completion.

Negative gains are the bribes we give ourselves when using defences.

If you like, negative gains are the means we use to justify actions which we are secretly embarrassed or ashamed of. Temporarily, they allow us to think we have addressed our conflict when, in fact, the use of a defence has only swept it under the carpet.

Thus, Judas may have used any of the following defences when justifying his betrayal of Jesus: 'He deserved it,' (critic) or 'I had no choice,' (victim) or 'I thought that was really what he wanted,' (helper) or 'I wanted him to prove himself; does he still love me?' (demander).

Understanding our negative gains puts us in touch with the mechanism we are using to hold ourselves back from doing the thing that is difficult – the thing we most want to do if we are going to break through the barriers which we have artificially constructed for ourselves. The nature of a negative gain is that it never solves the real problem, only deceives us, temporarily, that it has.

Negative gain is what it is because the behaviour binds up energy in continuing, unresolved conflict. It is like incurring negative equity, because it produces the opposite of what was intended.

As a concept, negative gain has its origin in game analysis, and the term 'payoff' is explained by Eric Berne (1966), in his book *The Games People Play*. He gives an example of the alcoholic who, desperate for attention and sympathy in daily life, gets what he wants as a consequence of his illness.

I have always found the word payoff a difficult one to use and have noticed that others can also be confused, usually because we suppose that payoff might be expected to be a good thing. I have chosen to employ the term negative gain which I have found generally makes the illusory nature of the behaviour clearer.

Examples of 'negative gains'

Behaviour	Negative gain
Not being as strong as I could be	I never get to find out if I'm a failure. (Helper – helping myself to fail)
Not being more proactive?	I avoid the possibility I might be rejected. (Demander – demanding you include me instead)
Not using my imagination?	People might laugh. I avoid looking silly. (Victim – people won't respect me)
Feeling guilty?	People feel I'm a nice person. (Helper – helping people like to me)
Helping others as much as I do?	I don't have time to deal with my problems. (Helper – helping others so I have a good excuse for not helping me)
Letting other people exploit me?	I feel I am making up for things I have been guilty of in the past. (Victim – people wouldn't like me if I didn't let them demand things of me)
Being sick	People show me how much I mean to them. I don't like myself, but this way I find out that others do. (Demander – you must pay attention to me)
Making a joke at your expense?	I look superior by putting you down. (Critic – I feel inferior so I displace my fear of looking stupid on to you)
Blaming you?	Take the attention off me. (Critic – I displace my fear on to you)
Blaming myself?	Try to head off or defuse the anger you may feel towards me. (Victim – I project – by telling myself I am stupid before you do)
Holding myself back	I put you first so I don't find out that I may not be wanted. (Helper – I identify that you feel you are not wanted)
Making sure that you include me	I head off the fear of not being important. (Demander – you compensate for my fear of not being significant)

The negative gain is what stops us confronting our fears. It appears, initially, to be a legitimate way for us to live with our guilt, our betrayal of ourself, of avoiding doing what we really want. It is a rationalization of our compromise.

The richness of our language and experience means that negative gains are expressed by individuals, uniquely. But the fact that they relate in a simple and structured way to our defences allows us to see that they are not at all unique. We all share them, indeed, we all use them. Using defences is a natural inclination, albeit one which is not enabling. It is worth remembering that defences are used unconsciously; it is this characteristic of them which causes the trouble.

Now, can we exchange the behaviours, such as the examples above, which lead to negative gains, for other behaviours which lead to rewards?

You might be able to do this more easily by rehearsing in your mind what would be the worst thing that could happen. Ask yourself, would it be so bad? What could you also do to ensure that the worst thing did not happen so that you are not dissuaded, lose confidence or revert to your old negative gains, but that you go on until you do get what you want?

For example, let us examine one of the behaviours above – holding back – and see how it may be working in terms of negative gains and how behaviour may be changed to obtain rewards instead.

CASE STUDY

HOLDING YOURSELF BACK (PERHAPS OUT OF FEAR OF 'APPEARING TO GET ABOVE YOURSELF' OR 'NOT WANTING TO UPSET SOMEONE')

Let us suppose you tell yourself that, 'People like me to be modest'. Are you sitting on some ideas or trying not to look too enthusiastic because you fear that you will appear to be 'self serving' or trying to ingratiate yourself? Perhaps you would prefer for your views to be asked for, so that this would relieve you of the worry about appearing too 'pushy'. Perhaps you feel your boss is the one who should set the scene and create the atmosphere in which things may begin to happen in the way you would like.

These possibilities suggest that you are behaving as something of a victim. They include an element of waiting for others to make it possible to help you to do what you want, so that it won't be obvious that that is what you would really like to do, but did not want to be embarrassed about by being obvious. Therefore, a different behaviour from withholding would be for you to take the initiative, create opportunities for yourself. Does it sound risky and unfamiliar? If you fear you are being too pushy, ask people if that is their perception of you. You may be imagining it. Or they may indeed see you as pushy, because they are being defensive about their own tendency to hold back! In fact, they may be talking more about themselves

> than about you. (Telepathically, they spot their own fear in you, and try to
> overcome it by attempting to make you feel the same way as them.)
>
> If you identify your feelings and talk about them to significant others,
> you will both loosen up the organization and create space for yourself. If
> people try to 'put you down' as a result, or try to make you 'toe the line',
> perhaps you should consider whether it is a problem for them to address
> rather than one you should be apologetic about, or try to head off, in
> advance.

LIVING 'CLOSE TO THE EDGE'

Confronting negative gains brings you to the point where you change behavioural habits that keep you rooted in your past, where you are doing no more than placating the fears that exist in your nightmares. It is the point at which you take the step that will prove that you can get where you want to go, that you can be the person you want to be. That is enjoyment.

Sometimes, being aware of our negative gains is enough to move us to alter them. But awareness alone is not always enough. We need to take control of that awareness and act upon it. Only through our actions can we truly say that our lives have a new direction, a new focus, and that we have 'moved on'.

What actions might you need to make in respect of new behaviours you want? For example, how do you actually go about doing it? The best thing is to rehearse what might take place in a variety of situations. Consider the following:

Example – beneath the surface level initiating

Behaviour	'Beneath the surface level' initiating
Don't be exploited.	'I think you are not considering me when you do that. I feel exploited.'
Be well	'I think it doesn't matter to you whether I am here or not. I think I allow myself to be sick in order to get you to notice me.'
Be regarded	'I feel left out.'
Be open	'I think you don't like me.'
Be aware	'Who am I really protecting or helping or criticising?'

THE 'MEXICAN STAND OFF'

This is a metaphor for waiting for someone else to go first so that you won't have to. The trouble is, the other person is also waiting. So nothing gets done, you both wait forever, waiting for the other person to go first. So neither of you ever get what you both want.

Suppose you say, 'He should tell me what he feels, it must be obvious what I'm feeling.' This is, of course, a negative gain which is being used to justify your avoidance. Actually, you are making him an excuse for not doing what you want to do. You are blaming him for something about which you feel guilty, using the defence of being a critic. The 'stand off' arises when neither wants to take responsibility. Neither party wants to take control. It is a crisis of apathy.

Sometimes people want to be social, but are frightened to include themselves in case they find out that nobody wants them. So they say, 'They'll come and get me or come and ask me if they want me.' That is being a demander, because they are asking people to do something for them they are frightened of doing themselves.

The trouble is, because we haven't asked, they may think we don't want. And because we are not then asked, we think we are justified in thinking we are not wanted. Poor me!

To deal with the conflict you might compensate, as mentioned already, by becoming a demander, or displace, becoming a critic, saying, 'I wouldn't want to be with them.' Or you might slip into the defence of becoming a victim or martyr, saying, 'I'm not good enough for people.' Or you might become a helper, saying, 'Nobody wants to be here.'

Inventing negative gains for ourselves in order to justify our defences always has a demanding aspect, because all the defences make the other person at fault rather than ourselves. We prefer to think that the other person has to be 'cured' or 'see the light', not us.

Being frightened of taking the initiative, it is easier to mix with people who initiate first. You might even 'help' them to feel good about 'helping' so much. Thus, two helpers 'help' each other to get nowhere very fast.

Although you may be relieved of the fear you have of initiating, the trouble is, you never lose your dependence upon others, and you never have the courage to take the initiative with other people you'd like to meet. You look for others to do for you what you are frightened of doing for yourself. You exist in their shadow. You have no life, no presence, no sense of self unless they recognize you and invite you in.

An aspect that is at first difficult to perceive in demanders is that they may say that they are becoming aware of the defence they are using, whereas they are not. They may even be able to discuss their defence intellectually in a way that may suggest they are overcoming it. Unfortunately, there is often a discrepancy between what they say and what they actually feel. Thus, they may assert that they have learned so much, whilst giving no evidence that they have in any way changed. But the way they signal that they are on the verge of, for example, acting upon your advice, ensures that they keep your commitment to them going. A way of expressing this is to say that they 'keep you on the hook'.

Being manipulated is something that you have to guard against if your inclination is to be a helper. Beware that, if you confront them with your feeling, the demander does not make themselves a victim and 'hook' you once again, saying, 'So, I was right all the time, you don't care about me after all,' – the helper in you rushes in and 'gets hooked' once again, reassuring the demander that, yes, of course you care about them!

Nothing happens because you are both using a defence. The truth is:

There is never a good reason for maintaining defences.

COLLUSION

When we go along with (try to ignore) a defence someone is using we may be said to be colluding. In fact, to tolerate their defence implies that we also begin to use a defence. For example, we might have made ourselves a helper because, by letting matters ride, we collude with them in helping them in the demands they make of us.

Someone may ask us to do something to 'help' them by making out they are an unwitting victim; we may deal with it by making ourselves a victim too, saying, 'But I'm worse off than you are, I couldn't be expected to help.' Or we might deal with it as a critic and say, 'You got yourself into this mess, now get yourself out of it.'

Often in a training group, someone says, 'I can't stand the way you are all picking on a particular person.' Maybe they have identified with the person concerned, feeling they would not like to be talked about that way if it were them. We find out whether it is identification or not by asking the person if they feel victimized. Usually they say, 'No, I thought people's comments were making me become aware.'

Collusion

If you allow yourself to become a:	If the defence the person is using is:			
	Critic	Victim	Helper	Demander
Critic	1. War	2. Punishment	4. Inertia	7. Dependency
Victim		3. Paralysis	5. Welfare	8. Vampirism
Helper			6. Stalemate	9. Exploitation
Demander				10. Destruction

Colluding

1. A critic displaces his feelings about himself onto another. In this situation, two critics blame each other.
2. A victim blames himself. In this situation, both the victim and the critic agree to blame the victim.
3. Victims identify blame in themselves. In this situation, both victims want to take the blame.
4. The helper identifies the critic's justification for blaming, whilst the critic blames the helper.
5. The helper identifies that the victim is to blame, and the victim agrees.
6. The helper identifies that the other helper is to blame, but does not perceive where they are to blame.
7. Compensation by demanding the other be a critic.
8. Compensation by demanding the other be a victim.
9. Demanding the other helps compensate for what the demander is not.
10. Demanding the other is (or is not) a demander.

It might be interesting to work out whether any of your own relationships fall into one or more headings in the above chart.

NEGATIVE GAINS FOR UNDER PERFORMANCE

What do you get out of saying you cannot cope, that you are no good? On the one hand, you get flattering comments as people rush to reassure you. (In fact, you have used the defence of demander – getting people to tell you what you are unwilling to believe in yourself.) On the other hand you create a 'hostage to fortune' because you are not surprised when you fail.

Ironically, having no self doubt would mean either that we really had attained perfection or that we are not letting ourself be aware of areas in which we doubt ourself. We would have stopped trying, become one of the 'living dead', almost.

Perhaps an element of self doubt is necessary for us to do anything at all. Too much self doubt and we give up before we start. Too little self doubt and things are happening to us in ways we are not aware.

'PEOPLE MAY NOT WANT TO HEAR'

If you think this, you give yourself a negative gain for doing nothing. The defence is being a helper. It is a projection of your fears onto others. You are, in fact, making up their minds for them, deciding what they may or may not want, what they may or may not be able to take. This is taking control from them (disempowering). It is best left up to them to decide.

CONFLICT

Conflicts are the most interesting part of meetings. Overcoming conflicts is the only way to get the task done.

What are we avoiding? What is happening here? Are there things beneath the surface which are holding us back? More to the point, what am **I** and what are **you** not saying that is holding us back?

Saying they wouldn't understand is a way of blaming them for making you not do what you say you want. Your defence is to be a critic.

HOW MUCH OPENNESS?

Are you obliged to tell everybody everything? The only obligation is to tell a person who is significant to you how you feel in their presence. Anything else is boring or intrusive.

The best thing to do is ask the person if they want to hear. Let them decide. Always allow the other person to feel they are in control. Rather than force the truth upon them, put them in control of deciding how much they want to hear and at which moment they want to hear it.

CASE STUDY

A subordinate was talking to her boss about a matter he had upon his mind about a behaviour in some of the staff which he could not understand. When she suggested that some people might be confused by his own behaviour in the same way, she experienced the atmosphere become distinctly cooler. The subject shifted to one that was less confrontational. She felt afterwards that she had not only lost the situation but that she had lost the relationship. She felt she had blundered and might not get another chance. Her instinct in reflecting back to her boss was correct, but her actual behaviour was too intrusive. He obviously did not want to hear the message and had the power to end the conversation. A pity, because this particular issue may have been crucial to his own personal development. His defensive behaviour suggests that this is highly probable. He may have been more amenable had she volunteered, 'Do you want me to comment upon how others may see your behaviour?' This leaves him in control. It implies she has an insight which might enable him, but lets him decide if he wants to hear it. He trusts her because he senses she cares enough about him to tread sensitively. Even though he may reply, 'Not just now,' the relationship is preserved at an optimum point, that is, the matter is left for possible reopening should he wish to take it up when ready.

Another thing she might have done is to call attention to the chill in the atmosphere, saying that she has a conflict. On the one hand, she does not want to upset her boss, but on the other she feels they are colluding in avoiding what is probably the most important issue. She experiences a conflict and is fearful of pointing it out because it makes it obvious that she handled the situation incompetently. She might almost prefer to say nothing, hoping the pain will go away – 'let sleeping dogs lie'. But she feels that they probably both noticed that 'something had happened'.

As it is, she experiences her lack of confrontation as failure. She tortures herself with the thought that she lost the relationship. But she may be imagining it all, not the situation, but what her boss feels about her. This is the real concern. If she can raise the subject again, and tell him how she feels at the beneath the surface level, she may get a quite different response: 'No, I did not think you were incompetent, it was just my own fear of talking about my weaknesses that made me clam up. I'm sorry I frightened you off. I didn't mean to. Actually, I would like to talk about it further, because it has been on my mind too.' Even if he says, 'Yes, you did go too far,' he will respect her competence in following up and completing on the issue.

This illustration makes another point. This story was told to me 6 months after it had happened. Such meaningful experiences don't go away even with time. The evidence that this one hadn't was the fact that she was still dwelling upon the event, still trying to find a way of dealing with it. Ghosts are exorcised when encountered at the beneath the surface level.

TIME

Maybe you allow things go on too long because you fear you may not be able to cope with the way people may be affected by what you do. Lack of time is the most common negative gain used in organizations. As Douglas Keir, from the Swiss Reinsurance Company, sagely observed, 'We tend to do what is urgent rather than what is important.'

Being in a rush is also a good way to avoid our fears. We become a victim of time, thus having an excuse for becoming brusque and bad tempered. As Robert Kriegel (1991) says, 'Speed sabotages teamwork and communication.'

If there is an incompatibility between people who have had an opportunity, they have not taken responsibility.

TRACING THE ORIGIN OF YOUR DEFENCES

As you will realize, we tend to use some defences more than others. These are the ones we have found reliable in dealing with earlier circumstances in our life. Thus, we continue to employ them in circumstances and to a degree that is no longer enabling us to cope and may in fact be increasingly inappropriate.

To understand our character and what we might regard as our limitations of character (those things we might want to do differently) it is useful to go back in our minds and consider people who had an influence upon our self development.

Perceiving what defences they used in their relationship with us may enable us to understand them and why we responded the way we did. What made us behave the way we did then need not limit us now, once we are aware of how the mechanisms worked.

Awareness is the first step of taking control of the process.

Example – exchanging negative gains for rewards	
The psychology of it:	What you say and do:
Surface level	For example:
	1. 'I am not happy with you' or
A negative	2. 'You worry me' or

feeling or
thought in a
relationship
(using a defence)

3. 'You make me feel uncertain' or
4. 'You make me feel depressed'
   Because _____

Your own
behaviour in the
relationship

For example:
1. 'I tend to ignore you to prevent you
   reminding me you are a problem to me' or
2. 'I avoid dealing with you because I'm not
   sure how you will react' or
3. 'I keep on coming to your rescue; I feel I'm
   wasting my time' or
4. 'I am always having to ask if what I do is
   good enough'

(What you do
that makes you
feel the way
you don't like)

Beneath the
surface level

For example:
1. 'You should change – *then I won't have to*'
   (critic) or
2. 'You should make it easier for me to cope
   with you – *then I won't have to*' (victim) or
3. 'You should sort yourself out – *then I won't
   have to*' (helper) or
4. 'You should give me more attention – *then
   I won't have to*' (demander)

What is your
negative gain?

What defence
are you using?

Awareness

For example:
Keep people happy.

What you are
avoiding by
using the defence

Don't let people see the way you really are.
Keep a part of yourself hidden that people
wouldn't approve of.
The fear of being out of control.
Parents or teachers made you frightened
about being disorderly. Perhaps you are taking
on their problems as your own. Fear of finding out you are different.
Living through other people rather than doing
what you want.

Resolution	Initiate by saying, for example: 1. 'I think you may feel that I haven't been happy with you' or
(What to do to change my behaviour in order to feel about myself the way I want)	2. 'I think you might feel that I was worrying about you' or 3. 'I think you may have felt I was uncertain about you' or 4. 'I think you may have felt I was depressed'
and after each statement	Be open about the behaviour you don't like in yourself and explain your negative gain.

SUMMARY

This chapter has shown that we become ourselves when we obtain rewards. In contrast, negative gains hold us back and confine us to our past. So, it is the negative gains we must encounter. Understanding why we choose negative gains is the key to changing old behaviours we do not want so that we can reward ourselves with behaviours which are more fulfilling.

Optional exercises

It would be interesting if the following exercises could enable you to 'catch yourself out' in spotting your negative gains, and also 'catch hold of' the defences you might use. These are elusive, having been designed to hide away in the shadows, so it is best to write them down in the spaces provided so that you can fix them with the beam of your conscious mind. When you study them, you may find that a pattern emerges. And you may find you begin to see how and why the pattern formed in the first place. It may become clear to you how your present character is only as it is because of the way you learned to cope with earlier situations in your life. This is all useful in creating the awareness of the negative gains which hold you back.

Exercise – negative gains

Instructions: Write in the behaviour you do not like. Then write in your negative gain, that is, what you hope to get out of behaving that way. The objective is to bring to your awareness those behaviours that are self defeating because they stop you being the self you are.

Behaviour (that I don't want)	Negative gain
_____	_____
_____	_____
_____	_____
_____	_____
_____	_____
_____	_____
_____	_____
_____	_____
_____	_____
_____	_____
_____	_____
_____	_____
_____	_____

Exercise – rewards

Some of the rewards you will give yourself by changing your behaviour:

Changed behaviour (replacing what you don't want with what you will do to get what you want)	Reward (for behaving the way you really want to)
eg Don't be sick (victim)	Feel self reliant. In control.

eg
Don't blame yourself   Feeling you can cope.
(critic)

eg
Don't let people exploit you   Feel good about yourself doing
(victim)   what you want to do.

eg
Don't keep asking for reassurance   Trust yourself.
(demander)

Others:

_____   _____

_____   _____

_____   _____

_____   _____

_____   _____

_____   _____

_____   _____

_____   _____

_____   _____

_____   _____

_____   _____

Exercise – initiating 'beneath the surface' statements

Instructions: In respect of someone's behaviour, or your own, write down what you would say in order to engage them in resolving your conflict. The objective is to make a statement about yourself, not about them. Examples have been given to you earlier in the chapter.

Behaviour	'Beneath the surface level' initiating
_____	_____
_____	_____
_____	_____
_____	_____
_____	_____
_____	_____
_____	_____
_____	_____
_____	_____
_____	_____
_____	_____
_____	_____

Exercise – exchanging negative gains for rewards

Instructions: Think about some behaviours of your own that you don't like. Write them down in the chart below. You do not have to be original: you can borrow some that have appeared in this chapter if you feel they are relevant. On the right hand side, write down the nature of your own, unique, negative gain you give yourself for behaving that way.

The psychology of it:	What you say and do:
Surface level	_____
	_____
A negative feeling or thought in a relationship	_____
	_____
(using a defence)	_____

Your own behaviour
in the relationship
which causes the
feeling or thought

_____

Beneath the surface
level

_____

What is your
negative gain?

_____

What defence
are you using?

_____

Awareness

_____

What you are
avoiding by using
the defence

_____

Resolution

_____

(What to do to
change my behaviour
in order to feel about
myself the way I want)

_____

And after each
statement

Be open about the behaviour you don't like in yourself and explain your negative gain.

9

Personal Agenda Setting

Being people have all the breaks. Becoming people are very unlucky, always in a tizzy. The becoming people are always having to make explanations or offer justifications to the being people. While the being people provoke these explanations.

Saul Bellow, *Henderson the Rain King*

INTRODUCTION

Total leadership rests upon being open to oneself and responsible to oneself. This is not a moral position. It is simply what works best in order to discover the law that exists in your situation. Nobody uses the words 'should', 'must', 'got to', 'expected' or similar. Moral imperatives are not enabling.

These words usually cover up a lot of things we don't know about beneath the surface in ourself and in others. They are difficult to challenge because they are presented to us us 'givens', or accepted wisdom. They are used in order to make us feel we are responsible for someone else's defences. The sense of moral obligation they impart, the outrage that we dare to challenge what we are expected to obey, really do make it difficult for us to take responsibility for ourself.

In suggesting that you focus upon yourself and how you want to be, this chapter may well be the most significant to you.

DOWN WITH MORAL IMPERATIVES!

The word 'should' and other 'gottas' were mentioned earlier (Chapter 3). By this stage in the book, you will no doubt have got the message: if 'should' arises internally as what you want for yourself, then act upon it; if you are behaving in a way due to a 'should' that is imposed externally, you are finding a negative gain for not being yourself. When you come across the word 'should' in this book, ask whether it is being used in a way which will fulfil your personal agenda, as opposed to someone else's.

I suggest that your 'best' choice is to behave in the way that makes you feel good about yourself, not as you think others would want you to behave. You may be imagining what they want incorrectly. And even if you are correct in your perception, it is a projection of them on to you, not what they really want for you. How can they know what is best for you, when they are behaving defensively and, thus, are unable to perceive themselves clearly?

If you behave in a way that is not you, because that is the way you think people will like you best, you will come over as unreal or, literally, as though you are 'acting a part'. The best way to be is yourself. If you are not aware of what this is, behave in the way that makes you like yourself more. Now you are on the way to being yourself!

The more you are yourself, the more people will like you. That is because they will see in you something that they also like to see in themselves.

The more you fear you are really an unpleasant person deep down, the more difficulty you will have with the previous statement. This is because your fear is: 'The more people get to know me, the more they will dislike me'. Strangely, people sometimes act in a friendly and pleasant way because they feel that they have to cover up and hide their real self, like using camouflage or a smoke screen, so that people will not see what they fear is the real, unlikeable person inside.

To change this, imagine you like yourself when you act pleasantly to people, even though you think it isn't the real you. Start off by liking the part of yourself that can behave in a way that allows people to like themselves. You can't be all bad, after all. Then do a bit more of it. You may make a great discovery: there may be more to like about yourself than you ever thought.

And you may make another astonishing discovery: the more you like yourself, the more genuine is your liking for others. You don't even have to act anymore. People seem to like being in your company. They seem to like themselves when they are with you, which means that they find you likeable and it seems that you probably are!

The person people like best, in the end, is the 'real' you, not necessarily the person you are now, but the person you can see yourself 'being'. It enables them, after all, because the more you can be yourself, the more they can be themselves. Instead of being cautious and covering up, everyone seems to be open, and having much more enjoyment.

DON'T PRETEND

What homo sapiens imagines, he may slowly convert himself to.
                              Saul Bellow, *Henderson the Rain King*

There is a useful concept in psychology which is the difference between the 'real' me, which is kept hidden, and that part of me I am prepared to let you see. It is called the anima and the persona. The anima represents all our potential and also all of our fears. The persona is that much of ourself we think is acceptable enough to others to safely reveal to the world.

Often, we hide the anima. It may be for all sorts of reasons, but mainly because we fear we will be vulnerable if we let others see us as we really are. The trouble is, we often don't know who we are ourself. If we did really know ourself, we would also know that there is nothing to be afraid of in being ourself, nothing we need fear, nothing we need hide from. The persona is the cloak we use to hide from our fears of being ourself. The persona is, in fact, the summary of all the defences we use.

People often perceive more of our real self than we care to think. They know that the image is a cover up for our underlying feelings of weakness. Sometimes they are deceived and think we really are tough, but that probably has more to do with the doubts they have about themselves – being confused about themselves, they do not perceive our conflict. Interestingly, the clearer we are about ourself, the more we seem able to 'see through' the defences others put up.

It takes a tremendous amount of energy to put up defences. And it is all negative, because our energy goes into covering up rather than enjoying. Projecting a persona means we are putting on an act. We have to remember our lines. Above all, we have to make sure that the 'mask' doesn't drop. Playing a part is in the end not very satisfactory, not, that is, when life has to be lived. People who engage with each other on the basis of their personas seem to have a shallow existence. And, if people see through us anyway, why do we so fearfully pretend to be somebody we are not?

The answer is down to our greatest fear: 'You wouldn't like me if you really knew me'. In fact, the reality is deeper and has little to do with what others may think about us at all – it has to do with our fear that we would not like ourself if we ever revealed ourselves to ourself.

It is a strange thing, but we sometimes fear that the real self we hide from may be destructive, violent, mean or hateful. And, of course, we would not like ourself that way. Therefore, we keep ourself hidden in the fear that it is better not to find out. How would we ever cope if we found out that, deep down we really are the self we fear we might be?

This sometimes arises from having too little practice at showing the world the self we really are. Maybe, as a child, you were rebuked when you did something you liked, but others thought you shouldn't do. Fearing that people would not like you, you learned to cope by suppressing your real self. Perhaps you coped by trying desperately hard to be nice, perhaps you coped by doing nasty things to test whether people still liked you. You may have even come to think that there is something innately wrong with you, that you were 'born evil'.

> We're inheritors, like everyone else, and because sometimes the only way to punish our parents is to imitate them.
> John LeCarre, *The Naive and Sentimental Lover*

The fear that our anima may be destructive and the fear that we would not like our anima is only fear. The fact that there were some people around at that point in your life who showed disapproval of you, withheld their love from you if you did not present a persona in the way they wanted, is unfortunate, but doesn't mean you need choose to go on being the way you have learned to cope. You may have to understand what those people were getting out of behaving to you the way they did. They had their own fears and projected them on to you. This is not to blame them, but only to understand how it all started – why the defences went up in the first place.

Bearing in mind that our objective is to be ourself by developing our feelings of self worth, this is the same as saying that we want to develop our anima rather than our persona. One way grows us and makes us feel good. The other way holds us back and makes what we do unfulfilling. How could it be any other way when it is 'not ourself' that is doing these things?

Conversely, the more we are ourself, the more we experience a sense of fulfilment. And we notice a strange and infinitely rewarding thing – the more we are ourself, the more others like us. People like us when we are ourself best.

You may in the past have experienced people who tried hard to make you someone who was not you, but did their behaviour towards you really make them any happier? As you will no doubt understand by now, their behaviour towards you was really a defence. Indeed, it was a part of themselves they did not like, but demanded you take responsibility for. They were confused about themselves and, no doubt, confused you as a result.

We enable others not to be confused by not being confused about ourself. If you perceive yourself clearly, you perceive others clearly too. The
more you allow your anima to be you, the more your persona falls away.
The more you are your anima, the more people like you. The more they like
you, the more they like themselves. The more they like themselves, the
more they feel confident in being their anima too.

Being our real self works best for ourself and works best for others too.
The only 'reason' we give ourself to behave differently is our fear. And
when we confront this, it turns out to be nothing, not what we anticipate
will happen, only fear.

> This above all: to thine own self be true,
> And it must follow, as the night the day,
> Thou canst not then be false to any man.
>
> Shakespeare, *Hamlet*

PROJECTING OUR FEELINGS ONTO OTHERS

We see others as reflections of ourself; we can only know another person to
the extent we know ourself. Ultimately, personal and professional success
rests upon our understanding of ourself.

> I both perceive the world in terms of who and what I am and project onto the
> world a great deal of who and what I am. If I know this, I ought to be able to
> escape the stupider kinds of illusion.
>
> Robertson Davies, *The Manticore*

REMEMBER YOU ARE SIGNIFICANT

Some leaders try to pretend to themselves that they are not as important to
others as they really are. In effect, they are trying to identify with the others, trying to 'belong' by attempting not to be different. But people expect
you to be different. It confuses them if you pretend to be otherwise.

Whether you are the actual leader or not, your very presence is significant to your colleagues. They are alert to the signs they pick up from your
every word and action. Suppose you distance yourself from people because
you do not want to intrude, or because you feel there is no task that brings
you together. Whilst you may be thinking that you are protecting them from

yourself, they feel that they are not important enough for you. Small wonder that you begin to get the 'cold shoulder' – it is only a way for them to protect themselves from feeling isolated by you.

If you are moving through an office where there are people, acknowledge them with a smile, nod or wave of the hand. Make a habit of looking around to see who is looking at you – and acknowledge them first. 'Small talk' is enjoyable to some, but not to others. Just the right amount of inclusion is essential. Thereafter, talking to no purpose when there is a task to be done is a waste of your time, and theirs too; generally, there is a common understanding that this sort of talking can be left to more appropriate times.

People will get to understand if you do not 'want to talk for the sake of talking'. (Such assumptions begin to be written into the psychological contract which is formed between you.) This does not matter at all, as long as they realize that you are aware of their presence and that if there is something important to mention, either party is able to take the initiative in engaging the other.

A simple acknowledgement conveys much more powerful signals than you realize; unfortunately, not acknowledging also sends powerful signals!

SELF BELIEF

People will treat you as you treat yourself; they will feel about you as you feel about yourself. They may perceive the real you – your anima – but they may collude to dance with only the bit you show – your persona. Unsatisfactory for both parties.

For example, if you fear that what you want to say may not be important to the other person, you transmit uncertainty. You show yourself as limp, so is it any wonder nobody takes much notice. If you believe in yourself, others also believe in you – it simply does not occur to them to do otherwise.

The way it works, psychologically, is that if you present yourself clearly, people feel about themselves in the same way. You have, in fact, eliminated their own doubts and fears about themselves. They like what they see in you, because that is how they like to feel about themselves. That is why they associate themselves with you so readily, not because you have a great idea, but because they feel better in the situation. In a climate of uncertainty, even the greatest great ideas will run into the sand.

Be sure you choose what you believe and know why you believe it, because if you don't choose your beliefs, you may be certain that some belief, and probably not a very creditable one, will choose you.

Robertson Davies, *The Manticore*

BURNOUT

The surest way to drive yourself into an early grave is to try to be the person you think others want you to be. It is a hopeless task, simply because they don't really want you to be the way you think they do – it is only you who thinks they do. What is happening is that you are trying to help them like you, by trying to be the sort of person you imagine you are not, but should be. This is a projection of you on to them.

At the same time, you are playing into their hands by colluding with what they project on to you. They are also getting you to be what they are afraid of being themselves. Your attempt to make up for their unconscious inadequacies is not a good thing for them, since it maintains their projection. It is not good for you either, since you get nowhere, and experience all the stress of burning yourself out. Being the person you want to be, getting yourself right first, is the only way truthfully to enable others – by helping them to help themselves.

THE SELF

The following chart shows the behaviour and feelings that are related to the self. Apart from the fact that it relates to the self, the behaviours and feelings are just the same as those with which we relate to others.

The 'self'

(after Will Schutz, 1994)

Feeling About myself	Significant	Competent	Likeable
	⇑	⇑	⇑
	⇓	⇓	⇓
Behaviour towards myself	Include Being present	Control Being self determining	Open Being aware

FEELINGS ABOUT ONESELF

Personal significance

That you feel you have a right to be here, that you can take your own place in the world. You expect to participate when you want to. Lack of personal significance may be accompanied by withdrawal from the world. Alternatively, a tendency to 'push oneself in' forcefully may indicate a fear of being left out. Robust feelings of significance allow you to say, 'People are not ignoring me deliberately,' and 'I'll join in as much as I feel is significant to me, not because I feel I have an obligation, or because I need to compensate for not feeling significant.'

Personal competence

Relates to your being able to live your life in the way you want. You are able to use your resources and achieve things in ways that make sense to you and are worthwhile. Competence also includes the way you deal with yourself and overcome internal conflicts. Competence means relating oneself to the outside world, as well as examining and ensuring the state of readiness of your body and mind. Robust feelings of competence allow you to overcome the occasional failure or setback, to learn from that experience and to examine what went wrong, not to give up for fear of humiliating yourself. Blaming others is usually a sign that one's own competence is fragile; surer foundations exist when you are able to laugh with others at your own mistakes.

Personal liking

An acceptance of oneself. It shows a tolerance for oneself even though you are less than perfect. This does not imply colluding in aspects that are unlikeable, but merely acknowledges your humanity. Nothing is condoned by this. But there is no point in beating yourself up for what one has done or been in the past (unless of course, we don't change as a result!). Even though we may have done or thought things we are ashamed of, we can like ourself for being aware of those things, and not repeating them, or not expressing them in ways which do not enable us to like ourself. It cannot be pointed out too often, that to the extent we like ourself, others who are with us like themselves.

I had a voice that said, I want, I want. I? It should have told me what *she* wants, *he* wants, *they* want. And moreover, it's love that makes reality reality. The opposite makes the opposite.

Saul Bellow, *Henderson the Rain King*

BEHAVIOUR TO ONESELF

Personal inclusion

This has to do with how much I allow myself to be in and engage with the world. Sometimes it is described as what you 'focus' upon, but the word I personally most resonate with is 'presence'. Being 'present' describes how much you are alive, active and involved in the 'here and now'. It has to do with the 'total use' of your being, where you are and in what is going on around you.

Sometimes people are present too much. We wish they would leave us alone and not interfere, that they would get on with their own business. For example, consider the case of the manager who feels incompetent when dealing with economic and strategic issues, so compensates by walking the shop floor to examine the correctness of tool settings or maintenance logs. We can say that he is present in what he is doing (too much 'present', we might feel), but that he is not present at the level and in the activity which should rightly be gaining his attention. He has 'switched off' or detached himself from what he either finds boring or cannot bear to face. Clearly, the organization is not receiving value from his contribution as he is misapplying himself as a resource. In his situation, he is probably unaware that he is not present, focused or engaged. He may justify his behaviour by choosing to think that subordinates should be more interested in what they are doing, so that he is 'forced' to keep a watch on them.

Another example is when someone is a member of a team but does not contribute as much as the rest of the team feel they could. Maybe they are regarded as the quiet or thoughtful member of the group. Different from the previous example, they are present physically, but are absent mentally. Of course, you may say that they are very present with themselves in their own thoughts. Nevertheless they are not present in the situation as they should be at this time. To the extent they are not with us, they do to all intents and purposes exclude us. This is not usually done intentionally, but from a fear of whether they are significant enough to take up the group's time with their own issues.

Sometimes people do not participate for another reason – because they feel they might swamp others and take over; they assume they are being most helpful by remaining quiet.

If someone is not present, because of a misperception of their self, their avoidance helps everybody to fail to discover the law of the situation.

You are expected to contribute at the level you fulfil yourself. If you weren't thought to be good enough to be on the board, on the committee or on the working party, you would not have been invited in. The fact that you are there means that you are expected to behave as an equal. Everyone perceives what you are capable of. You must give as fully as you can. And you must assist others to give as fully as they can. You do this by initiating on anything which you think may be blocking the process. This becomes a self monitoring system through which you can ensure that all members of the team are made aware when they are under present or over present.

By making them aware, I do not mean telling them to 'pipe down' or to 'shut up' but to consider the conflicts they have in the situation that is giving rise to the behaviour. When you examine this issue, you begin to gain insight into the workings of the team, its effectiveness and how to make it an even better one.

If someone is not present with you, it can make you consider whether you are significant to them, or if they have thoughts about you that they are withholding. Your suspicions, in turn, may make you withhold from them. In this situation, the relationship is at best superficial, but has the potential to become 'political'.

To confront the situation, say, 'When you say nothing it makes me think that you feel I am not worth bothering with or that you feel you cannot trust me,' or, 'When you take over it makes me feel that what I think or want to say isn't important, or that I'm not competent.' In both situations, you are probably thinking, 'Why am I bothering?'

Personal control

Strange as it may seem, effective control has very little relationship with the fact and content of what is actually done. It arises naturally from the emotional rather than from the intellectual, objective side of your being. It is when there is unresolved conflict that behaviour becomes disorganized or over organized, or unbalanced, which is the same thing.

For example, we try to organize ourself or others because we fear deep down that our slothfulness will get us into trouble. We think we should be organized, but fear that we are not. Where did the word 'should' come from? How did the fear arise in the first place?

CASE STUDY

A director of finance astounded his colleagues by confiding that he perceived himself as disorganized. They all perceived him as the most organized, punctilious person they had ever met. He said that he only appeared to be like that, but he wasn't really; he had to work hard at being organized to compensate for a lack he experienced in himself. It is often amazing that small 'slip ups' happen to such people, as though there is a suppressed, freer side to themselves that is trying to emerge and sometimes manages to catch them out! I know another manager who was equally surprised that his colleagues did not see him as well organized as he thought they would, and he thought he was. In his case, his attempts to compensate for the way he feared he was were seen through.

Often behaviour is a compensation for the way we don't actually feel. It is a way we attempt to compensate for our fears. Of course, having too much control is just as worrying to us as having too little. They are opposite sides of the same coin. The tightness and rigidity associated with too much control are a way of trying to compensate for what we fear we are not. The looseness and vagueness associated with too little control are a way of running away from our fears of what we are not. The first tactic is an attempt to force us to be the way we fear we are not, the second may allow others to take over and do for us what we fear we are not competent enough to do. Neither method allows us to examine why we learned to cope that way in the first place. The way to deal with it is to become aware of our negative gain for behaving that way.

Being open with oneself

'Awareness' is the special word used for this behaviour and 'beneath the surface level' is a good metaphor. Beneath the waves and their apparent direction are profound undercurrents. This is where what actually happens is determined, where the meeting actually goes.

The way to start is to experience your own thoughts and feelings fully. Ask yourself, 'How do I feel in this situation?' If you feel happy, fine. If not, do something about it! Does this mean you attack people because something they said got under your skin, or because someone spoke your brilliant thought before you did, or is not paying attention to you, or making you feel small because they are talking about something you don't understand or have an interest in?

There is another way. Allow yourself to be aware of what your conflict is. Then tell people what it is.

Example

Deepening awareness of the self

What is your negative gain for behaving the way you do?

Surface level A feeling you have about yourself you do not like	For example: 'I am not happy with myself.'
(Projection of you onto yourself)	Because
Behaviour What you do that makes you feel the way you don't like (or like)	For example: 1. 'I am too detail conscious' or 2. 'I am too judgmental' or 3. 'I am too quiet/or too noisy' or 4. 'I keep things to myself too much then get angry with people who want to help'
Beneath the surface level	1. 'I am covering up my fear of not being competent' (critic of myself) 2. 'I demand the highest standards to cover up my fear of not being in control'
What defence is used?	(critic of myself) (victim of my expectations of myself) 3. 'I run away from situations or make my presence felt because I'm uncertain I am significant' (victim of myself) 4. 'I am frightened of people who may help me get to know myself' (helper to myself – helping me not letting myself get to know me)

Awareness	
Negative gain	'What am I "getting out of" doubting the way I feel about myself?' (Example: 'I never risk finding out whether I really am insignificant, incompetent or unlikeable')
Why you feel about yourself the way you do	'What happened in my past, for example, with significant family members or teachers, to make me feel about myself the way I do?'
Resolution	'Ask my parents if I have perceived what they want from me correctly'
What to do to change your behaviour in order to feel about yourself the way you want	'Initiate to my parents, teacher, partner with how I feel they perceive me'
	'Do what I want and see if it makes me feel good'

HOW OTHER PEOPLE AFFECT US

Our stock of self esteem can quickly run out. No matter how strong our feelings are about ourself, the human condition is such that even a trivial remark can torment an old wound. We may have spent years having apparently forgotten an area of conflict and, in a second, we fall prey to the same feelings we experienced way back then. As our self esteem is threatened, we may withdraw, or maybe we make a caustic, defensive remark, the intention being to get our own back. And this has taken place in a split second; later on we probably regret that our emotions were so easily provoked.

If you fear you will not be regarded, you may defend yourself by asserting that the people are not worth bothering with, but your deeper fear is that you will be denied getting to know yourself through them.

MOVING ON

Changing jobs should arise because your fulfilment will be met by change. Change should not take place because of what you are running away from, but from a challenge you want to take up. In this situation, there is no reason for resentment between team members or in any part of the organization. Your going is therefore not hostile but amicable.

Moving on always involves risks. The biggest issue is how you will cope. It is getting the right balance so that you have a challenge in order that you can extend yourself, but don't get into a situation where you are confined. It is the difference between doing better or doing worse, going forwards or backwards, being happy or unhappy.

You attempt to reduce the risks by anticipating the situation in which you might find yourself. On your future stage you go through endless rehearsals with characters played by the people you have met who will be significant to you in that new situation. From their behaviour to you so far, and from the feelings they engender in you, you obtain impressions which make you feel positive or negative about the new situation. Here, your task is to become fully aware of your own feelings, denying nothing to yourself which may lead to the maintenance of any defence.

Of course, you will pay more attention to any negative impressions you have; it is certainly unwise to ignore these; pretending that everything will work out fine when you get there is probably too risky.

Where you feel negative, ask yourself whether it is you that has caused you to feel that way. If it is one of the people, you would do well to resolve the issue at this stage rather than after you take the job. Remember, the law of reciprocity states that what you perceive as a significant issue for you will also be an issue for the other people involved. Thus, if you clarify the issue that you have with them, you will be enabling them to clarify the same issue they have with you.

CASE STUDY

Having been 'head hunted' to be the Managing Director of a new factory, Peter Evans had an exciting, informal meeting with the man who would be his new boss, the Group Chief Executive, who was as keen to have Peter come to work with him as Peter was to sign his new contract.

As Peter prepared to give up his new job and take up his new position, he became a little taken aback that his new boss apparently found it so difficult to find time to see him. Peter was keen to establish his conditions of service before he finally left his old job, but the message he felt he was getting was: 'Just join us and start the job – you can trust us to make sure you are well paid.'

Peter felt he was beginning to be perceived as someone who was making unreasonable demands, in fact, that he was being seen as 'finicky' or 'too detail conscious', but he had no past experience of his new boss, and he felt he would be naive to 'trust' statements made during their original meeting. Peter's doubts were: 'How *significant* am I to you, because I think you are *ignoring* matters which are *important* to me?' and 'I don't think you are being *open* with me, because you are asking me to *trust* you, but I don't feel you are telling me what's on your mind.'

It got to the point where his new boss appeared frustrated that Peter would not commit himself and Peter felt that his reasonable demands were not being met. All these feelings were completely the opposite of those that had been experienced by both men at the initial meeting.

Happily, the situation was resolved when Peter insisted on a meeting in which he was able to initiate at the beneath surface level. His new boss was stunned that his behaviour had conveyed to Peter that he was not regarded as *significant*, in fact, his new boss wanted Peter to join him at any price, salary was irrelevant! He admitted he had a fault which was to expect that people knew what was in his mind, and thus seemed to make unreasonable demands upon people. Their difficulties were quickly resolved and they agreed to talk immediately about any possible misunderstanding in future.

PERSONAL DEVELOPMENT

Will people like me if I change? Is it proper to tell people about my conflicts? Shouldn't I be able to deal with them myself?

In the first place, don't be so unaware as to believe that others do not know that something is on your mind. The fact that you keep it to yourself carries the implication that nobody else is significant enough to share it with, or you don't think they are competent enough to trust, or you think they will not return your openness.

What sort of signal do you think your silence sends to others? It tells them they aren't good enough. Don't be surprised if they avoid you. Being with you does their ego no good at all. They want to be with someone who makes them feel fulfilled.

See how they change when you tell them there's something on your mind you can't cope with. It tells them that they are important to you, that you know they have the skills you need to get things worked out, and that you like them enough to trust them with something that involves your feelings. People respond enthusiastically. They think you are great, simply because you put them in a position where they feel good about themselves.

And even more to the point, their feelings about you mirror their own. You kept quiet because you feared seeming weak, but your openness comes over as being strong.

A strange thing is that, when we are prey to fears we don't express, we are dominated by them. They control us. Our happiness is fragile, our relationships evasive. At any rate, that is what happens when we are afraid. Actually, when we tell people about our conflicts we do not lose control, as we fear, but we put ourself in control. Dealing with the fears puts us right in the driving seat!

COMPLETING

The continuing endeavour of humankind is a state of being in which we experience ourselves as fulfilled. As we have seen, our fears polarize us, whilst feelings of significance, competence and likeability unify us. This is sufficient to explain all about motivation.

Whilst we may appear to be motivated by material reward, our ultimate satisfaction is to feel good about ourself. Our efforts, indeed all our behaviour, are directed towards feeling significant, competent and likeable, to the degree we want them. Provided rewards on the job are fair and equitable, it makes no sense to increase pay as a device to increase performance. Such inducements soon wear off.

The only lasting motivation is that which arises from being the person you want to be. Organizations should therefore concentrate upon what is inhibiting that development. Taking the brakes off is more effective than any amount of pushing and pulling. Motivation is about self esteem. It arises from the way in which we behave to ourself and the way we feel about ourself.

And in the end, the love you take, is equal to the love you make.

The Beatles

Finally, the most fundamental question for your personal agenda setting is: 'What can I do to like myself more?'

SUMMARY

To have confidence, have no fear and be yourself is easier than you think. This chapter has told you more about the enabling process, through which you can 'choose to be'. It is important to start with what you want, because you can go badly astray if you lead your life in the way you suppose others want. Paradoxically, living for yourself turns out to be the best way of living for others.

Optional exercises

Understanding how you can be, taking control and focusing on what you want is your agenda. These exercises assist you to recognize the fears that may prevent yourself fulfilment. The technique is to initiate reverse feedback with yourself.

At the same time, recognizing that you are what you are because of past experiences, you are asked to explore how your relationships affect your self perception. It is great if you are with people who enable you. If you are not, it may be possible for you to enable them to enable you.

There is an exercise – anticipating your new job – that you can do in relation to a possible job change. Work is one of those grand situations, like family, where we cannot easily go back upon the decisions we have chosen to make. You will see that this particular exercise contains a guide which is worth reading carefully before doing the exercise itself.

The final exercise – Where are you now? – is one you can use at any time to 'take stock' of the situation. If you completed this on a 3-monthly basis you could chart your progress. Before undertaking the exercise, experience what is happening to your body, as well as what is in your thoughts and what you feel. Remember, in Chapter 2 the point was made that conflict may be embodied and revealed as sickness as well as affecting our behaviour as defences. Therefore, in taking stock, be aware of all aspects of yourself.

Exercise – deepening awareness of the self

Instructions: Complete the spaces in respect of a behaviour of your own.

Surface level	Instance:
Write down a feeling you have about yourself you do not like	
(Projection of you onto yourself)	
	Because:
Behaviour	

What you do that makes you feel
the way you don't like

    _____

    _____

    _____

Beneath the surface level

    _____

1. How you fear you might be

    _____

2. Recognizing your defence

    _____

Resolution

    _____

What to do to change your
behaviour in order to feel
about yourself the way you want

    _____

    _____

Turning negative gains into rewards

    _____

    _____

Exercise – how other people affect you

Instructions: Think of some people who are important in your life. Write as many names, or initials, as you want under 1, 2, 3, etc.

Give each person a score from 0–9 for each of the statements. A score of 9 means complete agreement, 0 means absolute disagreement whilst 5 is about average.

When they have scored you in the same way, enter their scores for you in the second chart. If they are not with you, you can imagine what their scores might be and enter those.

Then, initiate a discussion at the beneath the surface level on the differences. You can check out how you may be colluding by giving each other the same scores. It is important you talk beforehand about this exercise with the people involved.

Chart One

How you feel about them	1	2	3	4	5
	___	___	___	___	___
These people make me feel significant	___	___	___	___	___

Competent   _____   _____   _____   _____   _____

Likeable   _____   _____   _____   _____   _____

These people
help me feel
present and alive   _____   _____   _____   _____   _____

These people
enable me to be in
control of my life   _____   _____   _____   _____   _____

These people
enable me to be
aware of myself   _____   _____   _____   _____   _____

I make them
feel significant   _____   _____   _____   _____   _____

Capable   _____   _____   _____   _____   _____

Likeable   _____   _____   _____   _____   _____

I make them
feel present
and alive   _____   _____   _____   _____   _____

You help me to
be in control of
my life   _____   _____   _____   _____   _____

You enable me to
be aware of
myself   _____   _____   _____   _____   _____

Exercise – anticipating the new job (use with following exercise)

From what you have learned about the people:	How you anticipate being treated and How you anticipate you will feel

I can be involved in the job	Is it a job in which you will feel alert, fully present and attentive to what is going on? Will you feel alive in the sense that you are engaged in a way that gives your life purpose and meaning? Have you a clear focus on where you are going and what you are aiming for? Alternatively, is there a part of you that may be bored, not fully engaged, thinking of other things or wanting to be elsewhere?
I can be in control in the job	Are you able to determine what you want to do and how to use yourself in the best way? Are you able to change things which make you feel dependent so that you feel you are in control of what is happening to you and what is going on? Can you take responsibility for yourself? Alternatively, is there a part of you that might feel out of control or that you cannot manage sensibly? Might too much be expected or not enough? Are you afraid of failure and what are the consequences?
I can be open with the people in the job	Are you able to tell people your feelings? Will they respond to your openness in initiating discussion of your conflicts? Will they tell you their doubts and fears before things get bad between you? Alternatively, do you get the impression that there is a preference to leave some difficult things unsaid? Do you doubt that people will discuss the defences they use with you?
I will feel I am significant	Will you feel that the job gives meaning to your life, that your experience of being in the job will allow you to have regard for yourself? Alternatively, is there any aspect or any time when you might

	feel you have less regard for yourself than you feel you would like to have?
I will feel I am competent	Can you feel that you can use your intelligence and experience in a way that makes you feel expert? Are you employing all of your skills in a way that creates respect for yourself? Are there challenges which stimulate you but which you know how to rise to? Alternatively, do you feel you are letting yourself down or that in some way you are being stupid?
I will feel I am likeable	Are you prepared to confront aspects of yourself that might threaten to hold you back or make you feel uncomfortable with yourself? Is the job one in which you like the person you are when you are in it? Alternatively, are there some aspects which make you feel angry, resentful or other negative feelings? If so, do you have a way to resolve these feelings?

Exercise – job change

Instructions: Use the previous chart as necessary to remind yourself of the psychology involved, but these are just guides: what the statements mean to you is what is most important.

On a scale of 0–9, where 9 means totally agree, 0 means not at all and 5 is around average, place a number which corresponds with how you anticipate feeling in the job. You can do this with one or more jobs, to help you resolve what is best for you.

From your experience of the people whom you will relate to in the job:	Job 1	Job 2	Job 3	Job 4
Name	____	____	____	____

I can be involved in the
job   ____   ____   ____   ____

I can be in control   ____   ____   ____   ____

I can be open   ____   ____   ____   ____

I will feel I am significant   ____   ____   ____   ____

I will feel I am competent   ____   ____   ____   ____

I will feel I am likeable   ____   ____   ____   ____

Where scores are less
than 9, write down your
reasons _____

_____

_____

_____

_____

From your reasons, write
down the probable defences
or negative gains of your own
or of the other people_____

_____

_____

_____

_____

Resolution: Initiate your negative gains and defences at the beneath the surface level with yourself and with the other people. Do this before you make the final decision about which job is for you.

Exercise – where are you now?

On a scale of 0–9, where 9 means totally agree, 0 means not at all and 5 is around average, place a number which corresponds with how you feel about yourself.

Score
0–9

Write a word or phrase which says how you feel:

I feel I am significant   _____

I feel I am competent   _____

I feel I am likeable   _____

I am allowing myself to be fully alive   _____

I am in control of myself   _____

I am aware of myself   _____

If any mark is less than 9, write down your negative gain for it being less than 9

Resolution: Your next step is what you do about it! Write down what you will initiate at the 'beneath the surface' level

10

Influencing Skills

Every misunderstanding has at its center a breakdown of language.
John Irving, *The Hotel New Hampshire*

INTRODUCTION

This chapter contains examples of situations we find ourselves in. They are in no particular order. In my work with individuals and with organizations, I have encountered them many times which suggests you may find them useful.

By this stage in the book, you will be aware that you cannot influence a person any more than they want to be influenced. True, they may unconsciously choose to allow you to influence them more than they are aware of, in the same way that people choose to be suggestible to stage hypnotists. But taking advantage of people who are unaware is not the purpose of this book, nor would it serve to attain the excellence in a working relationship that is possible when people are aware and in control of what they are doing. The skill is never to dupe, but rather to enable others to choose to be influenced. They will make that choice only when they perceive that your behaviour regards, respects and is open with them. This chapter, therefore, spurns the use of 'power over', and seeks to refine the skills of 'power with'.

The most influential person is also the most enabling.

WINNING PEOPLE OVER (TO THE GOOD SIDE OF THE FORCE!)

If influencing skills are ones which enable others, they will always enable you. They are effective only to the degree to which you take responsibility and are open; nothing which is enabling can ever exploit or take unfair advantage.

Do you have to work with someone who seems to be excessively critical, or subservient, or 'political', or evasive, or demanding, or justifying, or someone who seems contemptuous of change? It is worth remembering that these behaviours are defensive ones. It may be that people feel they will not be able to handle the situation, so they act in a manner which seems calculated to 'needle' you, and which can, if you are not careful, put you on the defensive in turn.

You might spend an inordinate amount of time trying to explain, placate and being reasonable. The defensiveness, however, may well be a tactic they choose, albeit unconsciously, to get back at you for the way they feel about themselves.

For example, your own enthusiasm and competence may make them feel weak, so they act out of fear that they might be 'shown up'. In the first place, it is no help to them if you go on carrying them – supporting them will never enable them to take responsibility for themselves. In the second place, and perhaps even more importantly, you are prevented from doing your own job properly, if you have to spend your time doing theirs as well.

A large part of your job is to break through the defences your colleagues have set themselves, if their defences are preventing you from accomplishing the task together. Furthermore, your job is not to collude with them in adopting their negative view of the world and their low regard for themselves.

The way to break through defences is to talk about your own conflicts rather than what you see as their problem. For example, tell them that you feel that they are, in effect, taking advantage of you – that, although you sympathize with them, doing their job for them does not make you feel that *you* are being competent. Tell them that going along with their view of the world – cynical, negative – does not make you feel good. How happy does it make them? Can you do anything to enable them do anything to feel positive? Note, you are not saying, 'What can I do for you?' They may well ask for a blank cheque, which is no solution. You are asking what you can do to help them help themselves. This is the essence of enabling, because it creates no dependency. In the end, it is what *they* do that is the essential thing, not what you can do for them. They are responsible for their own lives.

To resolve our difficulties, the emphasis needs to shift from blaming, or who is right or wrong, to what we can do about the situation, and how we can come to terms with those fears that limit our lives, if we let them. If those people then do not want to do anything about it, you will at least know that you have done everything you could have done. You can allow them to accept the consequences of their own attitudes or behaviour, without feeling guilt arising from your assumed responsibility for them.

DELEGATION

Maybe there are times you do not delegate enough, particularly those tasks which you think may be burdensome to others. It would be unfair to load others with the jobs you don't want to do, wouldn't it? On the other hand, it seems you are being more than a little over protective.

Furthermore, if you are really doing what should be done by others, you are using them inefficiently, while you are risking 'burn out'! Anyway, are you sure that what you regard as a burden, actually is a burden to others? It really depends upon how the burden is perceived. Be open about what has to be done as well as the fact that you do not know how to cope with it. The key message is that you need help to help yourself. People will respond and want to enable you: in the first place, they feel good about you because you have been open about your conflict, second because of the assumption that their competence will enable you to cope and third as a consequence of the significance they experience by being included with you. Remember, the law of reciprocity states that if people like themselves when with you, they will like you too.

If you anticipate that they will be demotivated by what you give them to do, because you would be if you were given it to do, they will be. But if you can engage them in solving the problem of how something is done, rather than what is done, they will feel motivated. This is not exploitation, because it does not get you off the hook; it will only work once, unless you fully initiate the conflict at the beneath the surface level. In this case, you have solved the matter on a permanent basis.

Be alert to people who turn down responsibility for important tasks. Maybe they feel, unconsciously, that they will let you down. Maybe they fear that they will be beholden to you in some way. It seems the issue is one for you to initiate at the beneath the surface level. Examples of how you might do this might be: that you think you feel you must be imposing upon them; that you think they don't want to be bothered to assist you; that you think that you are asking them to do something that they feel you should be doing yourself. Again, you are not wanting them to explain or provide excuses, but to find out what they feel you are doing wrongly in this situation.

This is your first task – to find out if there is something which they feel you could be doing better. If there isn't, then it is appropriate to ask them to tell you about their feelings of not being able to do the task you have agreed upon.

Establish the means by which it is clear to you both that the job is being done in the way you both want and agree upon. If then it is not done, you will know that you have done everything you can to enable the person successfully to manage the task, including asking yourself whether you have done everything you can to remove any barriers to his success, so that any failure is not due to your own lack of self awareness. Ultimately, there should be agreement that a person's lack of competence is not brought about by your own, unaware behaviour.

CLARITY

Many leaders imagine that they are an 'open book'. They are optimistic in thinking that 'It's obvious' or 'People will get the message'. Often, this is because of the leader's own lack of confidence in saying what is on his mind in case people ignore it or think it's not good enough.

However, if nothing is said, the danger is that people begin to interpret the silence through their own system of doubts or fears. They may begin to feel they are not important enough for the leader, or that he does not rate them or that he does not trust them.

You may feel you do not want to constrict them, that you'll support them in helping them do what *they* want. But this may be perceived as a lack of clarity on your part. You need to tell them what you want for yourself in this situation. And, equally, give them a chance to tell you what they want.

If you are not clear about what you want and where you are going, be clear about that too. It will communicate itself anyway, whether you are open about it or not. And your lack of clarity may be seen as blaming them or withholding from them; defensively they may regard you, with some justification, as a poor leader.

If you take them into your confidence and say where you stand, you will be a rock from which they can take their own bearings. Total leadership does not consist in always pointing the way; sometimes leaders have to begin by admitting they don't know the way. Pretending we know where we are and where we are going is unawareness.

Paradoxically, and strangely enough, admitting that we need to stop and find out where we are now can impart a sense of confidence – already there is a feeling of, 'We're on the way'.

You might worry that you will look as though you are dithering. It is some-times the perception people have of political leaders, whose thoughts and actions are inevitably perceived at a distance, and usually through some other, diffusing media, such as the press or television. What the public want is a dialogue that includes them directly, but this is what politics seems incapable of providing. Small wonder that we find politicians difficult to trust. Their problem is that they cannot develop a relationship with us that is as close as either party would like.

In an interview on the Clive Anderson 'All Talk Show', the ex-Labour leader, Neil Kinnock, said that, if he had one regret, it was that he would have like to have spoken personally to some of those people who had been abusive to himself and to his wife. No doubt Bill Clinton has similar feel-ings, as would many people for whom fame is inevitably accompanied by remoteness. Their problem is that everybody who knows of them cannot be known by them.

But this is the key: it is that those in the closest relationships – family, friends and colleagues – know what is in our hearts. Another way of say-ing this is that the people who are significant to leaders are defined by being included in their conflicts. It is in this intimate group that doubts need to be resolved. If this is achieved within an 'inner circle', what is presented to the world is certainty, continuity, uniformity. This is why leaders who have many reportees – a wide span of control – so often appear to be 'off balance'.

Although people always know when there is 'something going on' in your mind, unless you are clear about it, they may interpret through their own fears, attributing feelings to you about them that you don't have at all, at least, in the way they suspect, which is always the worst way.

You are deeper and more mysterious to others than you imagine. You think your ideas and behaviour are obvious. They are not. For example, maybe you are trying not to appear dictatorial in case you lose the commit-ment of others. To avoid appearing dictatorial you hope that people will see for themselves want you want. Then you will be relieved of the responsibil-ity for telling them.

In fact, people are more committed when you have included them by telling them what you want. The psychological mechanism is that you have included them in the first place, and made them feel significant by telling, as opposed to ignoring them. Incidentally, I have used the word 'telling' which I advised against in Chapter 2. In fact 'telling' is a good thing to do provided it is telling them about you rather than telling them about them-selves. The former is 'initiating', the latter is being a 'critic'.

So far, so good. But telling them what you want should not take away their control. It does not mean they should actually do what you want. This is disempowering, unless they want to do the same thing as well. Rather, your own declaration should lead to them saying what they want. Now you can see how both plans may be accommodated; the total leader's task is to see how what someone wants can be achieved as part of what he, the team and the organization wants.

'PARENTING'

Look after people when they need it. That is, when they choose to be enabled. This allows them to remain in control. Too often, we help people because of our needs, not theirs. Feeling that they are dependent upon us makes us feel good. For example, we feel wanted and appreciated. We might also feel smug that they can't manage without us.

It is better not to make assumptions about what is best for others; let them decide. What happens when we make decisions for others is that we are, implicitly, communicating that we don't think they are competent to run their own lives. Little wonder that our children ignore us, or do the opposite thing 'just to be naughty'. It is their way of paying us back for the way we make them feel about themselves.

'Parenting' happens at work as well as at home. Certainly, at work, you should not be doing other people's jobs for them. When training or practice has established a basis of competence, you are 'burning yourself out' if you continue to do for others what they are competent to do for themselves.

You may ask yourself what your negative gain is for treating them the way you do. The negative gain you are giving yourself, you will find, is that what appears to make you feel that you are looking after people and have their respect, in fact alienates you and is a source of stress.

So, what are you 'getting out of' allowing yourself to feel stressed? Do you tell yourself, unconsciously, that people appreciate the way you worry about them. In fact, they don't. They resent you for interfering and for not letting them use their own skills. Alienating them gives you a weak basis for assisting them in any fruitful way. If there is a fear in yourself that you do not feel they can be trusted, you need to be open with them about that.

What is it you fear so much about the possibility that they may make a little mistake? Deal with your fear of being out of control by deciding with them to give them the chance to take minor risks, but not major ones. Soon, they'll be managing the major ones as well. The longer you prevent them from taking risks the bigger the risk they'll take without telling you what they are doing.

Suppression always makes any situation worse. In all cases, it is your fear, not their competence, which is the major issue. You have to be competent enough to know that telling them of your fears will actually address the situation between you – and put you both firmly in control.

The other thing to do is to ask them if they need assistance. Letting them decide puts them in control, whilst you don't lose it. If they ask for your help you can give it, but they remain in control, so you are, in fact, enabling. This time you are achieving your objective by assisting them to succeed with something which you, for your own reasons, were concerned they might fail with.

We are not talking about 'life threatening' situations where, for example, children have to be held back from something of which they have no experience; we know when we are being 'bossy', even though we tell ourselves it is 'with the best of intentions'. Instead of 'parenting', replace the disabling 'adult to child' relationship with the mutually profitable 'adult to adult' one.

CONFRONTING THE ISSUES

Because of your own uncertainties, it is possible to allow yourself to be emotionally exploited. Be alert to the tactics others may use, albeit unconsciously. 'Tactics' are defences under another name. Your job is not to collude in the process, unless you choose to do so, temporarily, because you feel it would genuinely assist them (in which case it is not colluding), but to make them aware of the situation they are creating.

A person's seemingly vigorous certainty often deceives the gullible into compliance. But is the apparent certainty really a cover up for what is difficult to tackle? A person who has a fanaticism is using the defence of being a critic, because they are so vehement in pointing out what it is about people that is wrong and, of course, they have a 'divine insight' which makes them right.

> The best lack all conviction, while the worst
> Are full of passionate intensity.
>
> W B Yeats, *The Second Coming*

Due to your own doubts you become pliable, perhaps giving people so much rope, or you see so many sides of the story, that you are seen as aimless or vacuous. In this situation you are allowing yourself to be a victim, taking responsibility for what others dump on you.

Yet again, you are good at sorting problems out for others, whilst yours never seem to get sorted out. You are being a great helper, and no doubt people help you to feel good about helping them. Unfortunately, the last person you are helping is the one who needs it most – yourself.

A person might be a demander, because they insist upon your time and attention. It is frustrating and annoying, but the strength of their feeling appears to allow you no choice but to go along with their demands. They feed on your guilt, even your guilt about not knowing how to cope, in order to create advantage for themselves. They get you to do for them what they find difficult to do for themselves.

The way to deal with this is to make them aware of what they are doing. They would not do it if they were aware of the way they are distorting the situation and using you as a target for their own feelings of inadequacy.

Defences are only defences when used unconsciously. We are all enabled when we are made aware we are using them. This puts us in control instead of letting them control us. This is vital from the interpersonal perspective, because, otherwise, we will not complete the task successfully. From the personal point of view, whether a person wants to be aware of his defences is his choice; we take control from a person if we choose, on his behalf, that he should be aware.

Raising awareness in our relationship is our objective, and some suggestions as to how to do this follow.

Example

To the critic, say, 'I think you feel the problem is all me, but is there some way you make the problem?'

To the victim, say, 'I think you feel the problem is all you, but is there some way you make your problem?'

To the helper, say, 'I think you feel the problem is all me, but in what way does dealing with my problem mean that you do not deal with yours?'

To the demander, say, 'I think you feel you would not have a problem (or I would not have a problem) if you were like me (or I was like you) – is this really the answer to the problem?'

MEETINGS

Do you have a tendency to let discussions go on even though some people are showing signs of impatience, whilst others may have 'drifted off'? Some people may be wondering why we are still talking when the decision has been made, whilst others seem to take pleasure in bringing up minor points.

Trying to be helpful to everybody, you may be excessively tolerant to people, allowing them to speak because they do not normally do so, or because it would seem unkind to cut them off before they had finished. The psychological issue is with you not wanting to ignore one group whilst another group are feeling they are being ignored, hence their restlessness or 'switching off'.

Ask someone who is not fully 'with you' (that is, present) – someone who appears impatient or bored – what their feelings are. Do not be content when they state the facts of the discussion. That would be surface level talking. Get them to focus – repeat that you would like to understand their feelings.

A similar situation involves lateness. How 'genuine' is the excuse, or is this behaviour a way, albeit unconscious, of getting back at you for the way you make them feel? Blaming them does not resolve the conflict; until you engage in reverse feedback you may expect other behaviours signifying negative energy.

What you want to get at here is what is going wrong with the process if they are annoyed, disengaged or have anything else which is not fully involving them. Remember, the question (what are their feelings?) is not designed to blame them for what they feel, merely to establish why they have the feeling. It is almost bound to be the case that the reason for their feeling involves you as well as them. Blame is no solution.

Another way of approaching this situation is to 'bite the bullet' yourself. Suppose you reason that the fact some people in the meeting are not 'with you' is for you to do something about more than anyone else. After all, if you wait for others to include themselves, you may wait forever. Avoidance will be engaged if you use reverse feedback.

Why not state the obvious, which might be one of the following examples: 'I get the feeling that what I'm doing is not significant to you or that you don't feel I'm handling this meeting well – is that how you feel?' The issue is about how you feel, not apportioning blame to the other person for being at fault for making you feel that way.

You ask the other person to help you understand your feeling – it is for them to connect it with their own behaviour and choose to change their behaviour in order to prevent recurrence of your issue, if they choose to do so. At all times, they enable you best when they remain in control and are not being pressurized by you to change; they are most likely to change if they make the choice.

When they ask why you feel the way you do, then is the time to give examples of their behaviour: 'You seem to be bored, or show impatience, or make scoffing remarks, or talk to someone else as if I wasn't here.' They may become aware that they are also making a choice, unconsciously, to be impatient or bored in the meeting. Furthermore, what is their negative gain for choosing to be that way?

Culpability is always a collective responsibility. Getting to what is going on in the process is going to get everybody's attention. All of a sudden, you have an exciting meeting. When issues come out as to why people are impatient, bored, or feel negative for any reason, the efficiency and energy improve and, moreover, will bode well for enjoyable meetings in the future.

The aim is to establish that there is a process by which awareness is raised. For example, in wanting to please everybody, the difficulty is in getting the right balance, letting people have their say, whilst also wanting everybody to be involved. It may be that the speaker will want to think about why what they are saying is boring to some or makes others impatient. But letting the situation ride is the least likely method for assisting them to improve their delivery and saying something that others find interesting, or for getting all members of the group engaged with the process.

Until you allow the feelings to come out, people are unlikely to be committed to what is going on or to any decision which is made. This is true, whether the atmosphere is contentious or passive. The issue is hardly ever whether the correct decision has been made and that we should now go on to the next issue, but whether our feelings of being attended to and acknowledged have been taken into account.

Make sure you know what your own agenda is and make sure you know what others' agendas are. For example, you feel a failure if everyone in the meeting is not contributing. When you ask why, the person says they have nothing to say, although they want to be in the meeting. Really, it seems they are prepared to go from the meeting and carry out the execution, but not contribute to the decision. Make sure that it is not you who is demanding that they contribute to compensate for doubts about yourself. Although it appears to be their problem, the conflict is really yours. It is with how your leadership is regarded – you think that everybody should be contributing for the team to be an effective one.

If people want to be included, that is their choice. They also can make a decision to leave when they want to, for example, if they have more important things to do. Get on with the meeting with those who are involved and feel they are competent. As the decision is being made, ask the quiet person if they agree. If they say 'Yes,' that is fine, you have a 'concordant decision' (see the following chapter). If they say 'No,' they must be involved in the meeting. At that point they contribute why they are saying 'No'. In the end, people have to decide for themselves whether they are in or out of the meeting.

What do you do if people are talking when you are? What if they are talking to each other rather than being involved with what is going on in the meeting? How do you 'enforce discipline'?

The first thing is to be aware of your feelings in this situation. What you probably feel is that you are being ignored. Their behaviour excludes you. It communicates that their sub group meeting is more significant than your meeting.

Your issue is your doubts of your own significance. You might also feel incompetent because it must be a poor meeting if they are not attending to the issues you are dealing with. And it makes you feel rejected, because there is an element which is binding them together, making them seem close, but it isn't you. What they are discussing is so important that they are whispering together; they appear to have a secret that is not including you or the group.

It is no good getting angry or trying any form of discipline. The fact of the matter is that they are not with you. How do you bring them back?

You draw attention to how you feel in this situation. Say that their behaviour makes you feel you may be running a poor meeting. What do they want to do if the meeting is boring? Why are you not significant enough to be included? Being open at the beneath the surface level will make them present with you.

Actually, the issue is theirs as well. If the meeting is not giving them what they want, it would be enabling if they did something to change it. Why don't they take the lead? But if they don't, are you going to wait forever? You'd better do something, after all, you're the leader.

The other point to make is that everyone is aware that the meeting is fragmented. Do we just go along with it? Or do we confront it – 'I do not think I am contributing to this meeting; I feel that you may feel this is not important.' This is not being critical. It's just pointing out your own conflict, and what everybody perceives, but is afraid to comment upon.

Now that we are more aware of the situation, what can we do to make this exciting for everyone? What can you do to make it more exciting for yourself? Perhaps you have already done it – by living closer to the edge. Just by raising awareness of what is happening beneath the surface.

COMMUNICATING REGARD, RESPECT AND WARMTH

Smile as genuinely as you feel. If it is false, it turns people off. But if you really engage people with you, then you will begin to smile. Smiling arises from the feeling of identifying closely with someone and their, and your own, defence. At least partly, the smile arises because your own feelings are reflected in the person you perceive. It is not the act of smiling so much, which predominantly uses the lips. Smiling takes place also with the eyes and all the other facial muscles. It is impossible, when smiling with some-one, not to have engaged them in eye contact.

The message that passes between people at these times is, 'I recognize you, I am with you, I understand'. In other words, smiling enables you to be genuinely present with the person. It rates as one of the most valuable expe-riences, and it costs nothing to bring it about.

We distrust the salesman or the politician who smiles to a degree beyond that in which they have been included, because they are projecting an emotion they are not feel-ing.

If you are with someone and not smiling, part of you will seem to have stopped existing for them. They will not know what you are thinking and feeling about them. Consequently, they will begin to have doubts about themself. Fearing there may be something the matter with them, they will not like themselves in this situation, and so, as a consequence, will not like you. People like being with people who make them feel happy with them-selves.

If you are not clearly present with the person, you will appear detached and analytical. They will fear that you are having thoughts about them which you are not sharing. The fear of being left out or superfluous (ignored) is not a pleasant one. They will dread your company for making them feel this way, alternatively, they may try to force themselves upon you in order to get your attention, that is, to become significant enough to you for you to recognize them.

THE EMOTIONAL 'SUB TEXT'

We tend to respond to what people are saying and how they behave at the surface level; we should use our senses to experience what they are afraid of beneath the surface. Partly, it is to protect ourself that we do not listen fully, partly it may be because we think they prefer us to deal with their 'persona' rather than their 'anima'.

Our culture has put such a value upon the 'show of things' and upon intellectual argument, that we try in vain to follow the logic, and get hopelessly lost in the feelings. And, because we filter the 'logic' through our defences, it is not surprising that we do not agree with the 'logic' either.

To the extent a person feels defensive about even the most obvious and brilliant plans, he will find fault and be unmoved. He will deny the obvious, even though it stares him in the face. A person will disagree with you unless they feel 'as one' with you. That is, that their understanding of themself in the situation is identical to yours.

Listening carefully to the 'sub text' gives you clues as to the underlying conflict that you or the other person are experiencing. For example, the occasional 'loaded' or emotional word is thrown in as part of what is supposed to be an objective statement. Attend to what you or the person are feeling beneath the surface of their talking and their other behaviour. It is the emotional sub text where the story is actually being written.

GAINING RESPECT

Won't I lose respect if I do not direct others? The question arises out of your fear of losing control. It rests on a shaky idea of what control actually is. In fact, the more you try to preserve your respect, the less control you actually have; the more control you share, the more respect you have.

This sounds paradoxical, but it is true. If you are aware of the feeling you have, then you never lose power, or make yourself vulnerable, or any of the other things you fear, by telling others who are involved in the situation about it. Far from exposing you or robbing you of control, it puts you fully in control, because you are initiating what is necessary to resolve the conflict that is holding you and others up.

As a result of taking others into your confidence by telling them what conflict you experience, you have communicated that you find them likeable (why would you confide in someone you did not like?), competent (why would you reveal your problem to someone who was incompetent?) and significant (why else would you include them?). The feeling they now have about you is a reflection of the way you have made them feel about themselves.

Paradoxically, the more you give away, the more you get back.

INTIMIDATION

The senior person in the group has tremendous scope to ignore someone or make them look small. All they have to do is pretend they did not hear or just look doubtful whenever the other makes a suggestion. Intimidation arises when someone feels that they will be ignored, humiliated or rejected, if they draw attention to themselves or if they do not conform. A person may convey approval or disapproval by the slightest, oblique signals.

Most people deal with these unspoken, unacknowledged threats by saying nothing and remaining in the background. Even the senior person present may be intimidated by subordinates. Intimidation is used to make you say the things the other wants to hear, or to prevent you from saying the things they do not want to hear. Usually, these things are those which they fear, which, in turn, might make them feel ignored, humiliated or rejected. Intimidation is thus the means which is being chosen, without awareness, to protect themselves. It is the defence of the critic. Ask, 'Am I being intimidating? Perhaps it's because I'm frightened of hearing what you want to say – why would that be?'

CONFIDENCE

Lack of confidence arises from false anticipation of the consequences of acting upon our awareness. What happens is that we may have awareness, but we are afraid of focusing it. Fear often leads us to express our awareness in a manner which is not competent, so that the message does not get transmitted and, therefore, not received, in the way we intend. Feeling stupid, we lack the confidence to have another try.

You will always gain confidence when you gain the information you require to resolve your conflict. For example, rather than assume what you fear might be the case, ask people who matter to you whether you have let them down or might let them down, whether you have done a good job or not, and about anything which concerns you. Your lack of confidence almost always turns out to be imaginary. And if it turns out to be true, then you have something concrete to go on.

If people can enable you to overcome the reasons for your lack of confidence they will, because that way they also enable themselves. Nobody wants to see you unfulfilled – we are all losers to that extent. But be careful of becoming a demander – don't continually ask for reassurance as a substitute for understanding and taking responsibility. Initiating the conflict that is your lack of confidence is dealing with your situation.

SPEAKING 'TO THE POINT'

You will have experience of people who appear to speak a lot, but say very little of any substance. There are those that seem to be skimming over the surface, perhaps giving lots of information, very little of which seems significant enough to lodge with us.

Then there are those who make a point to which we would like to respond, but then go on to make another point, and another, ignoring the signals we are making that we would like to have our turn.

Listen carefully to the person who is speaking: Is it evasive? Is it pompous? Is it dismissive? Is it successful in communicating? Is it getting full attention? Is it the most important thing on our minds? Is there an unspoken conflict? What you experience may lead you to make an initiating statement about your conflict in the situation.

All sorts of devices may be used to keep the conversation light and on the surface. This is all right in a social situation, but not among people who need to understand each other well in order to work together. Notice that when people talk about what is really significant to them, their speech dramatically slows down as the quality and meaning of the communication deepens. This is always the character of beneath the surface level communicating.

DON'T BE EXPLOITED

Frequently, people offload onto someone else those things they are fearful of undertaking themselves. This is the case of two defences finding a convenient liaison – that of the demander enlisting a helper. If the self concept is inadequate, they may say, 'You are the best person to do this,' or 'This is your responsibility.' And because you want to be a good leader who is liked by everybody, you fall for it. Your own fear is that people won't like you if you don't help them with their burdens – so you 'pick up the cudgels' on their behalf.

Unfortunately, what is being created is a culture of dependency. You find yourself doing what others should be doing for themselves. You burn yourself out and they never learn that they are adult enough to sort out their own problems.

The total leader's job is not to challenge people on behalf of others, unless he is also involved with the issue himself. If subordinates see you as a failure (eg for not looking after them) it may be because they have failed themselves and are displacing on to you.

Confrontation is not about taking sides, but making sure that everybody is on the same side. Confrontation is about addressing the issue which separates us so that it brings us closer together; confrontation is never successful when it is about making someone else a loser.

People who have unreasonably high expectations of themselves can be their own worst enemy. If you are unsatisfied with yourself because you are less than perfect, you can make yourself a 'martyr' to other people's expectations. In fact, unwillingness to accept less than perfection in yourself leaves you exposed and vulnerable. You are your own worst critic, and you accept the judgement of others when they are critical of you. They know they can get away with it, and make even greater demands.

Your negative gain is that you think that, if they tell you you have done a good job, then maybe you can legitimately believe in yourself, that you have done a good job. The defence allows them to get the task done which they want, rather than the task you want. There has been no understanding in this situation.

The problem is your own self doubt. You are looking to others to reassure you for an aspect of yourself that you feel unsure of. If you make your feelings about yourself dependent upon what other people think, you will never be in control of your life.

'HIDDEN AGENDAS'

The 'hidden agenda' is not what bothers you. It is the fact that you think you are being excluded from something in which you feel you should be included. You are being left out, passed over, ignored or 'taken for a ride'. Perhaps you suspect that someone is taking advantage of you and you resent feeling gullible. If someone is not open with you, are they behaving more as an enemy than friend? Why trust, if you do not feel trust? Why 'let matters ride' when you experience doubt?

The thing is not to accuse the person of having a hidden agenda, because that would be 'surface level' relating, but to say at the beneath the surface level that you feel excluded. Perhaps you should say that you have a conflict because the person is making you think you should go along with them, but you feel you would be foolish to do so. If the other person engages with you, they will become aware of what it is about their behaviour that does not enable people to trust them the way they want.

UNLEASH OPPORTUNITIES

All you can do is create the circumstances in which people can develop their skills and talents, if they choose to do so. Do not feel that you are a failure (incompetent) if people do not respond the way you would yourself. Do not feel resentful (ignored) that they do not take the opportunities that you have created. Maybe you hoped for some recognition or thanks for your own efforts. Maybe you are tempted to say, 'Why did I bother?' Remember that you did what was right for you. Be pleased with yourself. Any appreciation may be a bonus, but don't expect it. Whether what you did is going to be right for others is for them to decide. You cannot make up their minds for them, in advance.

DON'T WAIT FOR RECOGNITION

You are wasting your time if you think that others are as aware of your qualities as you are. They may be, but do not assume so. Because if you do, you'll feel cheated when someone you consider inferior gets the promotion you think should rightfully be yours.

The truth of the matter is that you are wasting your time if you go about doing those things which you think will get you recognition in the first place. What you think is worthy of recognition, the people you are trying to get to recognize you may not. You are really playing at guessing games. The only sure thing to do is to do what is significant for you, not what you think ought to be significant to others.

If you address those issues which are significant to you, you will always succeed and you will never feel cheated. If others see what you do as significant, because it is significant to them, that is a bonus, but do not expect it to follow automatically. Of course, in a working relationship, you should be aware of what there is between you that needs to be initiated upon.

If you feel cheated, left out or passed over, find out from people what you need to do to have the significance to them that you want. For example, why have you not been considered for the job you wanted? If that will involve you in behaving in ways you also want to behave in, well and good, there is a congruence of aims. If it doesn't, the job, as defined by them, is not for you, your path lies elsewhere – in going the way and doing the things that will lead to self significance. That may be in continuing with your present job or in a modification or change which allows you to 'grow' in the ways that are meaningful to you.

Your role should not limit you. You cannot fulfil yourself if this depends upon the way in which you think others see your role. Instead, elaborate and extend your role in ways which have meaning for yourself. Do more things that make you feel you are liking yourself in your role.

DON'T HOLD BACK

You need to make sure that people really have understood the message you have been trying to tell them. Sometimes we think, 'I told them straight and clearly enough', when they were wondering what on earth we were rambling on about and when were we going to get to the point and say what we meant.

Another thing that can happen is that the person with whom we have raised an issue does not think we were as heated about the matter as they feared we might be. So they may tell themselves that it is not really significant to us, when it really *is* significant to us. You need to make sure that there is understanding between you. Of course, out of kindness you may try to protect the other person, but this may not in fact be the best way to enable them. Ask yourself who you are really trying to protect. Being easy on yourself doesn't get what you want either.

Do not hold back because you have some insight or knowledge you fear might be unfair to mention because it might influence them unduly. Let them be the judge of that. Not telling what you know or what you feel disempowers them. The only crime would be to insist that they saw things your way – giving them the knowledge and the freedom with which they may challenge your perception is no crime at all.

DON'T JUSTIFY

The border between an explanation and defensive justification is a very thin one. It may not even exist. It is easy to sound either angry, because of trying to make out that you are not understood, or apologetic, because of thinking that the other person might become upset.

Justification is a behaviour which takes place in an area of conflict as a result of an accusation that has been made, or to head off an accusation we think might be made.

For example, when giving feedback to a colleague, there is no need to preface your remarks with such 'hostages to fortune' as, 'Of course, I don't know you very well, so I might be wrong.' What is wanted is your perception of the person, that is, the truth as you see it. You may well turn out to be wrong, but expressing your perception is the only way to discover the whole truth.

If you express your feeling, rather than justify yourself, the other person is in the best position to assist in clarifying that perception – what he does, and you do, to create that perception. There is nothing about the perception that needs justification, it exists the way it is. Understanding the perception and how to deal with unconscious conflicts and unwanted behaviours that may arise from the perception is the much more meaningful task.

MISPERCEPTION

It pays to be honest about all this. Unless you know how you are perceived, how can you do anything to change the behaviours you do that cause a perception to arise that you do not want?

Suppose what you feel about someone is irritation, because they never complete what they say they will do. You see them as ignoring you. The feeling you have about them is annoyance. You recall an occasion when they said they would do something for you, but they dropped what they were doing for you in order to get on with something else instead. The thing is not to confront with, 'My perception of you is that you don't bother about letting people down or you never what you say you'll do.' Instead, at the beneath the surface level, create awareness, saying, 'The feeling I have is that you don't think I'm worth bothering with.' When they ask you to, 'Tell me why you feel that way', you can explain the behaviour that caused your perception to arise.

When you get on to discuss the way both of you feel about the incident that caused your feeling, the outcome might be that the other person thought you would realize and accept that he had some other priority which distracted him from attending to you. He is surprised to learn that you do not think he is reliable and that you think he is ignoring you. At the same time, he becomes aware that he cannot assume you know what he is thinking and why he is doing what he is. Sure, other things do come along which may have to take precedence, but you need to be involved in the decision when he switches his time from you to something else.

Without awareness the psychological contract is broken. The danger is that you will not seek his advice in future, even though the team structure and the demands of work necessitate that you should.

Example

'My perception of you is based on the feeling I have that you don't think I'm worth bothering with.'	'Tell me more. Will you tell me what I did to make you feel that way?'

'We had agreed you would...'

'We did agree. But I thought you would realize that... had to be done first.'

'I did not know you had to drop what you were doing for something else. I suppose I would have agreed it was more important if I had known. But you never explained or made it all right for me, so I just got the impression I couldn't rely on you.'

'I did intend to do what I promised, but the other thing came. I suppose I shouldn't have assumed you knew what was going on. Also, I suppose, I had a conflict because I didn't want to let you down. I didn't know what you might say. So I tried to avoid the conflict by saying nothing and just hoped that you would understand. I think you might have been irritated, or not bothered to ask me to help anymore.'

'That's a pity because by avoiding talking about the conflict you seem to be bringing about the situation you don't want – I certainly felt irritated. But it's interesting that you said you felt I might have got angry and that put you off telling me what was on your mind. I didn't realise that my attitude might prevent you from telling me your difficulties.'

'When I see you with your head down and obviously very busy, I think I'd better not bother you. Once before, when I wanted to tell you of a problem, you looked up and said, "Yes?" in a blunt way that told me you didn't want to be bothered and I was being a nuisance.'

'I must be aware that if I want you to keep me informed of any problem in the way we are working together, I'd better make it really clear that I'm really available to you and be aware that I'm not giving the impression I might bite your head off if you tell me some-thing I might not want to hear.'

'I shouldn't keep things to myself. I avoid what I think might be confrontational by telling myself you'll understand, although I can't expect you to unless I've made it clear. I'm afraid of letting people down, even though it's the opposite of what I intend. In future I'll tell you of any conflict I have. And if I feel that you are making me feel you don't want to bother with me, I'll tell you that too.'

THE 'PSYCHOLOGICAL CONTRACT'

This has been explained already in Chapter 1, but I am referring to it here because it is at the very core of 'influencing skills'. It is about our expectations of how we treat each other. It is essential to our culture and our vision of 'how things are done around here'. The 'contract' is all that is felt to be right between you. It is your mutual vision for self fulfilment.

It is worth remembering that you have influence only so far as you have understood your 'contract'. If you attempt to force an advantage, perhaps applying pressure beyond what has been psychologically understood, you may obtain a temporary compliance, but you will risk losing influence, permanently.

POSITIVE RELATIONSHIPS

Believe that meeting another person is going to be an experience that will make you feel good. The nature of motivation is such that people want what you do too. Welcome the chance to get what each of you want for yourselves, together.

> Has it ever occurred to you that other people see you in the same way you see them, as a collection of appearances and habits – and they never see your thoughts, to know how wonderful you really are? So that you seem as strange to them as they all appear to you.
>
> Kim Stanley Robinson, *The Wild Shore*

When you have an opportunity to praise someone, to give them 'the good news', don't be frightened of doing so. It is strange how often we avoid telling people how good we think they are. We say, 'They know, anyway,' or, 'They'll be embarrassed,' when it is really ourselves we are trying to save from embarrassment.

Sometimes we think, 'Don't want to get them used to it, they'll always expect it,' when really *we* should get used to it and, if they make us feel good, why shouldn't they expect to get it reflected back to them?

Another reason for withholding praise is that we think that, although they have made some improvement, our praise will make them feel they are already as good as we want them to be, although we would really like them to go further. You have to remind yourself that people are always more likely to do more of that behaviour that wins them praise; the psychological mechanism is, you like them, they like themselves, they want to do more of what eventually leads them to like themselves more, and so on.

Back to telling 'the bad news'. This is best not delayed, but done straight away. But do not act so hotly that you give 'the bad news' without awareness. Giving the bad news without awareness is either coldly indifferent or unfair. It would disregard the subject by ignoring your involvement in whatever has led to the bad news.

Giving the bad news with awareness means that we take responsibility for our own part in the situation. It is then impossible to impart the bad news with anything less than regard, respect and empathy. The way you approach them preserves their respect for themselves. You are not diminishing them, but treating them on equal terms. Your debate will deepen your mutual regard and, although the bad news may be for them to act upon, their capacity to deal with it is facilitated by the knowledge that you have sufficient respect for them to confront them on 'adult to adult' terms.

The manner in which you approach them may well determine the way they react to you. Blame them and you create hostility. Respect them and they respect you. That is the only way to come out of a situation in which you have given someone the bad news. Holding on to your integrity, thus giving someone a chance of maintaining theirs, means at least something good can come out of a situation which does not give anybody much of a chance to feel anything but negative.

PRAISE (POSITIVE REINFORCEMENT)

It often appears to be easier for people to criticise than praise. Thus, a parent scolds a child for being silly, but does not reward him for doing what is sensible. Interestingly, telling people off can have the effect of making them do what we don't want even more! With a child, the desire is usually to have the unconditional love of the parent, even though they are naughty. It is not so different at work from what happens when we are at school.

Praise always works positively in the direction you can predict, whilst criticism has potentially unpredictable consequences. Tell someone they've done a good job and they will feel good, wanting to do more of those things that have produced that good feeling. Telling someone they've done a bad job may have the effect of making them work harder to improve, or they may feel so put down that they hand in their notice, go sick without leave, neglect some essential maintenance or put a brick through the window of your car! I am not condoning such reactions, but am merely pointing out the potential damage arising from a predictable and manageable psychological situation.

At work we focus on those things we do badly. And it is essential that we should, otherwise, how can we get better? However, I am talking here, not about criticism, but reverse feedback, which is very different.

The purpose of reverse feedback is to understand how both parties created the situation, and seek a way to resolve it, not to blame, but to enjoy the process through which awareness is gained. It is demotivating for people to experience being 'told off' or 'carpeted'. This is the opposite of what we want.

We do not want confrontations which reduce us, but rather encounters which enhance us.

The question to answer in the case of thinking or feeling something is wrong is to ask yourself, 'What did I do to cause that situation?' Finding a truthful answer to this puts you in the right frame of mind to work positively with anyone else.

When someone has done something praiseworthy, do not tell yourself that praise is superfluous. You may think that the other person is bound to know that you think they did a great job. In fact, you cannot be sure. Your reserve may well add to their feelings of self doubt. It may undermine their confidence if they think that perhaps they should not feel so good about what they have done since, in your eyes, it's not even worth a comment. Your saying that they did a good job relieves their uncertainty. Even if they are not uncertain, you only confirm what you should, anyway.

Sometimes managers, teachers or parents hesitate about giving praise because they fear it will have a negative effect on others who are not being given praise. It won't, but if it does, then we have to look more deeply at the self concept of those who are jealous of those who are justly praised. If you give praise when it is due, everyone will be pleased; even those who are not praised rejoice in the situation: they know that when they deserve it, they will be praised too, their time will come.

Praise people as often as you can, but only when you mean it. False praise communicates that you really do not care enough for people in order to tell the truth. Or, false praise can appear sardonic.

Don't worry that giving praise means that you will be expected to go on giving it. The fear is that if people get used to praise and you stop giving it, they won't like you anymore, that you have started something that you can't continue. In fact, you'll only stop giving praise if they stop deserving praise, you don't have to justify your feelings. You may have to tell them your conflict: 'I feel you want me to praise you and I'm afraid of alienating you if I don't, but I'd be incompetent if I said something neither of us could believe.'

You may try to avoid giving praise because you tell yourself that people must know how you feel about them. You cannot assume this. To the extent that someone feels a lack of confidence, they may well interpret your silence as disapproval. There is the story of the man who thought that, since his boss made no comment upon his work, it could not be good enough. He began to avoid his boss, even develop a critical attitude towards her, which was 'picked up' by other employees. She could not understand why he was so difficult towards her, particularly when his work was so good. What was potentially a highly motivating relationship descended quite unnecessarily into mutual animosity.

Give praise when somebody makes you feel good about what they have done. Some people harbour their praise as if it is in short supply. In fact, it is a coin that never runs out. Praise always works well. Let the future look after itself. Praise has a snowball effect. Because people feel good about being praised, they'll try to do more of what you praise them for.

PERSONAL POWER

If your idea of personal power is to force others to do things that may be against their will – forget it. Such tactics only ever work in the short term and in the longer term leave an atmosphere of enmity which you may never resolve.

If your idea of personal power is to create a positive response to you, a desire to work with you and support you – then you have everything to go for.

The essential thing is how another person's feelings are disposed towards you. Do they want to assist you because they feel good about doing so, motivated by the opportunity of working with you? Or are they under duress, complying reluctantly? People may obey if you use official power, but it is a fragile thing. Reliance upon official power will give people unlimited scope to evade your orders, even undertake actions which are the very opposite of what you want. They may pretend they misheard you, or inveigle themselves with your superior so they can say that they got contradictory orders from your superior, or they may go absent, or find that the essential papers or tools are missing. There are billions of ways of 'paying you back' for the way you are making them feel. Reliance upon official power has enormous potential for making enemies, even among those whose success is dependent upon each other.

Whilst official power has unpredictable and potentially disastrous outcomes unless it is used in something approaching a 'police state', where there is inspection and punishment, personal power is always predictable and enforces itself. Personal power is self disciplining. The objective with personal power is to create the opportunity for the other person to become the sort of person they want to be when they are with you. Another way of putting this, which means exactly the same thing, is that being with you enables them to resolve their conflicts and experience enjoyment.

Consider very carefully your state of mind when you are about to meet someone. If you have any feelings of defensiveness, feelings of resentment, fear of not being able to cope, these will be transmitted to the other person. They may well interpret your feelings about yourself as a problem you have with them. You are already creating a situation in which doubts about themselves begin to arise. They will not enjoy being with you because they do not enjoy the feelings they have about themselves when they are with you. Unconsciously, they will resist assisting someone if, in doing so, they are unlikely to feel good about themselves.

Now, just imagine the quite opposite effect caused by your feeling that you are meeting a person who has characteristics you admire. In some way, you are going to feel good about meeting this person. Imagine that they are significant to you, that they have skills which you respect, that you can trust them to understand you in ways that are important to your feeling of well being. What you do is create an atmosphere which emanates warmth. You create an atmosphere in which the other person feels unthreatened, comfortable and in control. They see that being with you allows them to feel positive. Without a doubt, they will be motivated by you.

If you can make people like themselves when they are with you, they will like you. Everybody wins.

It is amazing how this works. And it is so simple it is surprising that we are not always aware of it. The simple truth is that people will feel about you the way they feel about themselves when they are with you. Suppose you engender the feeling in someone that you admire the skill with which they do something (competence). It doesn't matter what it may be, it could be anything from technical performance of some kind, to the way they handle their relationships. The feeling they have about their performance when they think about you is a memory in which you said, 'I liked and admired the way you do that.' Later on, perhaps weeks later, and in completely another context, someone asks them what they feel about you: they reply, 'I like him, he's very skilled.' Or, if you have been open with that person in the past, they say, when asked by another, 'He's OK, you can trust him, you'll like him.'

Ultimately, it does not depend upon you, it depends upon how people feel about you. The fact that it all depends upon you, in the first instance, to initiate and respond in the way that is going to work for you and them, gives you unlimited power. It is the only kind of power that will *always* work for you in the way you want. The wonderful thing is that it works for others just as powerfully as it does for you. Again, everybody wins.

Ask yourself, 'What is it about me that people do not like being with me for?' What don't they like about you – perhaps it's just because you're quiet, which seems innocuous enough. But your quietness may be interpreted as your not saying something that is significant to the other person. Because of their own self doubts, they fear it may be something about them or something they think they should know. Therefore, they think you have a secret about them which you are not sharing. Which must mean you don't like them, because if you did like them, you'd tell them!

Our task must be to assist other people to resolve their conflicts. If we sense they have some doubt or uncertainty we can empower them by asking if they have something on their mind we can help with. If they say, 'No,' at least we have communicated our willingness not to hide anything from them, so, even going so far is useful. And, they may have 'helped' us by making us aware how we were projecting our fear of 'helping' onto them.

Power is frequently associated with winning arguments. The 'powerful' people seem to be those who win, through intimidation or in some way outwitting the opposition through whatever means it takes. This is a false, illusory power.

Real power works for you as well as the other person. It is stable because it is not accompanied by threat. It grows because it establishes a climate of trust and openness in which both parties can feel safe. The only power that you can have control of arises from asking people why they feel the way they do, saying how you feel when they behave that way, enabling them to clarify the basis of their feelings and fears.

Clutching on to power creates conflict; sharing power creates harmony.

VULNERABILITY IS STRENGTH

Suppose you resist telling people what is really burdening you because you are afraid it makes you vulnerable. Unfortunately, in some organizations it may do so. It may be daft to tell someone you feel you are not coping with the work in the way you would like, if the next thing you hear is that your confidence has been passed to a third party. Bang go your chances of promotion, and you were only being open! Clearly, it depends upon the psychological contract you have with each other. Also, it depends upon an organizational climate that rewards and does not exploit openness.

However, don't forget the law of reciprocity. If you are open, the other person becomes open in turn. It makes for mutual reassurance because, if you think about the situation you have created at the beneath the surface level, what the other person knows about you, you also know about each other – there is no fear of exploitation.

You initiate openness, going just far enough so that you are taking a risk, but remain safe. You don't blurt everything out in a way that makes you naive. You go a little way down the track, and they go a little way down the track. Trusting each other so far and beginning to feel successful about what you are accomplishing together, you go a little further. And so do they. Perhaps, emboldened, they go a little further next time.

Saying what is really on your mind puts you in control. It is the absolute opposite of the vulnerability you might have feared. It focuses upon what is most important to you in your relationship with the other person at this moment. Doing anything else, such as avoiding the issue, colluding together to blame someone or something else, may appear to give you a semblance of control, but is not control at all, because it is not directed at dealing with what is most important.

In truth, avoidance means that you are being controlled, and overpowered, by your emotions, more than you know.

Suppressing emotions means that they are not dealt with, but remain hidden, secretly preventing us from achieving what we most want. This is to confront the issue we are afraid of, in order to rid ourself of the burden it imposes upon us. The only way we can really be in control is to confront the issue.

Talking about your feelings puts you in control.

CLARITY

If people do not know what you think of them, they fear the worst. Your silence is interpreted as implied criticism. It is better to say what feelings you have about someone than risk what can happen when you say nothing at all. Almost without exception, what you think about them is unlikely to be as bad as what they fear you think! At least, if you get it out in the open, they know where they stand. It gives them the power to do something about it.

If you feel something good about them, say that too, because even your good thoughts might not be perceived unless you make them clear. Your silence about the good things may be interpreted just as hurtfully as your silence about the bad things. All anybody else perceives is that you have something on your mind which you are not saying. They do not know whether it is good or bad until you make it clear.

That is being clear about 'them'. However, maybe you should start at a deeper level. Start with yourself. Instead of thinking about them, ask yourself what you feel about them. How have they behaved to make you feel about them the way you do? Then you can focus on what you can do about the feelings you have about yourself, recognizing that the feelings you have about them are, in some way, displacements of the feelings you have about yourself. It is not enabling to blame them for the way you feel, when your own behaviour has also contributed to the situation.

Total leadership is, first of all, to become aware of the issue which concerns yourself. Listen carefully to yourself, to those parts of your mind where there is energy, where your thoughts instinctively turn, unbidden, to the matter that is most significant to you. There you have the unfinished, disturbing issue that you want to complete upon, but are afraid of doing so.

The following process, if you work through it, may enable you to get you where you want to go. Read through the examples to see how the process works. If you want, you can try it yourself in the optional exercise at the end of this chapter.

Example – working out your relationship

What is my feeling about the person?	Examples (from billions):
Projection on to them	1. Annoyance?
	2. Loathing?
	3. Fear?
(about them, not about me)	4. Irritation?
	5. Resentment?

	6. Warmth?
	7. Admiration?
	8. Respect?
	9. Confusion?
What do I think they have done to make me feel this way?	1. Didn't listen
	2. Makes jokes at my or someone else's expense
	3. Put me 'on the spot'
	4. Kept interrupting
	5. Forgot my birthday
	6. Looked up and smiled when I came into the room
Intellectual justification	7. Took time to speak to me
	8. Said he wished he could hear more great suggestions like the one I made
	9. Avoids my eyes
How does this indicate they must feel about me?	1. I am not seen as useful
	2. I am seen as stupid
Realization	3. I am not capable of understanding
	4. I am not capable of adding anything
	5. I am not appreciated
	6. They feel kindly towards me
	7. I matter
	8. I am clever
	9. I am not liked (trying to keep something from me)
What do I do to be in control?	Say:
	1. 'I think you feel I'm useless.'
	2. 'I think that you feel I'm stupid.'
	3. 'I think you feel I'm not intelligent.'
	4. 'I think you feel that I have no competence.'
Initiation	5. 'I think it doesn't matter to you whether I am here or not.'
(About me, not about you)	6. 'It made me happy that you were kind.'
	7. 'It feels good to be important to you.'
	8. 'I appreciate what you did.'
	9. 'I feel that there is something about me which you don't like.'

CREATING THE 'BUZZ'

Often, people experience the 'buzz' when they start up a business, or start any organization or, privately, when they get to make plans to join with their partner. When you analyse it, what is present is the feeling of doing something for yourself and the feeling that what you are experiencing is shared.

It's really quite simple; the job is to discover and promote self fulfilment in all our relationships. Unfortunately, what happens is that the organization grows too big and the initial excitement is lost as it gets routine and into the 'maintenance' phase. As we push ourselves to succeed, little setbacks and reversals can make us feel defensive. We might feel let down, not appreciated for our efforts or think that the others don't bother as much as we do. There are hosts of reasons why the 'buzz' can get lost. However, it is recoverable. And it can become the 'norm', if you want it.

Remember what gets you excited about working with and through others.

First, it is your own feeling of doing something for yourself – doing something that excites you. You feel in control, you are extending yourself, you trust others to enable you to deal with any conflicts; problems are dissolved through your mutual willingness to support each other and overcome any difficulties. People do things for you, not because they are told, but because you are so much in their minds that they anticipate what you want. They seem to care as much about you as they do about themselves. You are significant to them. When you meet each other, there is a sharing of regard. You have a feeling of confidence. **You like yourself the way you are**.

Second, you admire, respect and like the people you are with. You would miss them if they weren't there. You can't think that you could have a better person or better people to be with. You can rely upon them. You enjoy it when they do something which makes them feel pleased with themselves. You witness and assist as their skills are manifested. They can talk to you about any doubt or difficulty they have. Resolving those makes you feel close to them. **They like you the way you are**.

Too frequently, relationships are given up on after the first flush of passion wears off. It is the same with organizations. It is perhaps unreasonable to expect things to go on being 'rosy'; life really may not be like that. We get to the point at which we have to work at it a little bit. It won't go on happening just by itself. We have to have a way of confronting and overcoming those doubts and fears which otherwise will inevitable slow us down and make our relationship less than it was.

The 'buzz' in the organization has all to do with the way people feel about themselves as members of it. If there is no feeling of personal growth, then relationships are merely tolerable. It becomes 'just a job', something we are scared to leave rather than something we are really included in.

All that has to be done is to take responsibility for not being satisfied with compromise. Don't give up, don't get bored. Instead, confront yourself with why you feel that way. What is your negative gain for feeling the way you do? What do you have to do to feel better about yourself?

Replace any feeling of burden with a feeling of doing what you want. Get people to join you by confronting them with any issue between you that is not the way you want it to be. Sure, you risk being vulnerable and humiliated. But, in reality, you feel very much in control. You are doing the essential thing – confronting what is difficult. And as your own burdens are dissolved, you become aware that they are dissolving for others. You discover that there is much more about them that appeals to you than you ever thought. You find a new depth of understanding, a common purpose. You feel good about each other. Hey! Here comes the 'buzz'!

The 'buzz' arises from extending your own feelings of self worth.

POWER SHARING

How can you trust people? How can you feel comfortable with releasing the controls? It is primarily about trusting yourself although, naturally, you only trust as far as you feel safe. It is daft to trust someone if you anticipate being let down. What has not yet been formed is a psychological contract in which you feel competent enough to engage your trust. But someone has to take the first step – if you wait for the other person to go first, you may wait forever. The best thing to do is to discuss your conflict about trusting at the beneath the surface level.

TELEPATHY

Your feelings about yourself are transmitted, though they may be misperceived due to the fears of the other person. For example, if you don't feel good about yourself, people may think there's something wrong with them. People do not want to perceive in you something they do not want to perceive in themselves. It leads them to have self doubt. What will happen is that they will not like themselves when they are with you. This may be transformed (displaced) into not liking you.

Your feelings about other people are, in some way, the same ones they have about you. 'I don't think he's a good boss,' is reflected by, 'I don't think he's a good subordinate.' Similarly, the things we want to see in other people are exactly the things we want to see in ourselves.

'I am afraid to tell her I would like our relationship to get closer. It might frighten her away.' This is exactly the fear that is on her mind; she never tells you what she feels about the relationship, in case you run away. She interprets your reserve as coolness. You see her as independent, but really she is frightened that she'll never mean more to you than just a friend. The truth is that she stays with you because behind your reserve she glimpses that you might have stronger feelings than you express. The solution is to initiate reverse feedback.

In fact, people always know what is in our minds and in our hearts. But because they doubt themselves, they are afraid that what they perceive may not be accurate. But if they do know, why do we pretend? That is why people always say, 'I knew that anyway,' or 'I'd sort of guessed,' or 'I'd hoped you might think that.'

PRESENCE

You may ask yourself, 'Should I be in this discussion?' Perhaps not: if it really doesn't interest or concern you, you really should be somewhere else, doing something more profitable, so that you feel more alive. Sometimes people sit in on a discussion because they think they ought to, or because they are afraid they might miss something, or because they are frightened they may offend someone if they get up and leave. All of these reasons indicate that you are wasting your time. It is your responsibility to ensure your time is used productively.

If the discussion really is irrelevant, because you are not involved with it or affected by the outcome, you should not be spending time with it. Sometimes doubts arise: Is it really the discussion, or is it me? Perhaps I'm missing the point, maybe I'm not as clever as the others. Maybe I should keep quiet and try to attend better. If you ask those around you to enable you to understand why you feel so remote from the issue, you will soon resolve your conflict in the situation.

In perceiving you are not present with them, the group may realize it has been going off the point. It may lead them to realize they are not using your expertise in the way they should be. Or, they may agree that you could be doing something else more significant to you. Whatever happens, you get more involved, with them or without them, in what you want to do.

ALLOWING OTHERS TO KNOW US

People know a lot more than they say. It is only self doubt that leads them to keep things to themselves. Doubts such as, 'Will people lose respect for me if I say what I feel?' or 'Will they like me?' Sometimes it seems as though the safest course is saying nothing. Saying nothing is risking nothing and risking nothing, leads to nothing. It gets you nowhere.

CHANGE AGENT

Change cannot be forced upon anybody, it has to be wanted. Change is never complete unless it is internalized. Otherwise, it is an oppressive yoke; people look willing, but their thoughts are rebellious. Change may be necessary, for example, due to economic circumstances, employment conditions or ways of working have to alter. But it is the *process* by which change takes place that is important in the end; it is the emotional repercussions that last the longest.

There is no point in change for change's sake. Change is not good of itself, only when we want it. The first task is to understand what the situation requires and then investigate our conflicts in relation to the situation in which we find ourselves.

Almost without fail, the difficulty with change is the fear of how you, personally, are able to cope with it. If you feel threatened, you become defensive – you prefer things the way they are and you resent others for interfering. If you feel you are in control of what happens, that you can influence any outcome for yourself, then you are able to welcome change as an opportunity, or, at least, you are able to look at it with detachment. As an observer whose emotions are not influencing your reaction you can ask, 'Is this change really necessary, or is it merely a defensive reaction on the part of some people, even a corporate reaction to an imaginary, internal confusion?'

Being a change agent is not the responsibility of those in the Human Resources department, or of our leaders, necessarily. The change process originates most successfully with any one of us. The question we should ask ourselves is, 'Do I feel good in the situation I'm in?' If the answer is 'Yes,' take time to make sure that you are not colluding in complacency, boredom, avoidance of doing something you think might be difficult, and so on. If your good feeling is not also accompanied by feelings of interest, excitement and of self enhancement, you are almost certainly deluding yourself. Standing still won't make you feel good for very long.

But, suppose you really, genuinely do feel good, then you are at a stage wherein there is nothing to change. Enjoy yourself, you are getting what you want. Ask yourself the same questions again tomorrow! You are likely to find that new vistas are opening up. Right then, you've done it before, you can feel the challenge once more, but you have the confidence to do it again. This is a natural checking and adjustment process.

And that is all any change agent is required to do. We start with our own lives, not with what we think others may want or with what is right. Check up on your own feelings; 'What am I stopping myself doing that I would like to do?' 'What am I afraid of?' 'How are those fears holding me back?'

The place to get to is a position in which you feel clear about yourself. Be aware of your own potential and how much of yourself you are using. Then, you are in a better position to take control of those aspects. Make a decision to determine your own life in ways that are going to make you feel good and get you where you want to be. Even if you don't know where you want to be yet, it doesn't matter: get the process right and the outcome will inevitably land you just where you want.

So, you are aware and are able to determine your behaviour and what happens to you. Now you can direct yourself in ways that are appropriate and efficient. You can focus on those things which are significant, not letting yourself be distracted or side tracked by the irrelevant, those things you previously feared might be significant, but now, you are aware, are not. The proper focus is upon those things which really matter to you, those things which, if not resolved, will block your living.

It is not surprising that we feel failures when we are not aware of our resources and have doubts about whether we are competent in determining our own lives. We go off in the wrong direction, or merely stay still, or even let somebody else run our lives for us! Having got our own focus right, we are in the best situation to enable others with their focus.

It is not that they should be leading their lives the same way as us, far from it. Rather, how can we enable them to become aware of themselves and what they are doing to cause themselves to have fears that are self limiting?

The change agent is not a driving force. The change agent asks, 'What can I do to enable this person to resolve any fears which may be limiting them?' This is not to presume that there must be some, either, just because their views and attitudes may be different. But it is useful to explore whether the feelings they have are leading to self growth.

Alternatively, is there energy which seems destructive, that is, turned in upon the self, or turned outwards and projected on to others? That, then, is negative energy. It helps nobody. How can it be changed to enable the person to grow? Perhaps to appreciate being enabled to discover what they 'can do'. Awareness of what they are holding back is usually the first step. Then the thought arises, 'I'd be letting myself down if I didn't use myself better.' Then there is the realization that only one person can lead their life best – themselves. Then they can decide what to focus on in order to express and complete on the resourcefulness that they have discovered within themselves. The route is always the same one – from *awareness* you gain *control* and with *control* you are able to improve *focus*.

The resource is always there, but sometimes we are so blind to ourselves, that we do not perceive ourself clearly. So frightened are we by what we have not yet become aware of, that we avoid it. And for those of us in whom it has been dormant for many years, there is the fear that it may explode, that we'll be out of control, that we won't be able to cope with the consequences. This is the result of not practising being ourself more often; it is like learning to be ourself all over again from the beginning.

By 'focus', of course, I mean behaviours, not physical objectives. I mean, for example, 'smile', not 'earn a million', I mean, 'tell people my feelings', not 'get my boss's job'. Get the behaviours right and the feelings will be rewarding enough by themselves. They are, as a matter of fact, also the best way to achieve those physical rewards, but let them arise as byproducts of the process – they are not so important, unless they are accompanied by good feelings as well. Remember that it is not the situation which needs to be changed, and not necessarily the task, but the feelings about where we are and what we are doing.

Other words for change agent are total leader. So, what prevents you from becoming a change agent?

CHECKING OUT OUR UNDERSTANDING

This is necessary for two reasons:

(a) Intellectually – we think of possibilities, have ideas and ask questions, before other people have had a chance to catch up and understand the process of our thinking. For fear of looking stupid, they may simply agree with what we say or suggest. Or, they may say nothing, which makes us ask ourselves if they are stupid or just not interested. We should have made the effort to mentally hold their hand along the way. If they do not want to come, maybe it is our fault for not making the path or the experience interesting enough.

(b) Emotionally – we do not check out our understanding for fear of finding out that people are not with us or, simply, that they disagree. We are emotionally wedded to an issue, so that 'backing down' carries the threat of finding out that what was significant to us is not to someone else, or that what we are doing is not as competent as we would like to think, or finding out that nobody really cares. We keep pushing the point as a means of trying preserving our self esteem.

Why not admit what everybody is feeling, but not saying – that it is not working, that we have lost each other, that you want to deal with the problems they have with the issue or deal with the issue that is on their minds first?

BACK OFF FROM DOING OTHER PEOPLE'S JOBS

If you are doing someone else's job, it is either because you are intruding on them or you are letting them intrude upon you. In the first situation you are indicating that you don't trust them, that they are not competent. This is all well and good if they are still being trained. Otherwise, it is a sure sign that you are making them dependent. Are you frightened to find out that they might be able to manage without you?

In the second situation, you are allowing them to avoid responsibility by continuing to make you responsible. What is your negative gain from allowing them to treat you this way? Perhaps it avoids your fear that you are not significant whilst allowing them to cope with their fear of failing by letting you do the work?

The other matter to consider is this: can you be doing your job properly if you are spending your time doing theirs? Perhaps you feel you can manage all right by putting some extra time in. But you know this is no answer. No one is competent in this situation. You are letting the situation ride instead of confronting it.

Example

Projected statement: 'They can't manage by themselves.'

Conflict: 'I don't want to deal with this, but I ought to show I care.'

Initiator	Receiver
You to	Boss, colleague, etc
'I'm frightened that, if I ask you to do this by yourself, you may think I don't care.'	'Tell me more about that.'
'Sometimes I think you expect me to be involved and will be disappointed if I'm not.	'I include you because I think you'll be disappointed if you're left out. Perhaps I impose a bit too, because I don't think I could do as well by myself.'
'I think you can, but I know I have trouble letting go. I suppose I'm fearful of any mistakes that might be made.'	'The trouble is that if I never do things myself, I'll never get better. I could always ask you to check what I've done until you feel you can back off without being worried.'
'It would help me if you could manage by yourself. I'll always be there if I'm truly needed.'	'It's good to have the opportunity. And you're right, I've got to stand on my own feet.'
'Actually, you're enabling me to stand on my feet. I feel that we will manage things better between us.'	'It's really good that you feel able to share things this way. We won't duplicate and it's good to know you have more confidence in me than I thought.'

AGREEING ACCOUNTABILITY

If people are in a facilitating environment, it is only natural they should seek accountability, or responsibility, if you prefer. If they are not taking accountability, maybe you think they are not ready, whilst they may or may not think they are. You should check out their perceptions in any case; perhaps you are underestimating them or perhaps they are overestimating themselves. Use reverse feedback: 'I do not feel I am being competent' or, 'You may not think I feel you are competent' or, 'You may not think you are as competent as I do.'

Let's assume that the fact they do not feel accountable is because you are over controlling. Why should they bother to take on responsibility when you won't let go? You may see your involvement as 'helping' them, they may perceive it as intrusive.

Because you are preventing them from doing what they feel they are competent to do, they may have doubts about their competence. They will resent you for making them feel this way. Your own fears of making errors are interpreted by others as a distrust of them. They may not perceive that it is really yourself that you don't trust.

Your behaviour would be more motivating if you gave them a chance to work in a way that they can have control over rather than in the way that is determined by you. But don't just give people accountability because you think you ought to; accountability without skill is a risky situation; you should remain in control as well until such time as you can confer account-ability – safely. Then you are both in control. Control is not a commodity that can be passed from one person to another, like a coin. Sometimes peo-ple fear that if they give control to another, they will have lost control them-selves. It is not like that, but like this:

When a person in control imparts control, it is not halved – it doubles.

The thing to be aware of is whether you are holding onto control because people are not competent, or whether you are holding on out of fear of let-ting go. In either case, check that people understand your behaviour, don't assume that they do. Especially tell them of any conflicts you experience about the issue, for example:

'I don't want to upset you, but I don't think you are capable.'

(critic)

'You tell me you want to manage by yourself, but I don't think you really do.'

(helper)

'I feel I should let you do the job, but I'd be foolish to let you.'

(critic)

'If I let you get on with this, you'll want to take over more and more.'

(victim)

'I'd like not to be involved, but I think you like me to check up for you.'

(helper)

'If I wasn't involved, you wouldn't see me as important or have respect for me.'

(demander)

SUMMARY

This chapter contains many examples of situations which illustrate how to use reverse feedback and practise total leadership. Using the process you may enable yourself and others to create a buzz in your relationships. Let the organization be warned – it is infectious!

Optional exercise

To influence others, you start from a position of clarity about yourself. Enabling others is mainly about enabling yourself. The exercises which follow are intended, first, to enable you to confront your perceived lack of influence and, second, to confront you with your negative gain for not influencing the way you want. After that, it may be difficult not to choose to be fulfilled!

Exercise – working out your relationship

Me _____   You _____

What is my feeling about you?   Write your feeling succinctly:

Projection on to you   _____

(about you, not about me)   _____

_____

What do I think you have done   Write down what has been done to
to make me feel this way?   you

_____

_____

_____

Intellectual justification   _____

_____

How does this indicate they must   Project onto them the feeling you
feel about me?   think they must have about you:

Realization   _____

_____

_____

_____

_____

What do I do to be in control?	Say, about my feeling:
Confrontation Asking them to help you be aware of what happens between you to make you feel the way you do (About me, not about you)	_____ _____ _____ _____ _____

Example – working out your own relationship

Guide to the following exercise

The numbers are intended to relate to each other, so that, for example, all the 1. numbers form a sequence.

What is my feeling about myself?	Examples (from billions):
Projection	1. Annoyance? 2. Loathing? 3. Fear? 4. Irritation? 5. Resentment? 6. Warmth? 7. Admiration? 8. Respect? 9. Confusion?
What do I think I have done to make me feel this way? Intellectual justification for behaviour	1. Didn't listen to myself or to someone 2. Makes jokes at my or someone else's expense 3. Let myself down 4. Never get around to doing anything 5. Allowed myself to be trodden upon 6. Lost my temper 7. Took time to thank someone 8. Insisted I told someone what I felt although I feared I was going to be rejected 9. Avoided the issue with my partner

How does this indicate I feel about myself? Realization	1. I am useless 2. I am stupid 3. I am not capable of understanding. 4. I am not capable of adding anything 5. I am not worthwhile 6. I feel kindly towards myself 7. I matter 8. I am clever 9. I do not like myself this way (trying to keep something from me)
What do I do to be in control? Initiation (about me, not about my defence)	Say: 1. 'What is my negative gain for pretending to be this way?' 2. 'Why do I choose to have this feeling?' 3. 'What am I gaining by pretending I'm not capable?' 4. 'How does this allow me to let myself down?' 5. 'What is my negative gain for not believing myself worthwhile?' 6. 'See, I can do more things this way.' 7. 'I want to feel significant more of the time.' 8. 'That shows how much ability I've got when I choose to use it.' 9. 'Am I really getting anything out of hiding from myself?'

Optional exercise – your relationship with yourself

What is my feeling about myself? Projection	Write down your feeling succinctly: _____ _____ _____

What do you think you have
done to make yourself feel this
way?

Intellectual justification for
behaviour

How does this indicate you feel
about yourself?

Realization

What do you do to be in control?

Initiation

(About the real me, not the defence)

11

Unity of Decision

Decisions which are made without feelings being taken into account are almost never implemented in the way intended.

INTRODUCTION

This chapter is about how the most effective decisions can be made, whether in pairs, teams, or organizations of any size. By 'most effective' is meant 'where there is no disagreement, so that everybody agrees and acts as one, that is, in unity'.

Decisions are the purpose of all organizations; the point at which a decision is made is the focus, and it demonstrates the extent to which the organization is aware and in control. If the organization has integrated all its parts, it will be totally effective, combining in a unity each individual's personal agenda with its own, corporate agenda.

CONCORDANCE

Having reasoned what needs to be done, considered alternative actions and judged the likely benefits, but being unaware of the defences which distort their thinking, individuals may be surprised that others are annoyed at what seems to them to be an eminently suitable, rational plan that 'nobody in their right mind would disagree with'.

Alternatively, they may anticipate possible objections from others and therefore act secretly, perhaps hoping that others will realize and accept the benefits once they see what has actually been done for them.

However justified they perceive themselves, the first instance is autocratic and the second is patronising. Both alienate the very people the action may have been intended to serve.

In organizations, individual actions are always risky. It is wiser to share the decision, through a committee, or a working party or to have a consultation in which more people can be involved. Though all these methods have some advantages, they still run the risk of alienating those when the outcome is not what some of the people want.

For example, we think it's a great committee when it agrees with our own view, otherwise we think it biased or doesn't know all of the facts. We resent being consulted if we think that our view was ignored in the end, and we reject what we perceive as 'just a public relations exercise'.

Some forms of decision making, such as consensus and majority voting, at least have the advantage that those who did not get what they want this time at least get a chance to get what they want next time. But both are unsatisfactory, because there are always unresolved conflicts within a minority which may continue to thwart the decision that the majority think has been made.

The truth is that, unless everybody who is affected by the decision agrees with it, the decision is unlikely to realize the benefits intended. The only way to make sure that everybody agrees with the decision and that nobody, even unconsciously, does not want to see it not carried out, is to resolve the conflicts *before the decision is made*. If you can do this, you have concordance – individuals acting as a group with the same power and conviction that an individual would if they were acting independently. In fact, a concordant decision is always more powerful than any individual's decision or even a majority decision, because it contains the skills, experience and motivation of *everybody*.

This area of personal psychology, group psychology and its applications is termed concordance by Will Schutz (1994) and is comprehensively explained by him in *The Human Element*. This chapter can do no more than offer my distillation and application of Will Schutz's ideas in my own experience of working within organizations. I recommend you read both *The Human Element* and *Profound Simplicity* to get at the rich, inspirational vein of these and many, many more ideas.

The unity of understanding and purpose that is found in concordance is the natural goal of the total leader. Concordance arises when everybody involved with the decision has engaged with everybody else at the beneath the surface level. It is through concordance that the law of the situation is properly and completely discovered and implemented to complete the task.

Concordance focuses upon the unique contribution that individuals make to teams and, due to the historical tolerance of our culture to individual differences, is a more powerful process than 'quality circles' or 'performance groups'.

CASE STUDY

During a 'team building' programme for the directors of a business, the members were asked what was the most important decision facing the team at that time. The answer was that they were finding it impossible to decide whether to make another appointment to the board, for a regional director. It was an issue about which they had had a number of meeting in the last 6 months. Invited to discuss the issue once again, there was some 'heat' in the debate, particularly between the Managing Director and the Operations Director. The latter was convinced there was not enough business in that area to develop and that financial and other resources would be stretched too far, whereas the former thought a new appointment was necessary in order to concentrate on growing the business. Others thought that the specific candidate in mind was not up to the job. Reasons differed widely, though all seemed to be logical and were often supported by financial and other analysis, yet nothing seemed to resolve opposing perspectives. After a while, there were signs of giving up, or else repeating the same old points, this time louder and more angrily. The meeting seemed doomed to fail, yet again, on the rocky shores of irritation, annoyance and frustration.

The Operations Director was asked to tell the Managing Director at the beneath the surface level what his conflict was, with results that surprised everyone: 'I think you feel I cannot manage to do the job, I think you feel that I am not worth listening to, I think you don't trust me – there's something on your mind you're not saying, I am frightened you want to bring in somebody to replace me.'

The Managing Director was surprised, because he thought the Operations Director was doing an excellent job and that an extra appointment would take some of the weight off his shoulders, thus allowing him to venture into other projects which they were planning. The Operations Director said he had misconstrued why his boss wanted the new appointment and he was glad to find out he really did have his boss's support. The Managing Director said that in order to expand rapidly he had been frightened of opening up his ideas to the group in case they acted as a brake on expansion but he could see that what he thought was obvious to him was seen as 'political' to others.

When the group told each other how they felt about each other they decided they were a great team and were having a great meeting. They used the 'yes method' (see below) and all clearly said 'yes' to appoint the Regional Director – in about 15 minutes!

THE 'CULTURE'

The word used to describe an individual member of an organization who is fully motivated is empowered. The word Will Schutz uses to describe an organizational culture in which everyone is empowered is concordant. It has been chosen carefully to reflect what happens in concordant relationships and in concordant decision making – that actions are carried out with the heart as well as the mind. At the beneath the surface level those doubts and fears that would have inhibited empowerment have been confronted and resolved by everybody acting as a total leader.

Most human relations practitioners, and probably most workers, recognize that actions arising from the heart are the powerful ones. Yet few organizations act in ways which indicate that they believe it. Most insist that feelings just 'get in the way' or are 'irrelevant'.

This is self deception: being 'businesslike' is, more often than not, a cloak under which feelings are hidden, but continue to operate, albeit unknowingly. It does no good to deny feelings – they are always, simply, there, and control our actions more than we think.

It seems to make sense to talk to each other at the beneath the surface level in order to discover, harness and use the power that is contained in those feelings – that is what really puts the power into em**power**ment.

THE 'HARD BITS'

I am sure I share with others who are involved with the psychology of how people behave in organizations, the experience of being told by 'hard headed' line managers, somewhat condescendingly, that my job is to deal with the 'soft bits'. I have come to realize that I am actually the one dealing with the 'hard bits'. To call them 'soft' is a convenient way to deny they are of sufficient significance to be taken seriously in the 'real world', and is counterproductive if it becomes a defence. For example, it is easy to pass the buck, blame or justify under the guise of being 'businesslike'.

TOTAL QUALITY IS INSIDE OUT

The pursuit of quality has swung the emphasis increasingly from the product to the process. It is now well understood that it is through the manner in which people work together that organizations will become demonstrably different and more successful than competitors. What is still not fully grasped is that 'total' quality cannot be imposed from the outside – to be total it must be generated inside out. (See 'Feelings and productivity', in Chapter 1, and Chapter 5.)

Total quality management (TQM) and concordance are synonymous with respect to their aims. What concordance adds is the process by which the aims can be most successfully achieved. Most systems for monitoring, appraising and rating of performance give plenty of evidence of how far there is to go; the monitoring structures too often inhibit what the quality concept seeks to achieve. The role of the organization should not be to impose, but to set up a concordant process in which people choose to be motivated (see Chapter 2).

ADAPTABLE AND SELF MONITORING

Nothing motivates more than the way people choose to be motivated. The effects of self ownership of performance can be consistently and reliably predicted. Self ownership is also self monitoring and adaptive. It needs no quality inspection. It is the perfect, complete solution to organizational problems. It works at the personal and team levels. Get the process right and the product will look after itself (see 'Subordinates know their job best, in Chapter 1).

OVERCOMING OBSTACLES

Merely saying that empowerment is a good thing does not bring it about. Many organizations seem to find obstacles that are difficult to overcome and abandon the principle of empowerment. This is a pity because its fullest expression – concordance – is practical and realizable once you know how! (see Openness and trust, in Chapter 2).

People have to want concordance; they have to see what's in it for them. This sounds like selfishness, but what is meant is self interest. These two states need to be made distinct: selfish means to deny another their share or to gain at the expense of another, whilst self interest means to start with oneself. It has no moral connotation and it recognizes a psychological truth: that people do what they do for their own sake, not for anyone else's.

It is time the old myth of selflessness was shown up for what it really is – it is a projection of helping myself through helping you. People are most motivated by self interest. Managing Director of UK Corrugated Windrush, John Potocsnak, told his staff, 'There is no way I can impose it [concordance] on you, though I'd like for us to have it – if you want it, you're the ones to decide.'

SELF INTEREST

Edward de Bono (1996) says that:
It could be argued that all our actions are 'selfish'. Even the most selfless
behaviour of a saint could be seen to be selfish for a number of reasons:
(1) It makes that person 'feel good' to be selfless and to help others. There is
a sense of mission, fulfilment, accomplishment and virtue.
(2) It makes that person feel good to know that he or she is pleasing God and
following God's will.
(3) It makes that person feel good to know that a good example has been
given to others who might also set about helping the less fortunate.

Self interest, unlike selfishness, does not demean human action and desire.
Far from it. In practice, self interest is indistinguishable from others' interests; what appears to be a self centred action actually becomes an other
centred action! Getting oneself right first is the best way of enabling anybody else.

SELF WORTH

A moment's thought about what composes feelings of self worth will dis-
pel any doubts about the value of the doctrine of self interest and its difference from selfishness. Acting in a way that makes a colleague feel ignored,
humiliated or rejected will rebound against the self. Self worth is incompatible with putting someone else down (see Chapter 9).

NEGATIVE ENERGY

It is not taking feelings into account that leads to the negativism which,
regrettably, so often seem to characterize organizational affairs. Negativism never arises from feelings of self worth, but rather from displaced
feelings of self doubt, such as: 'What I might have said is probably unimportant,' or 'I wasn't sure that what I wanted to say made sense,' or 'People
might not like me so much if I said what I think.'

The only good thing to say about negative energy is that it is merely the
opposite of positive energy: there are ways of turning it around. It is not
always understood that people see reflected in others what they see in
themselves.

The more people discover their self worth, the more they discover the same in others. The effect is to increase compatibility between co-workers. And there is a direct correlation between compatibility and productivity.

THE TASK OF MANAGEMENT

Self interest means that an individual is directed to becoming the person the individual wants to be. This is sometimes referred to as a personal 'vision'. The task of total leadership then consists of showing individuals how what they want for themselves can be achieved, through the realization of a corporate vision (see Chapter 6).

THE THREAT OF CHANGE

To obtain a concordant organization, it is necessary to start with the individual. Change one person and you change the whole organization

Actually, 'change' is the wrong word for what organizations should be trying to achieve. The word carries an implied threat – change, or else! – and it is really no wonder that people have been fearful or resistant to the idea. Rightly so: 'change' is probably not what is meant. Instead of telling his staff that they have got to change, Mike Foy, Regional Director of UK Corrugated, told his staff, 'No one is saying you should change, just be more the person you want to be.'

Putting change into a developmental context removes the threat and is the first step in the process of letting people participate fully in decisions which affect their lives – in other words, becoming empowered.

EVERYBODY ENJOYS

What, then, does an individual want? In fact, it is what everybody wants. It has been clear since the work of Maslow (1943), that a person works to their fullest potential to satisfy their self actualization needs. All other inducements, provided they are fair and equitable, are only temporary as motivators. The challenge of becoming one's self is the ultimate and continually evolving challenge to each one of us. All the organization needs to do is to create the circumstances in which its staff choose to make this happen – for themselves.

THE NATURE OF MOTIVATION

Motivation arises from being included when decisions are made, from having control of the decision and being able to express personal feelings openly about the decision. These few behaviours fulfil all that is necessary to the sense of self, self worth or well being. People respond positively to others who enable them to feel those ways, and in organizations in which people feel good about themselves and each other, success is inevitable (see Chapter 5).

THE SUCCESSFUL ORGANIZATION

In an unsuccessful organization, management squanders time and resources in trying to come up with plans to get people to do their jobs better. In contrast, the concordant organization starts with the recognition that, ultimately, people work to their fullest potential to satisfy themselves. Concordance harnesses this natural motivation:

First, it invites everybody who is or may be affected by the decision to include themselves if they want to.
Second, it includes those people who know most about the decision – usually the same people.
Third, and most important, it allows people to express their feelings openly about the decision.
Fourth, to arrive at concordance everybody says 'yes' to the decision, even though, had they been operating independently, they might have acted differently.

The key aspect of concordance is that people agree because their feelings about the matter have been understood; their reasons for what they think should be the correct decision are no longer blocks to carrying it out.

Openness ensures that feelings are dealt with before the decision is made, not after. Decisions which are made without feelings being taken into account are almost never implemented in the way intended.

All that we ask is to be understood

Jenny

THE MOST POWERFUL WAY TO MAKE DECISIONS

All the well known forms of so-called 'participative' decision making fail in some respects, because they exclude, deny control or withhold secrets from those affected by the decision. This is why none of them is as powerful as concordance.

Thus, consultation runs the risk of demotivating because of the suspicion that it is a sham. In majority voting, minority members remain rebellious. In government, democracy is increasingly perceived as an enfeebled process because it is, effectively, an abandonment of power by the majority. Consensus comes closest to concordance, but consensus does not overcome the danger that unexplored deep issues come to the surface later on.

In concordance, no decision is made until everybody agrees. To this extent, the conditions are similar to those which sometimes exist in socalled performance groups. But it is the open expression of feelings that makes concordance different from, and more effective than, any other form of decision making.

In concordance, we do not make every decision together, it is just that we have a process to ensure everybody agrees with the decision.

In the normal course of things, decisions have to be made all the time. We do not have the time or opportunity to consult everybody who is involved with every issue. Imagine a football team deciding who should be playing and who should be sitting on the bench! We have a manager or captain who decides. During the game we need to get on with play, we cannot continually review selection and strategy. But if we feel that they are not good at directing the game, we can meet with them afterwards to tell them what we feel about being left out, or being used in ways which make us feel incompetent. Reverse feedback may well raise awareness and resolve the situation. If we no longer trust them, feel they do not listen to us, or ignore our talents, we concordantly decide upon a new manager or captain.

OPENNESS

One of the biggest blocks to empowerment and hence of concordance is the difficulty of being open. Though espoused as a 'good idea' (how many attitude surveys have revealed the need for more openness to be the top priority?) it is very rarely practised. There appear to be so many fears associated with it: 'I'll be ignored,' 'I'll look stupid,' 'I may say something people don't like.'

Openness is sometimes feared because it is expected to lead to 'devastating' or 'brutal' 'honesty'. This is not really openness, but rather a means of blaming you for the way I feel – always a defensive tactic – which arises from too little awareness.

Openness has also been trivialized as in 'Must I bare my soul so that everybody knows all there is to know about me, warts and all?' Openness of this kind is, if anything, boring.

But openness about how effectively two people are working together is always vital and never boring. The thing to do then is to be open with each other about what there is in our working relationship which is preventing us from working effectively together (see 'The psychological contract', in Chapter 1).

What inhibits feelings of success at work is almost always the conflicts a person has about himself, which thereby distorts his perceptions of others. The breakthrough is never achieved by directing feelings at the other person, but through expressing the feeling about oneself. Communication and understanding deepen as a person talks less about the other person and more, at the beneath the surface level, about their own conflict (see Chapter 1).

Open expression of feeling at the beneath the surface level is the process by which co-workers become motivated by each other. It is also the way to settle industrial disputes, as well as daily misunderstandings in the office, and everywhere people have tasks to achieve together.

Ultimately, dispute is not about what has actually been decided, but about whether people feel rejected, humiliated or ignored during the process by which the decision is made.

Concordance ensures acceptance by specifically building in the initiation of feelings and resolution of conflict as part of the process.

AVOIDANCE

In conventional meetings, the pressure on getting the task done is often allowed as a 'genuine' reason not to spend time in discussing feelings about the issue. A red light should go on at this point – it is precisely at such times that it is essential that feelings should be discussed! Concordance is the only way to ensure that hasty decisions – that is, made without taking the feelings of those who care into account – do not return to haunt later on.

FORMALLY

Failure to take feelings into account in all areas of activity in finance, strategy, operations, labour negotiations and all our affairs is massively costly and unnecessary. Typically, disagreements and difficult decisions arise from a lack of awareness of defensive feelings. When feelings are expressed, people realize that the conflicts which separated them almost always arise from nothing more concrete than misperceptions. Understanding of feelings ensures a solid foundation upon which decisions can rest; the decision is easy, since people are willing to go along with it, once their feelings have been understood.

... AND INFORMALLY

Concordance can be used informally and with great effect at an interpersonal level wherever and whenever people work together. It requires only that an individual should ask himself what feelings he has about the decision he wants to make. If there is a sense that others could possibly feel in some way negative about what he wants to do, he involves them specifically. If he is unsure, he issues a general invitation – just in case. This is completely the opposite of trying to get what you want through misinformation, pretending ignorance, winning over allies, or making the decision quickly before anyone realizes what is happening.

Setting specific time aside to 'have a meeting' is a somewhat 'heavy' process which is sometimes used too much; issues can be addressed as they arise whenever people come across each other; to check out your conflict with the other person can take just a few moments, a ponderous, serious, encounter is rarely required.

A simple rule of thumb for making sure that concordance is being used is to ask oneself, 'Have I been open with everybody who might care?' and 'What conflict do I have that I am trying to avoid?'

HONESTY

Confronting the issues that avoid or impair concordant decision making makes for exciting, motivating relationships. Withholding something that is significant, especially the feelings experienced about the matter, really is tedious, often confusing and always slows decision making down.

Being open releases energy productively. Being less than honest – that is, withholding – has the same effect that secrecy and containment always have – making matters worse than they need be. Everyone always feels better when the issues are out in the open.

UPWARDS LEADERSHIP

The total leader asks subordinates, who generally know best how their job should be done, as well as how their boss should be doing his job, for feedback. The best way to ensure they get honest feedback is to initiate the reverse feedback process.

Honest feedback involves telling those uncomfortable things which we debate with ourselves whether we should say. It is 'honest' because it seeks to overcome any defence.

The total leader does not assume that the lack of feedback from others means that his performance is all right. He initiates any doubt he has about himself with the people who matter. He is not vulnerable as is often feared, but competently taking control of the essential issue that relates to the task – that is, any misperception that may reduce compatibility and therefore risk reduced productivity. He begins to create a climate in which truth telling is trusted. After a while, subordinates initiate their own conflicts in the situation in which they are with him.

In a concordant organization, each individual takes responsibility for leadership. The prime responsibility is to lead the person you report to. The traditional dependency/authority relationship is divisive and defensive – it lets the manager take the blame for mistakes. The truth is that my manager's failure is also my failure.

The team always makes better decisions than an individual manager. And, if things do go wrong, we ask ourselves how we each contributed to the situation, not look for someone convenient to blame (see 'Agreement from the bottom up', in Chapter 1).

This approach is expounded by John Engestrom, Managing Director of Liberty Reinsurance, who states, 'I will know I have become successful when I no longer have to make decisions.' He recognizes that the quality of his effectiveness is entirely dependent upon the quality of the decision making of his staff. Leaders also need to be empowered!

The same objective can be shared between co-workers who recognize that their personal power is not diluted, but increased when others take power. Everyone then becomes a total leader.

The good manager recognizes that it is ultimately through his staff that he is effective. Therefore he seeks feedback as to how he can increase his effectiveness. And the effective subordinate takes responsibility for his superior's success – upwards leadership.

STRUCTURE

In organizations which practise total leadership and concordant decision making, it is difficult to tell who the appointed leaders are. This is because decisions are taken by the people who are affected *whatever their level*. It can hardly be said that levels exist – people simply do their jobs the way they know how to do them best and as a result of enabling by colleagues. The organization therefore has the flattest possible structure – in effect, everybody is at the same level. There is no difference between individuals except on the basis of who is included in order that the best decision is made.

All that remains is a small group – the directors – who sign legal documents on behalf of the organization. However, their legal obligations, which threaten to make them an elite, are only about compliance, they do not require a decision making forum. Necessary legal actions require only the ratification of what has previously been concordantly agreed.

A 'YES' MEETING

In many meetings, members are there only because they are appointed on the committee. They may have nothing to contribute, they may even want to be somewhere else, but they are afraid of missing something, or that, if they are absent, they will be perceived as lacking team spirit.

In a concordance meeting, people are there because they want to be. Those who are not attending agree to abide by the decision of those who do attend. The agenda permits discussion only of those items on the agenda, thus avoiding the fear of non attendees that something may come up that they may miss out on.

Everybody is asked whether they can say 'yes' to the proposed decision. If even one member disagrees with the decision, it is revisited until all doubts are erased. Everyone listens very carefully indeed to the manner in which people say 'yes' in order to make sure that they are convinced that they really do mean it. Any sign of reservation is taken as 'no' until everyone is sure that 'yes' is being said with the whole heart, that is, conflicts about the decision really have been resolved. Barry Remington, when he was Business Manager at Mercantile and General, said to a fellow team member, 'What would it take for you to be able to say "Yes?"'

The condition for concordance is that when everyone says they agree with the decision they really do mean 'yes'.

My own method to establish whether there are remaining issues is to ask, 'Do we have a unity?' This seems to draw into our awareness those issues upon which we remain polarized. We value individuals who polarize the issues, and take the necessary time to scour until we feel we are experiencing unity.

UNITY

The feeling experienced by members of a team who successfully engage in a concordant decision is the same as that experienced by an individual as self fulfilment. The only difference is that the parts that constitute the organization are different people instead of differentiated parts of the self. In a team setting, concordance is the stage on which each individual's natural endeavour may be fulfilled at the personal and social levels at the same time.

Unity arises only as a result of the process which specifically seeks to polarize differences between parts. Therefore, all conflicts are resolved at the beneath the surface level. It is inevitable that in almost every decision making situation there will be conflicts, but having a process through which differences are first polarized, then integrated, is fulfilling. In unity, total leadership discovers its fullest expression.

AUTHORITY

Through concordance, a decision is made at the level of the authority of the most senior person present. It cannot overturn that person's authority, because he has to concord, just like everyone else. Neither is it an abdication, rather it is empowerment, since he also gains the support of those present. Role power is replaced by personal power. And because everybody agrees, he needs no secret police, quality inspectors or other devices to push implementation through, or to deal with resistance. 'Back door diplomacy' becomes a thing of the past (see 'The Situation', in Chapter 1).

SUMMARY

Concordant decisions, having involved the resources of everyone, are likely to be more creative than anything the leader or any other individual might have decided by himself. The phenomenon of concordance decision making is how willing people are to support the decision, even though they may have opposed the decision on an individual basis, once their feelings have been understood. Empowerment, total leadership, concordance, the law of the situation and unity all mean the same thing.

In concordance, a group feels and behaves with unity, as if it were a single aware individual.

The substance of this chapter first appeared in *The Occupational Psychologist* (1995) with the title, 'Concordance – the only way to go for empowering organisations'.

12

Organizations

The purpose of an organization is to make decisions; resolution of conflict is essential for optimum performance.

INTRODUCTION

Total leadership makes use of natural motivation, enabling individuals to fulfil themselves if they choose, and in so doing, fulfil the vision of the organization to which they choose to belong. The more the success of an organization depends upon the feelings of the people within it, the more the principles of total leadership hold true.

BUSINESS

Any business becomes increasingly successful as individuals within it see their work as a way to fulfil themselves.

Where total leadership is practised, individuals behave with a level of responsibility which is normally associated with ownership. At all levels, individuals make the best decision at any moment for the company as if it were their own company.

Integrity is founded upon self esteem, this being incompatible with any behaviour which is disenabling to themself or to others. Work is fulfilling, not only in the completion of the task, but in the enjoyment of resolving conflicts which arise. In this process, individuals constantly overcome blocks which prevent their being. Businesses which are run this way are robust and creative, whilst adaptability to changing commercial and other situations is assured.

COMMUNITY

The sense of community arises from an identification with people in a local geographical area. It involves a sharing of local services and facilities which seem to 'belong' to the community. The community feels strongly about what its priorities are and has sufficient control to do something about them.

Within the community there are meetings of groups with shared interests, formal such as shared schooling, welfare and other public resources, or informal, such as social encounters.

A community contains an awareness of who lives within it, even though individuals do not necessarily know each other personally. For example, people who do not know each other greet each other as though they might know each other.

The sense of community diminishes when there are more people in the geographical area than can be recognized by the people that live in it. Psychologically, 'inclusion' has been replaced by 'intrusion'. There is a saturation point at which there are too many people to include, and people behave as though they are not included, for example, people are not acknowledged and do not greet each other. Rather, the number of 'strangers' is such that people ignore each other. As there is no sense of sharing, neither is there a sense of responsibility for services and facilities. These are now offered on a commercial basis rather than provided on a social basis.

Apathy, neglect and vandalism are the inevitable consequences of the absence of society's failure to find the right balance of inclusion.

EDUCATION

Perhaps the major failure of education is that it takes place between people who do not understand each other. Teachers cannot understand pupils when there are so many to include. To cope, teachers detach themselves, often becoming harsh and austere in an attempt to cope. This is not behaving as they are, but how they think they 'should' behave in order to maintain regard and respect. Pupils behave badly to their teachers because they do not perceive their teacher as having feelings. Or, recognizing those feelings, displace their defences because of the way they feel. They are merely compensating for the way they feel as a result of the way they perceive their teachers.

Learning arises almost in spite of the demands that teachers and pupils have for each other. It is particularly hard for teachers who set out as helpers. Unfortunately, although they want to include the pupils, the pupils often do not want to include them. The teacher's inclusion is prevented by the volume of unnecessary material they are expected to instil in order to meet requirements which have not been made concordantly with them. A further, major block to inclusion is class size. The circumstances in which education is expected to take place tend to be demotivating, creating a feeling in teachers and pupils alike of, 'Why bother, who really cares about us?'

For there to be real communication and real learning, teacher and pupil have to understand each other. There must be a way for them to resolve the conflicts which prevent them from achieving the task together. In particular, the conflicts about learning and conflicts in their situation which prevent learning should be addressed. Education takes place most effectively in an atmosphere of regard, respect and warmth. All that is required is to ask ourselves what is required to create these conditions.

The greatest aid to learning is allowing the pupil to be himself, that is, significant, competent and likeable. At present, the education systems we have in place create blocks to those feelings, not opportunities to enjoy.

EMPLOYMENT

Who, reading this book, would not want their own child to have the opportunity for employment.

Within our family, we want our children to feel regard, respect and warmth if only because, to the extent that they do not, we cannot feel those ways about ourselves – we know that we will have failed as parents.

So with society. It is only a family on a larger scale. Yet, somehow, tolerance of unemployment indicates how far our grip upon the situation has weakened.

Unemployment is a dismal example of how unaware society is of itself. The sub culture of drugs is another. The control of society is inevitably fragile whilst there is so much of itself it is not using. Where there are conflicts it does not resolve there can be small wonder at the high costs of welfare which are required to prop up the system, serving only to maintain the situation.

Full employment is the only way in which society finds its correct focus. Unemployment is also the result of organizations reducing staff who do not appear to contribute to profit. But whilst individual organizations appear to flourish as a consequence of the profit motive, the larger organization, society, gets sick.

A dependency culture denies the value of responsibility to its individual parts and thus to itself. Yet any of us, looking around us, at our organizations, at our environment, see so many valuable jobs to do which are neglected for cost cutting reasons. The truth is that much of what is called 'cost cutting' creates other, possibly greater, costs, elsewhere in society. Let us be less focused upon cost and more upon value. We will all be more fulfilled in a situation of full employment.

FAMILY

Perhaps the most fundamental issue for our future is that we should want our children. Yet even parents who appear to have chosen to have their children sometimes behave in ways which suggest to their children that they are not wanted and not loved. Writing in *The Independent*, Susan Emmett (1996) quoted a study in *The British Journal of Psychiatry* which says, 'Being unwanted is two and a half times more common in schizophrenics... If a pregnancy is unwanted, this is more likely to put a child at risk of a psychological disorder'. Being unwanted is another way of saying, 'Do we want to include this person? How significant do we feel they are? Will we like them, when they are with us?'

And later, after birth, children should be involved in decisions which affect them. Like anybody else, they do want their feelings taken into account. It is part of taking responsibility for leading their own lives; we treat them as though they are not competent at our peril. Understandably, they get upset when decisions are sprung upon them – like moving house, or even marital break up, because they have been ignored. They have an inkling of awareness that 'something is going on,' and resent not being included.

All that is necessary is to tell them our conflict when it enters our mind that we should not. In other words, as soon as we find ourselves searching for a negative gain such as, 'I don't want to hurt them', or 'They wouldn't understand', then is the time to initiate at the beneath the surface level, with the conflict we have about including them. More often than not they say, 'It's all right, I know there's a problem, but you'll work it out – I'll go along with what you say.' If they don't understand or react with hostility, you haven't told them about the other conflicts you have.

Hitting a child, like hitting anyone else, is an abuse of power. It takes away their control. Often, such violence is 'justified' as fair punishment for a misdemeanour. But hitting is never justified' because it is not dealing with the real issues. Hitting is only a displacement of the hitter's incompetence.

For a start, children do not intentionally commit misdemeanours. If they break something, it is either accidental, in which case they feel bad themselves about their carelessness, they don't need to be hit; alternatively, their 'bad' behaviour is to 'get back' for the way they feel. But the feeling they have did not just appear. Who made them feel resentful or hurt in the first place?

To examine this further, let us take the two situations in which 'smacking' takes place and see what happens in more detail. The smack might be reactive, so that the parent has lost control, hitting out as a result of annoyance or anger. Although the child might be blamed for having 'provoked' the smack, the parent is really hitting out as a result of feeling ignored, humiliated or rejected. They are 'displacing' their own feeling on to the child, in effect saying, 'You are to blame for making me feel this way.' They are not taking responsibility for what they have done that also contributed to the situation.

The other way of punishing is to institutionalize or ritualize it. This is supposed to make the proceedings more formal, objective and therefore 'just'. Admittedly, there has been a restraint upon the immediate, emotional reaction of lashing out. But the child still gets punished for what they have done. The parents do not get blamed for the way they have colluded to bring about the behaviour in the child that supposedly warrants the punishment.

This more formal, considered approach to punishment which purports to be detached and fair is neither detached nor fair. To be fair, both child and parent should understand the feelings of each other in the situation. Then, awareness would make punishment irrelevant. As it is, one of the parties becomes critic and the other becomes victim. No amount of justification can excuse the failure of punishment.

Sometimes people justify the treatment they received from their parents by saying, 'It never did me any harm.' This is not to be trusted. It is an after the event rationalization which seeks to excuse their own and their parents' collusion. It is an exercise in the denial of feeling. The emotions caused by the events were confused at the time and no doubt still remain confused below the apparently rational surface. One of the dangers of such supposed rationalization is that a continuing regime of punishment is perpetuated among successive generations of children.

The truth is that the aggressor in any situation is always the loser. The aggressor is just another name for critic. However 'justly' he may displace his feeling on to another, and however much institutions collude with him to provide a legal sanction, his behaviour remains a defence. It is negative energy arising from his failure to resolve his own conflict.

What can a parent have more at heart than the good opinion of his child?
Mary Shelley, *The Last Men*

GOVERNMENT AND ADMINISTRATION

Some responsibilities are best handled at a national level, some at an international level and others at a local level. A general rule would be to devolve power for decision making to the most personal and local level that people want it. This is what is happening in our most efficient, flexible organizations. There is every reason to expect that it would be also be the best model for our governmental apparatus as well.

Not surprisingly, people feel estranged by decisions which they have no influence over, but which adversely affect their lives. In Europe, nations fear they may lose their voice in a 'super' state. In individual countries, such as Spain and the United Kingdom, the move to devolution is pronounced.

CASE STUDY

Having received vociferous opposition against a planning application to build a hypermarket within its boundaries, a borough council conceded to the wishes of its citizens and refused planning permission. The developers approached a higher, national authority which overturned the local decision. The feeling among local people was that they were going to be plagued with a shopping mall, with all the road building and other infrastructure, which they did not want. There was a feeling that whoever made the decision at the national level could not know the local issues, including local feelings, and in any case did not seem to care. There was suspicion of why the decision was made – for whose benefit was it actually? – certainly people within the community perceived none. This is so often the case with government: things are done, supposedly for the benefit of the people, but actions are so often patronizing, because they disempower those whom they are meant to serve.

The more that control is pushed upwards from local to county, to central, to national, to international level, the more apathy on behalf of citizens. In this situation, groups of revolutionaries appear and struggle for local influence. Thus, when the situation is inclusive, but where there is no feeling of inclusion, where people feel they have no influence, and there is no openness, they begin to express themselves in the only way possible – as a pressure group.

What so often happens in this situation is that, instead of listening to what is happening and seeking to understand the feedback they are offered, governments attempt to suppress and deny local action. They should see local action as an opportunity to gain awareness, resolve conflict, and emerge as more effective leaders. A government which practised total leadership would recognize that they were behaving in a way that was not allowing citizens to feel they were understood. Talking at the beneath the surface level would inevitably allow access to the influence that the minority felt was withheld from them, whilst the government simultaneously relinquished the control that was experienced as abusive.

The establishment of trust is the best antidote to violence. Total leadership is the opposite of totalitarianism.

The most powerful body for decision making should be at the parish level. Issues which involve more than one parish, such as major roads, higher education buildings, hospitals, and so on, should be decided at county level, with representatives from the parishes who have been chosen through the concordant process. National issues, such as defence, railways and other communication systems, for example, should be decided by county representatives who have the concordance of their colleagues at that level.

As Geoff Mulgan (1997) wrote in 'On the brink of a new society', 'a government that is serious about solving problems has to decentralise... the best virtue of letting towns and cities make their own solutions, and letting them bid for the funds to get things done, is that this is the best way to tap into the remarkable amount of innovation that is already taking place.'

Profound and lasting change is always best brought about at the molecular level, that is, the smallest unit appropriate in any situation.

An imposed 'culture' is always fragile because it attempts to include people who do not want to be, or does not include people who do. A robust culture is one which creates the conditions in which people choose for themselves what they want.

Change takes place first of all with the individual; to the extent that one person chooses to change their feelings, the whole organization is changed. Similarly, within society, changes are best brought about when influence is conferred progressively from local to national level.

LAW

Will Schutz (1979) said that there is only one crime – to prevent someone else make the choices they want. Of course, any choice they want which interferes with the choices others might want would also be a crime. Thus would society regulate itself.

A crime is only ever undertaken by a person who does not understand the person against whom he is committing the crime. In this situation, the criminal has no identification with the person who suffers, and suppresses awareness of the consequences. The victim has been 'dehumanized' by the offender, who 'dehumanizes' himself in the process.

The most effective treatment of criminals consists of enabling them to become aware of the feelings of the person they have offended against. Crimes against people and property are rare in communities where awareness of others and the sense of inclusion are strong. Crimes are increasingly common where the population numbers provide anonymity and detachment from the consequences of antisocial behaviour – in other words, there is a situation of alienation, that is, low inclusion.

Crimes among people who know each other well also arise from misunderstanding. It is failure to resolve conflicts at the beneath the surface level which lead to crimes within the family.

All crimes are the consequence of negative energy. People with self esteem do not commit crimes. The only way to abolish crime is to resolve those situations in which a person feels the absence of significance, competence and likeability. Crimes are manifestations of the defences people employ to 'get back at' or 'restore the balance' for their weak self concept. Punishment generally confirms the weak self concept of the offender, because it attempts to humiliate and it excludes from society. Punishment is an 'after the event solution' similar to medical intervention for illness resulting from poor diet or psychosomatic problems.

This is not to propose a 'soft option' which tolerates criminals. But the point needs to be made that the only way to eradicate crime is to tackle those situations which make criminals. Preventative treatments would look at issues of resolving conflict where the concept of self worth is established, most obviously within the family, and also in education.

POLITICS

It is not surprising that electorates in democracies feel so much apathy about politics. Issues seem so often to be shams, whilst politicians are viewed with mistrust. Although the freedom to vote is an undoubted privilege, it is often not used by many of the electorate. Often, the percentage of an eligible electorate which actually votes is not much over 50 per cent.

In an article in *The Independent* Suzanne Moore (1997) makes the point that, 'Direct action comes out of a legitimate frustration with traditional political processes. As consumers we are offered more and more choice; as voters we are offered less and less.' Writing just before the election in Britain in 1997, Moore observed, 'The numbers of people who won't vote this time around are read as a sign of electoral apathy rather than political failure.'

It is easy to understand: people feel that if their vote 'does not matter, why bother?' They are included, since they have the right to vote. But they do not feel they have influence upon what is done on their behalf by whichever party they vote for. Nor do they feel that their politicians have been open with them.

If their vote contains any power at all, why give it to people they cannot trust? The wise thing to do in these circumstances seems to be to retain a semblance of one's power by withholding one's vote, thus denying the significance of the electoral process.

In a democracy, people are included. Thereafter, people have very little personal influence since they have handed control to their representatives. Though openness is often an espoused policy, there is precious little openness of information, let alone openness of the beneath the surface issues. The adversarial system in which political parties accuse and denounce each other, and in which they pretend that right is always on their side, and never on the side of any other party, is the continuing failure of our political system.

This could all be changed if political parties worked together in the same way that individuals can, for the good of all parties. The fear here is that all the parties would become the same and therefore that a single party would abuse its power.

This fear might well be realized if the parties continued to relate to each other at a surface level. It cannot happen if they relate to each other at the beneath the surface level, because the checks on the abuse of power are self adjusting. In other words, exploitation and manipulation of others are prevented by resolution of conflict at the beneath the surface level. Additionally, although the task is to get agreement, beneath the surface talking is the surest way to preserve the separate interests of different parties. In this situation, they remain distinct, but find the law which allows them to work together in unity for the benefit of all.

The tasks before us are manifold and manifestly obvious: education, deprivation, the environment, peace. The task of politicians is no different from that faced by anyone else. It is to ensure that beneath the surface level conflicts are encountered and resolved, because completion of the task is dependent upon this. They, or the political party to which they belong, do not lose their identity. Far from it. In fact, through the process described in this book, they assume a clearer identity and a greater individuality, since unity values a polarization of differences. Political parties can continue to contribute their own experience and their own philosophy in just the same way as individuals do in dealing with the situation before them. In finding the law that exists in the situation, they come to value the difference that their partners can bring. And the key word here is partnership, as opposed to partisan, adversary, enemy or opponent.

You only get people's attention if they want to attend, their compliance if they want to comply. Banging on the table creates passivity or hostility, not acceptance. And just because people appear to agree on the surface does not necessarily mean that their hearts are with you. Leadership is fragile unless those who are led are also the leaders.

Can those who are led also be the leaders? This is the subject of Chapter 1.

FINALE – UNITY

The endeavour of humankind is always the same. Several terms have been used to describe it in this book: fulfilment, wholeness, motivation, concordance and unity. It exists at every level of organization, whether individual, dyad, group or society.

It cannot be emphasized strongly enough how essential it is to find unity at all these levels. Though we think of them separately and distinctly, they do not exist separately or distinctly at all. Thus, to the extent that an individual is excluded, society is not a unity. To the extent that a member of the group allows themself to be unwell, or says, 'no,' you also remain diminished, unfulfilled.

Resolving our differences is only to be achieved by first differentiating between the parts which appear to separate us, then seeking those connections which create awareness of our unity. The action for the individual is to initiate what he or she is aware of; the action for the member of any organization is total leadership.

All roads lead in the end to unity. This may be discovered, not at the intellectual, surface level, but at the emotional, beneath the surface level, where all our apparent differences are resolved into oneness.

Glossary

'Loaded words' recur throughout the text and I want to draw attention to them wherever they occur. Here are the major ones:

Alive Being aware, in control and in the present
Avoid Failure to initiate conflict at the beneath the surface level
Aware Identifying the cause of conflict

Behaviour Including, controlling and being open
Being One's fulfilled self
Beneath the surface level Where conflicts are identified

Competence Feeling of being in control
Compromise Controlled by a defence
Conflict Unresolved discrepancy between a feeling and a thought
Control Balance between awareness and action
Coping Mechanism for dealing with fears

Defences Unconscious mechanisms used in an attempt to preserve self esteem
Denial Rationalization or justification used as a defence to avoid awareness
Distortion Ascribing feelings about the self to another
Doubt The human condition

Enable Assisting another without employing a defence
Encounter Meet with another at the beneath the surface level
Endeavour Search for unity
Engage Encounter at the beneath the surface level, behaving to another with regard, respect and warmth
Enjoyment Overcome fears, be yourself
Excuse Lying or withholding the truth

Fear Not able to cope with exclusion, humiliation or rejection
Feeling Emotional experience, absence or presence of significance, competence or likeability
Focus Initiating behaviour that is aware and controlled

Guilt/shame Suppressed conflict between a feeling and a thought

Include Do things with, share
Initiator Expressing conflict at the beneath the surface level

Insight	Awareness of the impact of conflict upon feeling and behaviour
Integrity	Wholeness of awareness, control and focus
Justification	A defence in which failure is projected as rational
Law of reciprocal psychology	Human beings are emotional mirrors of each other
Law of the situation	Natural consequence of understanding
Leader	One who initiates their conflict
Like	Feeling most fully expressed in love
Listener	Choosing to respond to an initiator at the beneath the surface level
Motivation	Wanting to feel significant, competent and likeable
Negative (energy)	Behaviour arising from unawareness
Negative gain	Illusory benefit from employing a defence
Open	Disclosing conflict
Participate	Include
Perception	What is experienced
Positive (energy)	Behaviour arising from awareness
Present	Fully alive, using oneself in the world in the way that is wanted
Process	Relating at the beneath the surface level
Rationalization	Using intelligence to deny the truth
Receiver	Person who engages with initiator beneath the surface level
Regard	Awareness of significance
Respect	Awareness of competence
Responsible	Ownership of conflict
Reverse feedback	Disclosure of one's conflict in such a way as to engage the other person in the situation
Self esteem	Feelings of self significance, competence and likeability
Significance	Feeling of importance and regard
Situation	Thoughts and feelings which affect completion of the task
Surface level	Superficial level of relating in which defences distort perception
Trust	Choice imparting influence or control
Understanding	Agreement of the situation
Unity	Connecting polarized elements (total leadership, law of the situation)
Vision	Something imaginable which, were it achieved, would imbue feelings of significance, competence or likeability
Warmth	Awareness of likeability
Well	All parts integrated in a unity
Withholding	Awareness without initiating

References

Achterberg, J (1985) *Imagery in Healing*, New Science Library.

Bailes, F W (1941) *Your Mind Can Heal You*, Dodd, Mead & Co, New York.

Bayly (1958) out of print.

Berne E (1966) *The Games People Play*, André Deutsch, London.

de Bono, E (1996) *Textbook of Wisdom*, Viking, London.

Clark, L (1974) *Help Yourself to Health*, Pyramid Books, New York.

Dethlefsen, T and Dahlke R, (1990) *The Healing Power of Illness – The Meaning of Symptoms and How to Interpret Them*, Element, Dorset.

Dimbleby, J (1997) A sense of betrayel, *The Sunday Times*, 6 July.

Dixon, N F (1994) Disastrous decisions, *The Psychologist*, July, London.

Drury, N (1989) *The Elements of Human Potential*, Element Books, Dorset.

Emmett, S (1996) Schizophrenia risk rises for unwanted child, *The Independent*, 1 November.

Follett, M P (1941) *Dynamic Administration*, Pitman, London.

Goleman, D (1996) *Emotional Intelligence*, Bloomsbury, London.

Gordon, T (1977) *Leader Effectiveness Training*, Futura, London.

Hawkins, P and Miller E (1994) Psychotherapy in and with organisations, in *The Handbook of Psychotherapy*, (eds P Clarkson and M Pokorny), Routledge, London.

Jaques, E and Clement, S D (1994) *Executive Leadership*, Blackwell, Oxford.

Jones, H (1996) Jester bit of corporate fun, *Evening Standard*, 20 November, London.

Kriegel, R (1991) *If it ain't broke… Break it*, Warner Books, New York.

Lawrence, J (1997) Put workers in control to cut disease, *The Independent*, 25 August.

McLuhan, M and Fiore, Q (1967) *The Medium is the Massage*, Penguin, London.

Mansfield, P (1992) *The Bates Method*, Optima.

Maslow, A H (1943) A theory of human motivation, *Psychological Review*, **50**, no 4.

Matthews, A (1989) *Being Happy*, IN Books, Media Masters Pte.

Miln Smith, D and Leicester, S (1996) *Hug the Monster*, Rider, London.

Moore, S (1997) No wonder politics is nothing to rave about, *The Independent*, March.

Mulgan, G (1997) On the brink of a real society, *The Guardian*, 1 February.

Mullahy, P (1955) *Oedipus Myth and Complex*, Grove Press, New York.

Murray, I (1997) Back pain caused by discontent with work conditions, *The Times*, 29 April.

Ouspensky, P D (1974) *The Psychology of Man's Possible Evolution*, Vintage, London.

Powell, J (1995) *Why I am Afraid to Tell You Who I Am*, Fount, London.

Schutz, W (1960) *The Interpersonal Underworld*, Science and Behaviour Books.

Schutz, W (1967) *The Bates Method*, Optima.

Schutz, W (1979) *Profound Simplicity*, Will Schutz Associates, Muir Beach.

Schutz, W (1984) *The Truth Option*, Ten Speed Press.

Schutz, W (1994) *The Human Element*, Jossey-Bass, San Francisco, CA.

Sheldrake, R (1997) Are you looking at me? *New Scientist*, 26 July.

Wilson, G A (1963) '*Emotions in Sickness*' (out of print). In Clark, L (1974) *Help Yourself to Health*, Pyramid, New York.

Yalom, I D (1991) *Love's Executioner*, Penguin, London.

Index